D1063216

Social Working:

AN ETHNOGRAPHY OF FRONT-LINE PRACTICE

In this unique work, Gerald A.J. de Montigny maintains that social workers, along with other professionals, create an institutional reality through their day-to-day practices. He traces the practical ways that social workers, when involved in child protection, struggle to produce a world which can be ordered, systematized, and subjected to their powers. It is a penetrating and sensitive analysis of how social workers in their everyday practice make sense of a confusing collection of case details to create organizationally defined problems and cases.

De Montigny uses the tension between his experience of growing up 'working class' and the difficult process of becoming a social worker to explore the practical activities professionals use to secure organizational power and authority over clients. This tension has forced him to confront the dilemma of how to stand on the side of the client when facing professional and organizational realities.

In the first half of the book, de Montigny focuses on the practices social workers use to produce a universalized professional form of knowledge. He examines social workers' use of ideological practices; fetishization of the social work profession; insertion of details from clients' lives into discursive order; accounting for front-line practice as a problem-solving scientific practice; and naming of their own frustrations, conflicts, tensions, and pain as professionally manageable phenomena. In the second half of the book, based on his own work in child protection, he systematically examines how such reality-producing practices come to be expressed as child protection and develops a synthetic account of his social work interventions in cases of child abuse and neglect.

This book should be read by all practitioners and students of social work. It is an original and practical application of theoretical arguments to the everyday reality of social work.

GERALD A.J. DE MONTIGNY is a member of the School of Social Work, Carleton University.

GERALD A.J. DE MONTIGNY

Social Working: An Ethnography of Front-Line Practice

UNIVERSITY OF TORONTO PRESS
Toronto Buffalo London

12-17-96

© University of Toronto Press Incorporated 1995
Toronto Buffalo London
Printed in Canada

ISBN 0-8020-2845-4 (cloth)
ISBN 0-8020-7726-9 (paper)

Printed on acid-free paper

Canadian Cataloguing in Publication Data

De Montigny, Gerald A.J.
Social working :
an ethnography of front-line practice

Includes bibliographical references and index.
ISBN 0-8020-2845-4 (bound)   ISBN 0-8020-7726-9 (pbk.)

1. Social service. 2. Social service – Vocational
guidance. 3. Social workers. I. Title.

HV40.D45 1995   361.3   C95-930308-1

University of Toronto Press acknowledges
the financial assistance to its publishing program
of the Canada Council and the Ontario Arts Council.

This book has been published with the help of a
grant from the Social Science Federation of Canada,
using funds provided by the Social Sciences and
Humanities Research Council of Canada.

To Andrea Trudel

Contents

Preface

As Hegel explained in the *Phenomenology of Mind*, it is 'inappropriate and misleading to begin as writers usually do in a preface, by explaining the end the author had in mind, the circumstances which gave rise to the work, and the relation in which the writer takes it to stand to other treatises on the same subject, written by his predecessors or his contemporaries' (1967: 67). Clearly, writing a preface is a peculiar exercise. The preface is a short story about a longer story, a putative synthesis, and a fragment claiming to represent the whole. As we all know, the preface comes at the beginning of the book, yet it is written after almost everything else. How then are we to approach the preface? Can we violate Hegel's arguments and treat it as a short story about the writing process or even as a synthesis of the text to follow? Can we scan the preface in the hope of peering through the author's reflections to the deeper waters of purpose and meaning? Can the preface illuminate the dark purposes of the author and the text? Can the preface make the text transparent for the readers?

The preface before you claims to speak with authority about the text. The authority of the preface arises not intentionally as such, but as an artefact of its organization in the spaces of the text, that is, as written by the author of the text as his preface, to his work, thereby invoking a form of proprietary ownership and authority, and as placed at the front of the text, and in the text as part of the text. Even as I write this preface, I recognize that the authority, which at this moment I seek to repudiate, but which the preface claims on my behalf as the author of the text, submerges me into the very sort of problematic that impelled the work of the text itself. Whether as an author or as a social worker, I find myself implicated, or as Althusser would have said, 'interpellated' into forms of social order that not only begin outside me, but that transform the meanings of my immediate actions into transcendentally realizable shapes and forms, which in their outer worldliness conflict with the impetus of my innermost desires.

The problem of the preface is not just with its authority or with the concept of authority, but with the very real social organization of authority in the text. The problem awakened by the preface is that of an authority which is enlivened through adherence to conventional forms, protocols, and rules. Just as I can play, and am playing with the writing of the preface, social workers can play, and do play with rules. The ad hocing that accomplishes the application of a rule in daily routines is always full of equivocation, ambiguity, and play. Good social work, like good writing, breaks the rules. Good social workers play with their clients by distancing themselves from the rigidity of the rules, the pull of protocol, and the limits of legislation.

As a social work student, I was told that I had 'a problem with authority,' and indeed, my enemy, and the implicit enemy pursued through the pages of the text, although cloaked by shadows, and speeding through the fleeting cracks of common sense, is the authority of truth, the commands of power, and the certitude of objectivity. So it seems curious, indeed, that I, as the author of the text, am expected to make authoritative pronouncements about what the text means. As I leafed through the pages of the manuscript, I was struck by the semblance of order, control, and rational argument. However, just as the smoothly polished surface of an oak chair belies the trembling muscles of the artisan, the finished character of the text belies the trembling synapses and emotions of its author. The certitude of the text belies my own confusion, forgetting, stumbling errors, and intellectual and emotional turmoil. However, I needed to write a preface. I searched for some order, pattern, or prevailing themes, only to hear the echoes below the printed words of stories and narratives conjured from my past. Thus, the stories I have chosen to share in this preface are the safe ones, the ones I have rehearsed, and replayed for students, colleagues, and for the audiences I will never meet. I must confess, and in confessing I invoke the compulsions of my art as a social worker, that there are deeper, private, and personal compulsions that impelled me to pursue this work and to track down the trail of sense making that produces mainstream social work. These secret stories, that which is left unsaid, comprise an essential mystery and secret of my life, just as such stories comprise the mysteries and secrets of the lives of my clients. It is essential that readers, social workers, and writers recognize that the attempt to invoke closure and certitude on the stories of our lives or the lives of our clients is a form of intellectual authoritarianism. This text, this preface, and the social work practice that I believe in are marked by profound uncertainties, confusion, partiality, incompleteness, and humility. Therefore, for the purposes of the preface, the best I can hope for is that the narratives that follow will open up the spaces of the mysteries from out of which I struggled for sense.

The mysteries that created this book are those of confusion. At the centre of this confusion are the ruptures, tensions, and conflicts I experienced as a student social worker. The genesis of this book began as a flight from the knowledge that I encountered when doing my work for the Master of Social Work degree at the University of Toronto School of Social Work from 1976 to 1978. I had moved to Toronto from British Columbia where I had been actively involved in student politics and where I had completed a Bachelor of Arts degree in history. The freedom I had in the history department at the University of British Columbia allowed me to work through a dialogue of Marxist concepts and theories. Such freedom was denied me in the School of Social Work. In the School of Social Work, my attempts to use standard Marxist concepts such as class, capitalism, exploitation, ideology, fetishization, and so forth, were understood by faculty members to be outside the recognized boundaries of professional social work. The social work faculty treated my analysis as missing the point of their exercises, as not addressing the concerns of social work, or as demonstrating my failure to orient myself properly to the profession of social work.

Against my Marxism and against the burgeoning Marxist scholarship in social work, I encountered the banal and simplistic analyses of mainstream social work. Although Pincus and Minahan explained, 'Some societal systems have been granted the authority to serve as agents of social control' (1973: 32), and Siporin pronounced, 'Social workers are sanctioned by society' (1975: 25), I wondered who had the power, practically speaking, to sanction social work and to grant social workers their authority? Did the workers on a picket line grant to the police the authority to break their line? Did the prisoners in a jail grant to the guards the authority to do body searches, to rip apart their cells, and to stand guard over them with loaded shotguns? Did the psychiatric patients lined up in the morning for electro-convulsive therapy grant to the doctors the authority to 'treat' them? Similarly, when I read Compton and Galaway, who noted, 'the general assignment for the social work profession is to mediate the process through which the individual and his society reach out for each other through a mutual need for self-fulfilment,' I wondered if the clients I saw standing in a line-up outside a welfare office saw themselves as reaching out for welfare to ensure their own self-fulfilment and that of the social workers they met?

It was clear to me was that these texts, relied on methods for divorcing the author's words, and the words in their texts, from the practical, everyday, and situated realities of people's lives. The grand, abstracted, and universalized language of these texts with their depoliticized, clinical, and professional focus was itself a particular art form. This was an art form or a form of practice that I could not accept as valid on its own terms.

Although repudiation provided a powerful point of departure, my intellectual survival demanded more than a position of pure negativity. Beyond repudiation I needed an alternative. I needed a source for a positive knowledge. Fortunately, my immersion in Marxist literature provided a beginning, for I had latched onto a core of powerful concepts for sorting through the world around me. I clearly recognized the forces of class in the people around me, whether expressed immediately in their dress, their grammar, their accents, their physical appearance, or, more abstractly, through their life opportunities, their dreams, and their desires. A focus on class allowed me to begin to develop a positive terrain for the analysis of social work and social problems. However, I remained plagued by the problem that if I repudiated objectivity, authority, and power, would I be reduced to naked powerlessness? What sources of validation could I claim for my beliefs? Certainly, relying on my lived experience seemed like a strong beginning.

As I ploughed through my course readings, my sense of my own experience led me to rail against the erasure of people's lived worlds. I had worked in provincial prisons and provincial psychiatric hospitals. When I read the controlled, regulated, and orderly words of social work texts, I felt compelled to spit out a response. My brain was too full of real people, real images, and real memories to accept that 'the social functioning of people, individually and collectively, is understood to be the outcome of a dynamic, transactional process between a human unit and its social physical environment' (Siporin, 1975: 125). My 'human units' had names, felt pain, and lived in actual places. I could not forget the hot blood coursing down Frank's face, as he stood in his cell on the protective custody floor, having just plucked out his eye. I recalled the quiet desperation of Nelson, who was always brilliant. Nelson played chess with me one evening, won, thanked me for the game, then left the ward and, hurled himself off a bridge a few hours later. I remembered Jimmy, with his obsessively rubbed bald spot. A charge nurse dragged Jimmy by the remaining strands of hair on his head down a flight of stairs, and pulled him against his will to the occupational therapy unit, because 'It is good for him.' I could not forget John, a sixty-year-old man, the smell of his feces covering the walls, covering his face, standing in the shower as I hosed him off. I could not forget that John had been left to starve and twitch on the floor of the hallway, placed on 'extinction,' as part of his therapy in the behaviour modification ward. Against the fine words of social work scholars, I wondered what really gave a charge nurse, psychologists, social workers, and hospital staff the power to deprive the patients on the ward of grounds privileges, snacks, meals, bedding, television, and visitors?

Usually, after I had read through social work texts, the margins were crowded with hurriedly scrawled and angry comments; however, beyond my initial reactions, I felt a deep sense of fear and dread that such people could intervene in the lives of others. I recognized that these professionals had the power to deny the actual organization of people's daily lives in the exploitative, oppressive, and dehumanizing social relations of a capitalist society. Furthermore, these professional social workers had the power to deny power itself and to disguise it as a mutual, transactional process. They had the power to then promote their analyses as 'truth,' 'knowledge,' 'right,' and 'objective science.' As writers, researchers, professors, and practitioners theirs was the power to rewrite people's lives and experiences.

Fortunately, I eventually began working with Dorothy Smith, and it was she who gave me the tools to not only build on my Marxism and to deconstruct the power of these texts, but to develop an alternative methodology for speaking from a standpoint in a lived world. Through Smith I explored the problem of ideology, and I learned how to analyse the claims of expertise, truth, and objectivity as themselves ideological. Through Smith I learned how to search beneath the calm surface of the words, to find the logic and order of the text, as a practical accomplishment in itself.

Dorothy Smith's analysis of ideology provided an important beginning for the work that produced this text, as she inverted the conventional sense of the term as designating a 'deviant inverse of an objective inquiry' (1990: 32), to focus on objective inquiry as itself ideological. Ideology points us not to deviations from objectivity, but to examine the peculiar practices for producing knowledge that presents itself as objective. However, the redirection turns our gaze not simply to objectivity as object, but objectivity as a practical product, as something produced by living women and men. The key is to focus our gaze on what actual men and women are doing, that is, on their practical and socially organized day-to-day activities. For Smith, ideology targets whatever methods, moves, tactics, and manoeuvres intellectuals engage in to erase their knowing presence and to produce a knowledge that claims to stand alone and apart from its human creators. It follows, then, that the antipode to ideology is not the creation of a knowledge that claims an ultimate truth, but rather a knowledge that is self-reflexive and transparently produced, in that the fundamental inseparability of the knower and the known is visible in its claims. Now, within the hegemonic discourses of the various professions, such a knowledge is plagued with the problem of being treated as not legitimate, not authoritative, and not truthful. Such a knowledge is easily dismissed by those in power as partial, subjective, located, interested, political, and biased. Yet, it is precisely such charges that underscore what is of value in such knowledge – and that is its humanity.

Certainly, there is something extremely peculiar about a 'knowledge' or a series of claims that purport to stand apart and separate from those who espouse them, think them, and fabricate them. Indeed, the peculiarity of this 'knowledge,' or this type of human product, had been recognized by Marx, not only in *The German Ideology*, but in *Capital* when he discussed the problem of the fetishization of commodities (1887). Ideology then opens up as problematic the actual practices, moves, and techniques employed by intellectuals to generate authoritative, expert, and professional accounts. Ideology, as taken up by Smith and as used in this book, is not about incorrect ideas or about lies as opposed to truth, but about a focus on those actual intellectual practices, actual situated ways of making sense, that operate to obliterate, erase, and obscure the connections between knower and known.

The focus on ideological method represents not a closure or an answer, but a beginning. It represents a line of enquiry that searches for the practices and social organization of knowledge production. The problem, as Marx argued so convincingly in *Capital*, is that the social organization of our society results in a process of fetishization that defines the core of our daily lives. The problem for social workers is that fetishization is imbricated not only in the forms of their day-to-day work, but in the problems of their own lives and the lives of their clients. In summary, what I found through my work with Dorothy Smith was a validation of my standpoint in the class relations of capitalist society and, closely related, the validity of combining political activity with scholarship.

After the effort of completing a BA, MSW, and MA, and the course work for a PhD over a ten-year period, I needed escape from university life. I felt compelled to work for social change. Furthermore, whenever I thought of the PhD thesis I could not think of a topic that seemed worth doing. In 1981 I began working in child protection. This work brought me face to face with the pain in the lives of those children and family members involved with child welfare systems. In this work I discovered a thesis topic worth pursuing. As I went to my job day after day, flew into small isolated communities, drove through the night to emergency call-outs, waited hour after hour in the hallways of the courthouse, argued, fought, and worked with clients, I experienced the disjunctures between the sterile academic discourse of mainstream social work and the dynamic, mysterious, challenging nature of everyday practice. By working alongside my colleagues and doing the job myself, I learned that good social work is not marked by confident pronouncements, certain decisions, and resolute action, but by an openness to dialogue, self-reflection, self-doubt, and humility.

Despite our recognition of what was necessary for doing good work, my colleagues and I found ourselves impelled by organizational forms that demanded a practice that violated the core of our desires. It was this problematic of the disjuncture between desire and the actual forms of practice that provided the initial insights into this work. I could see the disjuncture when I bundled three children into my car and drove them off to a receiving home. I certainly did not want to apprehend children, but neither did I have the material resources to keep these children in their homes. We could not put a homemaker into their homes. We could not pay for single mothers to receive job training or to pursue a college or university education. Parents who wanted to work could not find decent-paying or secure jobs. Adequate and affordable housing was not available for many clients. In the absence of resources, individual parents were held to be responsible for failing to provide adequately for their children. In the absence of resources, my practice hinged on blaming parents. As a front-line social worker, I needed to understand how my practice could be distorted and shaped in ways beyond my control and beyond the boundaries of my desire. I needed to understand how my location in extra-local and extended forms of social organization corrupted my desire.

I suppose that if there is a lesson to be learned from this book, it is that social workers cannot easily reshape their practice into an ideal or progressive political form, nor can they morally accept a nihilistic retreat into passivity and acceptance. Indeed, social work practice is always Janus-faced, that is, on the one side it arises as actual social workers' living, breathing, and situated activities, and on the other, it must articulate extra-local forms of authority and discursively organized power. The struggle for social workers is not won by retreat and denial of the other which is in themselves, but by engagement, explication, and efforts towards transformation.

Acknowledgments

After feeling bruised by my encounter with social work, Dorothy Smith proved that there are intellectuals who have the courage of their convictions, are prepared to dig beneath surface effects, can think critically, and, most importantly, take a side. On the foundation of my trust in Dorothy Smith's scholarship and politics, I was able to learn the craft of sociology.

I was fortunate to have had the opportunity to work in child protection with many capable colleagues. Unfortunately, to protect the confidentiality of clients, I can acknowledge former colleagues only by their first names and initials. However, I want to thank: Conrad H. for arriving at work wearing yellow rain gear covered in dirt and engine grease; he was the perfect antidote to the social worker in Scarborough who 'dressed up' for work because 'it is important to let these people know who we are.' Skip A. who, despite her claim that 'I don't always understand what you mean,' always said good things about my work with clients; Skip insisted that 'we all walk with clay feet.' Wally S., for winter days fishing for spring. Dale C. for his friendship and wit. Mardi L. for her scrupulous paperwork and her desire to be with clients. Barb P. for her Christian faith and integrity.

In 1985 I was hired by the University of Manitoba to teach in the affirmative action Bachelor of Social Work program in Thompson, Manitoba. The Faculty of Social Work provided both financial aid and time off from teaching to complete the PhD thesis that comprises the core of this book.

Since 1990 I have been employed at Carleton University in the School of Social Work, where faculty members prove that social work can be a vibrant, challenging, and socially transformative occupation.

Colleagues in the school have been extremely supportive of my work. In particular, I want to thank Allan Moscovitch, Gillian Walker, Colleen Lundy, Gale Wills, Peter Findlay, and Jim Albert. The text has benefited from the opportunity I have had of being able to teach with scholars and political activitists who are committed to a socialist vision.

Financial support for the publication of the book has been provided by the Social Science Federation of Canada, Aid to Scholarly Publications program. Special thanks goes to Leslie E. Butters who shepherded the book and me through the maze.

Virgil Duff at the University of Toronto Press has been a solid adviser. His faith in my abilities and dedication to this work have been heartily appreciated. I also want to thank Kate Baltais, the editor assigned to work on my manuscript by University of Toronto Press, for her thorough attention to detail and for her skilful editing.

Most importantly, I want to acknowledge the continual support of Andrea Trudel, my wife and partner for the past twenty-two years.

Whatever hope this book holds is grounded for me in the lives of our three children, Brendan, Julia, and Sarah.

SOCIAL WORKING:
AN ETHNOGRAPHY OF FRONT-LINE PRACTICE

1

Introduction

All men are intellectuals, one could therefore say: but not all men in
society have the function of intellectuals. (Gramsci, 1971: 8)

SPINNING COCOONS

Warm air blew from the car heater, lifting ammonia quills off our
damp pant cuffs, wafting them up to prick my nose. I did not really
mind their sharpness. They cleared my head of the dry smoke from
my father's cigarette. Perhaps I was too tired to care, but that night
even his cigarette seemed tolerable. Its familiarity was almost comforting. Glancing upward, I watched the speedometer's light paint a
green hue along the cigarette drooping from my father's mouth,
ending in the red fire of the smoking ember. As we drove through the
night, I nestled myself against his warm body, wrapped by his right
arm. Between the spaces of comfort and fatigue I was lulled by the
tires clicking over asphalt keeping rhythm with the motor's song. As
my father spoke about going home, having supper, seeing mum, his
voice quieted the echoes of clanking washbucket wringers, gurgling
black water spilling into buckets, and gritty mops swishing over
grimy floors. The gentle colours washing the inside of our car con-
trasted painfully with the glaring banks of fluorescent lights we had
left behind in the office. Back there were so many miles of criss-
crossing brown and beige nine-by-nine tiles, countless sweeps of wet
mops, dry mops, and wax mops, yet finally it was back there. We
were returning to our place, to our home, driving together through a
cool autumn night.

'Look at the sky, Gerry,' my father urged, 'the stars are so beautiful tonight.' Because I was only eleven and small for my age, I craned my neck to tilt my gaze over the high painted steel dash of the 1949 Plymouth. Outside, past the charcoal silhouettes of pines and beyond, I focused on a void punctuated by stars. I marvelled at the night, at the magically suspended crystals, at a heaven cleaner and more magnificent than all the miles of scrubbed floors imaginable. Beyond our moving cocoon, beyond this moment of safety, I sensed a whispered promise of freedom and yet, backward in the time of memory, I felt my own fatigue. I recoiled from the invisible chains that bound me to push, lift, soak, and wring a leaden mop. I stared at the sky feeling lost in its infinity and yet feeling imprisoned within. From this confusion I wondered aloud, wanting my voice to dispel my dizzying malaise. I asked my father, 'How were the stars made?' From the stars we moved to consider why we were alive. Why did we have to work so hard? What would our futures be like? During that drive home, through my naive questions, born from confusion and the awe of the possible, I who was a child, we who were 'only' janitors, 'only' workers became philosophers. We grappled with a contradictory everyday world as we encountered it directly through our experience. My questions and the dialogue that followed, most of which I can no longer remember, arose from our participation in social relations that extended beyond the immediacy of our cocoon. The everyday routines of work, feeling fatigued, and driving an old car home arose from our place as workers within a capitalist society. Our experiences, our questions, and our dialogue, existed within broad social relations of production, exchange, regulation, and organization. These background social relations organized our apparently private and personal dialogue.

CELEBRATING ILLEGITIMATE KNOWLEDGE

More than two decades later I remain concerned with philosophy and the problematic character of the everyday world in which I live. I have grown up confused by my world. As a social work student, I was confused by professional ways of talking, writing, analysing, and describing people's lives. I could see that the ways professionals addressed the lives of clients were shaped by their place inside organizational power and class privilege. Even after graduating and working as a front-line social worker, I remained unable to muster the authority of my education and the power of my organizational mandate to make 'true' pronouncements, to produce unequivocal case 'facts,' and to work with certainty and confidence in my authority and power. I remained confused by the worlds of my clients. Their lives remained out of my control and even outside of their own control. Perhaps it was my own keen sense of being confused, and thereby of being fallible, that continued to make me angry when I heard the pretentious authority and certainty that accompanied the pronouncements of experts and officials.

I grew up in a family where I learned to see myself as 'working class.' Both of my parents, and even both sets of grandparents had strong socialist beliefs. Growing up in my family meant growing up with a strong sense of class membership. Growing up meant developing a keen eye for injustice and a deep distrust of authority. Growing up meant listening to my grandparents' and parents' tales of the Great Depression, the persecution of union activists, the injustice of wealth, the corruption of big business, and the danger of state power. As I grew up inside my family, I learned that the world was a place truly divided between two warring classes. As E.P. Thompson observed: 'We cannot have two distinct classes, each with an independent being, and then bring them into relationship with each other. We cannot have love without lovers, nor deference without squires and labourers. And class happens when some men, as a result of common experiences (inherited or shared), feel and articulate the identity of their interests as between themselves, and as against other men whose interests are different from (and usually opposed to) theirs' (1963: 9). Even as a child I could see the gulf between my view of the world and the 'reality' produced by people in power. Perhaps it was walking union picket lines with my father? Perhaps it was the strikes against his employer? Perhaps it was innumerable talks around the kitchen table about wealth, power, justice, and social change? Yet, perhaps my class consciousness developed more subtly? Perhaps, as E.P. Thompson suggests, my class consciousness developed in the spaces and the obvious distances between the lives of working people, such as myself and family members, and the lives of the rich and powerful. These were distances I recognized in the pages of primary school readers, novels, biographies, movies, and plays. In textual and media representations, I encountered lives that were different from my own and those of my family. The lives of people in the books and on television counted. Our lives did not. When I looked at my own life, the life of my father who was 'only a janitor,' and my mother who was 'only a cook,' what I saw was of little value. The devaluation of our lives created a hunger for value, for validation, and for a different world.

As I grew older, I came to find names for my nagging senses of hunger, desire, frustration. By developing what I understood to be class consciousness, I was able to manage the longing for wealth and power instilled in all of us and to envision a different kind of world and different ways of being. By developing class consciousness, I was able to name my experience, to order events in my life, and to thereby preserve a sense of personal integrity. By naming the everyday experiences of disjuncture between representation and my daily life as 'class,' I was able to construct a buffer to protect me and those I loved.

The analysis developed in this book hinges on the development of class consciousness and class transition as both a personal experience and as an experience embedded in a set of social and historical relations and struggles. When I address issues of class, class consciousness, and class location, that is, working class, ruling class, intellectual class, and so forth, I am not talking about 'objective' phenomena that can be scientifically tested, dissected, and defined. Once again, following from E.P. Thompson, class is not treated in this work as a thing. As Thompson notes, 'It does not exist, either to have an ideal interest or consciousness, or to lie as a patient on the Adjustor's table' (1963: 11). Quite simply, class became a part of my life as I lived in relation with others and with the representations of others around me. By describing myself as working class, I produced sensible, cogent, and affirming accounts of day-to-day life experiences. By producing an explicit class identity, I brought myself into close association and shared identity with family members, a friendship network, and a supportive leftist literature. However, by defining myself as working class, I was not giving voice to some ultimate truth as scientifically calculated or to some true form of class consciousness as deduced by those authorized to assign class membership.

To a young man who saw himself as working class, the knowledge I encountered when entering university did precious little to dispel my confusion about the world in which I lived. Instead, it assaulted and, indeed, insulted those few propositions that I had come to believe with some sense of certainty. For example, having grown up inside a socialist household, I knew that Canada was a class society divided between the few rich and the many poor. As a grocery clerk for Canada Safeway – a grocery store chain with head offices in California – I knew that capitalist production exploited my labour as a working person. From my day-to-day experiences as a worker, I knew that it was my labour and that of those 'like me' that produced all value and wealth. From my days and nights walking picket lines, I knew that there is class conflict between capitalists and workers. Through my work in unions and the New Democratic Party, I knew that, although working people must struggle for socialism, the forces of ruling class hegemony[1] constantly serve to distort the images of the world held by working people.

As I moved through my BA and my MSW I encountered professors, supervisors, and other people of power who claimed that their knowledge was objective, real, non-judgmental, and unaffected by their situation in a class society. I refused to believe the claims of authority they made for their knowledge. It seemed to me that the wise, the learned, and the powerful had a place inside a class standpoint that permeated the very foundations of their knowledge. To counter their authority, I argued that their knowledge was really ideology.

Certainly, as a young working class man, I had been told all too often, and I knew all too well, that my own knowledge was partial, incomplete, and situated. I could not speak with the power of objective facts. I did not possess the whole story. I could not see from all sides. I could not be impartial. What I knew was ineluctably conditioned and limited by my standpoint in a working class, while the knowledge of the learned and the mighty was somehow exempted from the earthly limitations that plagued me. From a stubbornness fed by class anger, I refused to concede to social scientists that their knowledge was either superior or more 'objective' than that of working people. I knew that just as I was embodied and situated, so, too, were the authorized 'intellectuals,'[2] such as teachers, professors, administrators, journalists, or counsellors. They too were conditioned and limited by their class standpoint. Indeed, with youthful arrogance, I believed that there were intellectuals within the working class, for example, my own father, my grandfather, my grandmother, my fellow workers, and my union president.

As a young man I marvelled at the wisdom and strength of my maternal grandmother. She had been born in Hungary into a peasant family at the turn of the century. She suffered the loss of both her parents by age fourteen. To survive she emigrated to the United

States and worked in the textile mills of New York. After three years she arranged, through her church, to travel to Canada to marry my grandfather. As a Hungarian immigrant (part of that dangerous Eastern European underclass), a farm wife, and mother of six daughters, my grandmother lived in poverty. She and her family survived by working at backbreaking and low-paying jobs. She, and later her daughters, worked picking hops and berries, hoeing fields, planting crops, caring for trees in orchards, and other menial jobs. Despite her grinding poverty, the obligation to raise six children and, in later years, to run a farm (which was never economically viable), my grandmother built a world of love, caring, and warmth for her children and grandchildren. In her day-to-day practice, my grandmother built relations with others that affirmed her Christian beliefs. My grandmother was certainly an intellectual. She struggled to make sense. She built what she knew to be a supportive, caring world for those around her, despite her oppression, and despite her social situation in a world whose forces were largely beyond her control. From her religious, moral, and personal beliefs, she developed a version of the world that allowed her to survive, to raise a family, and to find meaning and purpose in her life.

A CLASS ACT

As I moved through university, I could not purge my memory of the experience of growing up within a world where class was painfully real. I could not erase knowledge derived from what I knew to be a standpoint in the working class. Just as I could not erase my memory, I could not deaden those senses which related that world to me. Yet to survive, and to succeed in university – which in my youth I recognized as an alien world of 'bourgeois culture' – I had to learn consciously how to manufacture a self that itself felt alien. I had to learn new ways of learning, new vocabularies, and even new ways of acting in social situations. Like the lads Willis studied in his book *Learning to Labour*, I too had to learn the 'right attitude' (1977: 69). I had to make myself over to graduate, to be a university-educated professional, and to be a front-line social worker. To administer, manage, govern, order, and make sense out of the lives of clients, I had to develop a professional attitude towards the world.

To become properly middle class, I had to conceal my anger, disbelief, and disdain for official and objective versions of reality. This was not an easy task. Even as a child, I had learned to distrust the bosses, supervisors, experts, newspapers, radio, and television. As my father talked about problems at work, he continuously framed events in the broader terms of class struggle. When the media raged with hysterical commentary about the Soviet menace during the Cuban missile crisis, my father spoke of U.S. propaganda. He argued, 'We hear only one side.' When the Americans were waging war in Vietnam, he said, 'They have no right being there.' Through my father, I learned to reject official truth. As a young man, I routinely pronounced any statement I disagreed with 'bullshit.' I reacted with thinly veiled disdain to those with authority. In professional language, 'I had a problem with authority.'

My problem with authority was necessary, however, for salvaging my ego when I was confronted by abusive bosses who insulted my abilities, teachers who saw me as just another punk, and media versions of my (working class) reality that insulted and blamed people for their predicaments. From my father, and from my explicit identification as working class, I acquired a repertoire of class-based devices for criticizing, disputing, or rejecting 'bourgeois ideology.' However, these devices also served to distance me from the knowledge I encountered in university, not to mention the unhealthy side-effects of diffused paranoia and generalized anger they created. Yet, university knowledge and the ways of thinking necessary for its production were essential if I were to perform middle class work. It was clear to me that administrative and managerial work required specific ways of thinking, talking, and acting. These were ways of being that felt alien to me. They were located in forms of life outside those of my lived world.

As I passed through university, like Garfinkel's transsexual, Agnes (1967), I passed from one class to another, one standpoint to another, one consciousness to another, and one reality to another. Passing from one class to another, like passing from one sex to another, made visible the practical activities for marking off social domains.[3] In the pain of passing myself off as middle class, I acquired insights into the art of 'doing' a middle class life.

Just as a strong sense of class identification was important for survival, so, too, was my encounter with Karl Marx and Frederick Engels. Early in my academic career, through encouragement from my father, I began to read their works, notably *Capital*, *The Communist Manifesto*, *The German Ideology*, and *The Condition of the Work-*

ing Class in England. Through Marx and Engels, I found an affirmation of knowledge embedded in the standpoint of working people. Additionally, I found affirmation for my gut sense that working people were not stupid, but oppressed. In *Capital*, I learned that when working people suffered in poverty it did not mean that they had failed, but that it was capitalism itself that produced poverty.

Even from my first reading of Marx's *Capital* at age nineteen, I realized the basic 'truth' – from my standpoint as a labourer – of the 'labour theory of value.' I could plainly see that it is labour (power) which creates value, that it is the working class which produces the wealth of a nation, that capitalism is founded in the private appropriation of wealth produced by a working class, and that the social arrangements of our society work to continue the exploitation of the working class by capital.

Marx and Engels provided more than an affirmation of the experience of being working class and a critique of capitalism. They provided me with a method. In 1972 I became part of a Saturday morning reading group that plunged into the intellectual depths of *The German Ideology.* Reading *The German Ideology* was electrifying, for it provided a series of principles, axioms, or 'rules' for making sense of the world. Again and again, albeit in different words, Marx and Engels repeated that a proper method is comprised 'not of setting out from what men say, imagine, conceive, ... but setting out from real, active men, and on the basis of their real life-process' (Marx and Engels, 1976: 36). By following this simple axiom, that reality was produced through active life processes of actual individuals in a social world, I began to see beyond the mystifications and reifications of academic language about 'systems operations' and 'organizational functions.' Following Marx, I wanted to examine the flesh-and-blood people and their real world and socially organized activities that made 'systems operate' and 'organizations function.' What was important, what was 'real,' and what was worth studying were actual people's socially organized practices. After reading *The German Ideology*, I was convinced that what mattered was what real people did day by day. Whatever people thought, whatever they called consciousness, theory, or even science had to be tied to what they did, how they did it, and how their activities were socially organized.

I stubbornly adhered to Marx's account of capitalist exploitation, class conflict, and power, and to the methods he and Engels developed, even while I moved through a very clinical and individualistic program for my Master of Social Work. Marx and Engels provided a framework for rejecting social workers' stories about individual and family pathology, the altruism of the helping enterprise, the humanity of the social welfare system, and the progressive advancement of caring. My socialism allowed me to recognize that social workers' practices were fully implicated in the social relations of accumulation, legitimization, control, and coercion (Cohen, 1985; O'Connor, 1973). I recognized that scholarly accounts of social work could not be accepted at face value. Indeed, social work scholarship was thoroughly implicated in social relations of power and control, and the failure of scholars to recognize these relations have produced accounts of the profession that are deeply mystifying.

Another intellectual turning point occurred for me after I managed to survive the School of Social Work and began to study under Dorothy Smith in 1977. Through Smith's work, I discovered a Marxist method that affirmed a focus on people's 'actual' activities as socially organized. By participating in Smith's lectures and by reading her papers, I learned how to think through people's lived worlds differently, hence, in a way that addressed socially organized practice, lived activities, and actual forms of work. Smith's work allowed me not only to recognize the problematic nature of phrases like 'social work believes' and the 'organization is mandated' but to pull apart the intellectual and organizational practices essential for giving these phrases their sense. Smith's work provided me with a method to dig into these phrases and to ask: Who are the living people that actually believe? What is the social organization of their experiences that allows them to write over their active and embodied lives, to constitute themselves in the abstract as social workers, and to attribute what they know, feel, and believe to this abstraction? What forms of life are necessary for producing these forms of knowledge and the consciousness that follows?

After the years of being attacked because of my socialist politics and my attempt to use Marxist methods, I found a place of refuge working with Dorothy Smith. I saw a parallel between the 'standpoint of women' (1987) as a critical standpoint and my self-identified standpoint in the working class. Smith also saw the parallel between my concerns and hers, and over the years that I worked with her, she proved herself to be a trustworthy and active supporter of my work. Indeed, over the years I have developed a steadily deepening trust not just in Smith's methods of working, but in her political commitment to socialist struggle.

MANAGING CLASS

As a social work student and later as a social worker for several government ministries, departments, agencies, and hospitals, I constantly bridged the conflict between two apparently distinct worlds. I bridged the gap between the world of my experience and the world that denied my experience, a world of my thoughts and beliefs and a world that demanded that I perform other people's thoughts and beliefs – spoken through operational directives, policies, and legislation. As a social worker, I bridged a flesh-and-blood world of embodied or immediate being and a textually cold world of disembodied or institutional being. To survive as a social worker, I struggled to appear to colleagues as another professional, that is, as an objective and non-judgmental social worker. I struggled to perform so that colleagues would recognize that my ways of thinking, talking, judging, and making sense matched their own and the generalized forms of the profession. I had to seem committed to the values of the profession, the knowledge of the profession, and the practices of the profession. In the process of professional education, what I was needed to be erased. I was repackaged, and I repackaged myself. In the process of becoming professional, I learned how to reframe, rename, and re-experience experience. Personal problems and conflicts were reframed as attempting to grow, transcending anger, and working through emotional barriers.

In 1981 I began working full time in a child protection ministry in a northern community, just in time to meet the victims of the recession. As a social worker for a child welfare office, my principal function was child protection, although I also provided family service, services to children in care, foster-home co-ordination, adoption services, and child paternity and support services. In addition, like other social workers in our office, I also carried some general welfare or income assistance cases – these were usually 'Family and Child Services' cases on our caseload.

Upon arriving at the office in the morning, particularly near month's end, I would walk past ten to thirty people lined up waiting for an appointment to apply for welfare. I easily imagined myself, my family, and my friends standing in that line. I could see the range of emotions in people's faces, the quiet withdrawal and turned-down faces signifying shame, the too loud conversations conveying anger, and the nervous laughter of anxiety. As a social worker for the organization, I had to walk past the line, put my key in the door, and enter the office. Their turn would come to enter the office, but they would wait in the reception area on one side of the counter, while I worked on the other side in my office.

FRAGMENTED REALITIES

Each day as a social worker, I experienced a serious split between my sense of personal integrity and the work that violated my beliefs about good social work practice. On the one hand, I continued to meet face to face with clients whose lives were being destroyed by generalized economic forces, on the other, policy and legislation forced me to treat these people as if they were personally and individually responsible for their situation. Being a professional demanded smoothing over the fissures between social workers and clients, front-line workers and supervisors, generalized policy and particular crises, claims to help, and interventions that blamed and stigmatized. Being a professional demanded a synthetically smooth self not racked by the pains of doubt, anxiety, and self-betrayal. It required a managed self and a polished self that lived inside an 'ordinary life.'

Although doing social work was usually limited to eight hours a day for five days a week, being professional was a full-time occupation. Although doing social work was a finite piece of daily life, what Schutz has called a 'finite province of meaning' (1973: 230), being a professional received a primary valorization, and thereby dominance as the source of truth, reason, and understanding. To pass as a social worker, the professional reality becomes the paramount reality (ibid.).

How could such a professionally constituted segment come to represent our truth, our totality? A partial answer lies in the moves of professional practice for producing knowledge. Professional knowledge is marked by the systematic subordination of the equivocal, uncertain, confusing, and, at times, mysterious domain of the flesh (Merleau-Ponty, 1968). It was as flesh that our bodies moved about in the fluid intercourse of daily life. It was in the embodied forms of our practice that we produced a self-alienation, and a self-negation, such that we ourselves became instruments of the organization. Through the forms of our practice, we realized the profession and the organization.

The professional self is a fractured self, a piece of the self exchanged for a salary, and once exchanged it finds 'itself' a participant in production guided and directed by commands, forms of order, relevances, and discourses that transcend the spheres of immediate experience. Kovel addresses the consequences that follow from the social organization of this form of working:

Thus work, the sustaining principle of necessity and the foundation of society, is no longer equivalent to the whole person's activity; it becomes the province of part of the self, a part that must be made enumerable for purposes of exchange – and the self has to be split in order to allow this exchange to take place ... Abstraction and splitting are the essential features of capitalist culture as it becomes marked with the identity of production. A personal side and a thing side, made by human activity but each apparently having a life of its own, seem to wander separately through the totality. The ruthless motion towards abstraction creates in the Cartesian split a disembodied human consciousness and a material, mechanical body, the repository of nature. (1981: 56)

The tension that arises from the social relations of work in capitalist society creates stress, distress, neurosis, and even madness – or the possibility of a critical analysis. Developing an analysis requires that we begin with our own experiences. It demands that we recognize our pain, discomfort, and anger as legitimate social phenomena warranting analytic explication, not therapy.

THE PROBLEMATIC OF THE EVERYDAY WORLD

Dorothy Smith has outlined a Marxist strategy that explores the social organization of everyday experience. By beginning with the tensions embodied in experience as socially organized, we can unfold social dimensions inherent in the seemingly personal. Smith notes: 'It is posed by actual properties of the social organization of the everyday world in contemporary society, namely that its social organization is only partially discoverable within its scope and the scope of the individual's daily activities. Its local organization is determined by the social relation of an immensely complex division of labour knitting local lives and local settings to national and international social, economic, and political processes. Here, then, is where the sociologist enters' (1987: 154).

Although she begins with personal experience, Smith recognizes that the world of daily life, as a matrix of experience, is organized by people's concrete relations to an extra-local ruling apparatus and by extra-local social relations, notably the relations of the state and the economy. The local sites in which people live their lives – their homes, their neighbourhoods, and their places of work – are subject to laws, policies, and rules that are purposefully designed to operate independently of these particular localities.

The problematic of the everyday world values our efforts to give voice to our places and our experiences in the social world. Our pain and confusion and the questions that emerge from our daily lives are not merely idiosyncratic, but are socially located and socially organized. We live and work within a society where our activities are regulated and managed by a complex of agencies, organizations, corporations, and bureaucracies. Through our unending contact with this institutional apparatus, both our own and clients' realities become reportable, accountable, and visible in its terms. Our accounts of clients' lives smooth out rough spots. We file away troublesome edges until what emerges are relatively uniform accounts, which to the degree that they represent a smoothly constructed object can be sorted out and fit back together through various forms of rehabilitation, teaching, healing, or correction.

People resist being smoothed over. They experience rage when their stories are rewritten into the organizational files. They complain about bureaucratic insensitivity, red tape, bureaucratic bungling, invasions of privacy, and violations of personal rights. Similarly, even those who effect the translation of daily life into institutional realities suffer the effects of the work as frustration, anger, guilt, resentment, rigidity, and burn-out.[4]

THE CASES

I worked with hundreds of welfare clients, children in care, parents, and other professionals. To make these people's lives understandable and manageable, both for myself and for them, and to develop interventions to deal with their personal suffering, pain, and needs, I had to confront the conflicts in my own position. On the one hand, I was a social worker doing child protection for a bureaucratic organization; on the other, I was a child of working class parents. This book uses case narratives and case examples to reveal social workers' techniques, moves, and devices for producing warranted sense. The lives of the people who became 'cases' are not presented as topics in themselves. Nor is the focus on the cases in themselves. Rather, the focus is on the practices of social workers for producing cases and the social relations through which these practices are accomplished. In developing cases and other practice examples, I have safeguarded the confidentiality of information about individual clients and co-workers. First, to guarantee the confidentiality of those people who were my clients, I have presented people's situations not as they 'actually' were, but as expressions of social work practice. The apparent character of this or that case, its particulars, facts, and actors' histories, arise through a work process and are creations of organizationally grounded practice. Accordingly, I have not only altered all identifying information, including names, addresses, city of residence, dates and so forth, but I have 'imaginatively elaborated' (Kovel, 1981: xiv) cases to draw out certain arguments and points. This technique recognizes not only that the particulars of individual cases often overlap, are similar to, represent the same dynamics, and forces, but that the case itself is an artefact of organizational work and that its structures are organized by the relevances of professional discourse. The client situation at hand is professionally read through the forms of an institutional reality.

The authors of traditional social work texts accompany case presentations with a standard disclaimer. An author notes that identifying facts of the case have been changed to prevent the identification of the clients, for example, name, location, agency name, or unique identifying characteristics. I have adopted this disclaimer only provisionally, as I argue that social workers' accounts about clients are institutionally mediated constructions (Pfohl, 1985). The claim that social workers know their clients is bracketed.[5] Insofar as my imaginatively elaborated constructions correspond to the case accounts produced by other social workers in the field, the cases I present can properly be understood as reflecting social work practice. My fabrications are neither arbitrary nor fanciful. Rather, my case examples proceed according to the forms of proper social work practice, accounts, and professional discourse. I expect that for readers skilled in social work, there will be a verisimilitude or congruence between the cases I present and the cases they may have encountered through their own practice.

The second concern is with ownership and property rights over the material. Certainly, in a society founded on property rights, the question of ownership of the data poses an even greater threat to ethical integrity. As a social worker, I was an employee working for a state organization. My reports, my running records, the forms I completed, and the files I produced were not my own. They belonged to the agency for which I worked. Therefore, when I present an example of a report to the court, this cannot be an actual case, taken from an actual record, but only an example reconstructed according to the protocol of a generalized blank documentary form. Accordingly, I have constructed documentary facsimiles in this work to reveal what any competent social worker, regardless of geographical location or organization would know to be an adequate account. Therefore, I have not identified either the province or the offices where my work occurred.

Analysis of social workers' practice of child protection has also relied on a range of public documents. To conceal the location of my practice, I will not provide references for quotes from legislation, policy manuals, departmental reports (for example, annual reports, ombudsman reports), operational directives, news releases, and protocol manuals. Quotes will be presented as they appeared in the original documents, with the exception that any information that could reveal the province where I practised will be deleted or altered. Child protection legislation is referred to in this work as the 'act' rather than by its actual name. I have used XX, xx, YY, yy as substitutes for the section numbers of legislation. Finally, to protect the confidentiality of clients, I have used XX wherever reference is made to the dates of a client's birth, the dates of case particulars, or the dates of legislation and documents used in case examples. Additionally, I have employed materials from other provincial jurisdictions and have incorporated these into some examples, with the hope of more effectively concealing the location of my practice. To reconstruct case examples, I have employed blank forms used by child welfare departments, but again, I have changed details as necessary. Like most other writers, I have relied on an extra-local professional discourse embodied in seminars, workshops, journal articles, monographs, and authoritative texts.

HEGEMONY AND SOCIAL WORK

This book examines some of the practical ways that social workers transform situated and local activities into coordinated professional accounts, and to thereby construct a distinctive professional reality. The sense-making and accounting practices used by social workers are examined as embedded in extended social relations, themselves marked by dynamics of unequal power and authority. For front-line social workers, the demand to manage, order, and account for the lives of those others who become clients requires the use of complex practices for bridging everyday worlds with organizational and discursive imperatives. These bridging operations which establish links between situated events and complex organizational settings – police stations, court houses, probation offices, community hospitals, psychiatric facilities, group homes – simultaneously disconnect the experiences and the voices of clients from their locations in everyday lived realities.

Social workers' power to connect their professional voices to an extended discourse and to disconnect clients' situated voices is best understood as a form of hegemony. Thus, hegemony designates two distinct but related moments or movements. First, hegemony directs attention to the practical exercises of sense-making and control, which social workers exercise day after day through the absorbtion of details from clients' lives into professional discourse, and the resulting imposition of professional accounts onto the lives of clients. Second, hegemony directs our attention to the voices that arise outside the organizations of power and to people's struggles to resist, oppose, and critique organizational power and professional discourses.

Although professionals may seek to exercise their powers to redefine the worlds of clients' lives, and indeed their own lives, the worlds of daily life remain profoundly intractable, chaotic, and uncontrollable. Furthermore, the possibility of recognizing hegemonic practices presupposes disturbance, disequilibrium, resistance, and opposition. Simply put, those subjected to the terms of organizational and professional hegemony rarely 'go quietly.' Hegemony directs us to focus not only on the differences of power and authority between clients and experts, professionals, and the powerful, but on the struggles over what counts as common sense. These struggles for hegemony, perhaps over hegemony, must themselves be understood as articulating the actual social organization, social forms, and social locations of the contestants. Hegemony directs our attention to the multiform separations, differential locations, and class divisions effected between those who administer the lives of others and those who are subject to this administration. Yet, wherever hegemony arises as a visible problem, hence, wherever its problematic is given voice, there must also be spaces and forms of resistance. Indeed, the possibilities of a book such as this, of radical social work, of client rebellion, of anti-poverty organizations, of self-help groups, of trade unions, and of left political activists, are rooted in the problematic of hegemony.

Attention to hegemony demands addressing the real-world activities and social relations that shape 'intellectual production.' Intellectual production and thereby hegemony, once understood to be carried out by a diverse cadre of living 'intellectuals,' who are themselves embodied, and actually situated in specific spaces and places, cannot be reified as a 'singleness of the nodal hegemonic point' (Laclau and Mouffe, 1985: 139). Simply put, the hegemony of ruling ideas, which for social workers are expressed as the power of their professional accounts, a power realized day after day in case decisions, court proceedings, and interventions, refutes the notion of 'a process without a subject' (Althusser, 1971: 124). Indeed, it is precisely this focus on subjects who perceive, investigate, assess, record, inscribe, interpret, and work that produces hegemony. Just as it is living subjects or actual actors who in the course of doing professional and organizational work bring the effects of their divergent locations, life histories, motivational imperatives, and intentionalities to the work, what emerges from the work as hegemony will itself express divergence. Although hegemony may from time to time appear to express an apparent stability, singleness of voice, and smooth tonality, hegemony as the living production of authority, control, and power, must also express deeper structures of profound discordance, opposition, and struggle. The hegemony of ruling ideas is never 'over-determined' by state or social structures,[6] nor is hegemony ever a singularity or unitary field. Rather, the hegemony of ruling ideas, as developed in this book, points towards the difficulties of coordinating cacophonous voices and real opposition and struggle into the semblance of coordinated activities, hence, into a putative singularity. This book takes up the practical problems faced by one group of intellectuals, social workers, and the challenges they face in producing professional and organizational realities that appear to be singular, ordered, managed, governed by rules, and controlled.

THE ORGANIZATION OF THE BOOK

In the chapters to follow, I trace the practical ways that social workers struggle to produce a world that can be ordered, systematized, and subjected to their powers. It is in the exercise of their powers that social workers actively produce professional and social realities, that is, worlds that are knowable, sensible, orderable, and, most importantly, intervenable. In the first half of this book, I examine the specific forms of the powers of social workers as reality producing. Hence, I focus on the use by social workers of ideological practices, professional location, discursive realities, scientific practice, and professional good sense to produce a distinctive 'reality.' In the second half of the book I turn to examine how these 'reality producing' powers are expressed as child welfare practice. The second half of the book follows the chronological order of social work involving a case of child protection. This section begins with the call to the agency and then moves to examine the investigation the report to the court, and the court hearing. Finally, the conclusion represents a circular movement back to a simple narrative, where once again I find myself encountering questions of meaning and purpose, although no longer as a child – but as an adult and as a professional social work educator.

2

Ideological Practice

Somehow he had got hold of a book of matches and was setting his sheets
on fire.

Something inside me snapped. I hadn't beaten him for a long time ... I
ran at him and started hitting him with my fists until my arms were
tired. He didn't cry.

How in the world could I impress upon him the danger of fire? I had
told him so many times what fire could do to a person ... but nothing got
through to him. An insane thought came into my head. Without stopping
to think I ran into the bathroom and turned on the hot water and let it
run ... I would show him what kind of pain he was letting himself and
others in for.

I dragged him into the bathroom and shoved his hands under the running water and held them there ... I felt nothing, stared straight ahead,
seeing only a white haze. His screams of agony penetrated through the
haze and I let go of him.

I had no idea how long I had held his hands under the water. I fell
down on the floor, vomited and blacked out. When I came out of it, I
picked him up and carried him to his bedroom and laid him on his bed ... I
picked up his hands; the skin was peeling back. (Camden, 1984: 109–10)

THE SYNONYMY

This incident is from Elizabeth Camden's autobiographical book, *If
He Comes Back He's Mine: A Mother's Story of Child Abuse* (1984).
The story is about an unusual or remarkable series of events in her
life. Clearly, for Elizabeth Camden and for most readers, her actions
are visible as child abuse. The evident good sense of Elizabeth

Camden's narrative as a story about child abuse, however, relies on her having answered a series of background questions. For example, how should she sort out the details worth telling? How should she order the facts of her story? How should she develop a temporal sequence for the story? How should she connect this incident and similar incidents ('I hadn't beaten him for a long time')? Elizabeth Camden's answers to these questions, like our own answers, arise against background frames and work processes for producing cases of child abuse.

This incident is a noteworthy fragment of the life of Elizabeth Camden. This fragment becomes worth telling and worth confessing within the problematic of child abuse.[1] Although on the surface this story is 'obviously' about an incident of child abuse and is told by a woman who understands that she 'really' did abuse her child, the good sense of the account arises from background knowledge about organizational and professional work processes for identifying, categorizing, and managing child abuse. Despite the shocking power of the story, its good sense is organized by a discourse 'which intends its own description of the event' (Griffith, 1984: 29). This story, with its very personal and immediately felt confusion, pain, and tragedy, is organized by, and, accordingly, becomes an exemplar of, the category of child abuse. Hence, the category of child abuse organized this story as worth telling.

The shift between hitting a child, shoving a child's hand under water, and child abuse is similar to that which Smith observed between the statements 'she killed herself' and 'she committed suicide' (1990). While, in our everyday talk, we often substitute such phrases for each other as if they mean the same thing, Smith explains that they do not mean the same thing. She argues that there are profound differences in how these statements are socially organized. While the statement 'she killed herself' is located in people's everyday language, the statement 'she committed suicide' is an artefact of complex organizational work processes conducted by police in police departments, coroners in coroners' offices, nurses and doctors in hospitals, and so on, which 'objectively' determine cause of death (Smith, 1990: 143). By analogy, there are profound differences between the social relations which allow Elizabeth Camden to say, 'I dragged him into the bathroom and shoved his hands under the running water and held them there' and the statement, 'I abused my child.' The first statement is derived from a lived moment in the historical fabric of Elizabeth and Keith's lives. It speaks to the embodied and immediate actions of Elizabeth and Keith and their ground (Bologh, 1979) in a particular setting. It speaks to a context, an actual apartment, bathroom, water heater, tap, and time. It speaks to activities and events grounded in Elizabeth and Keith's day-to-day worlds. The second statement – 'I abused my child' – speaks to the insertion of this lived reality into an institutional category defined in legislation and in professional discourse.

For Elizabeth and Keith the meaning of the occasion – playing with matches, snapping, running hands under scalding water, and collapsing – is inextricably embedded in the social contexts and spaces of their daily lives. What sets this moment apart as remarkable or unusual in their ongoing stream of life is organized for Elizabeth and Keith by their organic history and situation, by the painful violations of 'relationship' that this incident created, by the deep sense of betrayal and guilt. Elizabeth and Keith have a history together, or as Schutz has said, they 'grow older together' (1973: 220). Whatever 'snapped' means for Elizabeth, and however she 'snaps,' is woven into her life history and its day-to-day enactments with her son Keith. How Elizabeth snapped is rooted in other moments of 'snapping' or near 'snapping.'

What makes Elizabeth's account of 'snapping' worth telling is organized both by her desire to be a good mum, to love her child, to protect her child, and by the narrative structure of 'child abuse.' There is a gap between these two structures, between the immediate and the discursive; in the spaces of the gap, the latter promises healing, resolution, management, and containment of the former. Elizabeth finds herself running Keith's hands under scalding water. She finds herself being a bad mum by hurting her child. When the hot water ran over Keith's hands, he felt the pain in his hand. He was not just a boy in a text. Keith lived in a flesh-and-blood body. He was thoroughly tied to that body, that moment, that pain. However, in the text, as his mother tells the story of child abuse, we can only imagine Keith's experience. We do not know what he screamed, for her account of 'child abuse' is so powerful an organizing force that it silences not only Keith, but her own voice as well.

As readers, we can guess at Keith's terrified anticipation of being hurt. We can picture his frantic struggle to break free. We can imagine the hot pain in his hands, the tears on his face, and his desire to escape. After the event is over, Keith may want mum to love him,

mum to promise not to hurt him, to be a good boy, to make everything okay, and to be forgiven. His mother's story of child abuse
provides for organizational intervention and an organizational course
of action, and this silences Keith's experiences and desires. Even as
Elizabeth frames her own life, and remakes her story into one of child
abuse, she transforms her experiences into a problem that requires
social work intervention.

Any competent social worker would identify the events relayed in
this story as child abuse. However, a social worker's identification of
child abuse is organized by concerns outside of Elizabeth and Keith's
lives. The identification of child abuse relies on a child protection
discourse and the work processes of child protection organizations.
However, for Elizabeth, the problem of hurting Keith is not abstract
or universal, but immediate. For her the problem is not one of child
abuse in the abstract, but rather the turmoil and pain that mark her
immediate relationship with her son. For Elizabeth the pain she feels
and her sense of guilt and betrayal weld her stories to those of a
professional discourse that promises to help her become a good mum,
to have some sense of control, to manage her anger, to pass beyond
her sense of failure, betrayal, and self-hatred. For Elizabeth the
meaning of shoving Keith's hands under the water is necessarily
rooted in the visceral memories of his birth, in the soft touch of her
hand on his head, walking the floor with him as he cried, and so on.
For Elizabeth the problem of child abuse is poised inside knots, hot
flashes, sinking guilt, and ringing dizziness. The problem arises as
her love and longing for her child fall into rage and rejection.

THE POWER TO TELL

Properly executed social work practice requires producing stories that
erase the splits between lived realities and organizational categories.
Accordingly, proper social work is a process that continuously masks
the differences between the realities of daily life and institutional
reality. Pfohl outlines:

The material and definitional actualities of child abuse of any 'thing' else are
bound together in an indeterminate relation that 'is' the effect of a
transformative displacement of one set of social structuring practices by some
other(s). From within this collision or collusion of structuring practices arises
a 'true' story – the 'real facts' of the matter, the self evidence of 'things' and

the like ... To make something 'truly' present is to make absent something other. 'Things,' thus become 'real' only in a socially differentiated act of silencing. This (categorically) imperial exclusion marks the historical production of 'things in themselves.' Yet this is exactly what they are not. They are nothing but the cultural, political and material effects of a struggle for the organization of power in (and as) history. (1985: 230)

Pfohl draws our attention to the power relations inherent in those professional practices that bring phenomena into focus and into being. When, as social workers, we craft our stories about child abuse, we redirect attention away from the contexts of parents' lives; deny the impossible demands of being a parent; and silence the rage, the protests, and the visions that prefigure different ways of raising children.

As social workers, our textual accounts silence the deep craziness of daily life. Our stories black out the domain on the other side of common sense. Our stories select out the possibilities of a sane, sensible, manageable, and controlled social world. Our work converts the equivocal domains of daily life, with their chaos, uncertainty, confusion, and slippage into discursively fabricated and ordered accounts. Accordingly, even the ruptures, and the deep voids of madness, become manageable as social problems to be categorically defined and mastered, for example, child abuse and neglect, domestic violence, wife battering, mental retardation, and mental illness. Social workers, psychologists, psychiatrists, and other 'helpers' know how to discover these categories in the world, as though these are natural phenomena independent of their specialized work (Smith, 1990).

The stories social workers tell about their clients combine details from clients' lives with organizational and professional categories, theories, and themes. People's lives become the raw material lifted out of spoken words, carried across the distances between the apartment and the office, and reworked under the glare of the florescent light, over the office desk, and onto the officially sanctioned forms. A person's life, once inserted into a social work story, becomes an individual case of child abuse, child neglect, domestic violence, or mental illness. The person becomes a client who in turn is a child abuser, a neglectful parent, an alcoholic, or a mental patient. Once the person's story is shaped by that person's assignment to the terms of a recognized category that person becomes subject to the themes, patterns, types, and interventions best designed to address the problem category. For example, a person's abusive behaviours might be explained as resulting from a 'cycle of violence,' lack of 'life skills,' or inadequate 'mother–infant bonding,' and each of these in turn is suggestive of specialized forms of intervention.

People's lives, difficulties, conflicts, and problems provide raw materials to be inserted into professional frames and theories to produce the case. The transformation of the everyday into the extended discourses of professional social work comprises a taken-for-granted bedrock for social work intervention. For example, Louise Johnson in an introductory social work text states: 'A social work assessment is a picture (however incomplete) made up of all the available facts, fit together within a particular frame of reference for a particular purpose' (Johnson, 1986: 277). Johnson's account seems straightforward enough, however, it is clear that for her 'pictures,' available 'facts,' and 'particular frame(s) of reference' are not problematic notions. Indeed, for social workers in general, their training allows them to treat 'pictures,' 'facts,' and 'frames' as naturally occurring phenomena, yet this treatment bypasses critical questions about how pictures are drawn, how facts are produced, and how frames are selected.

When a social worker arrives at a client's doorstep, she brings with her the 'frames' for the picture she will see. As the picture is framed, cast in the light of her eye, and as the 'facts' emerge through her activities, these details will be recorded in her memory, daily log, or running records to be recalled, rearranged, and restated in reports and testimony. Her experience as work assumes an organizational work process. The social worker's activities on the doorstep are structured by an organizational question: 'Is this a case of child neglect or abuse?' The social worker's focus on this question bypasses questions about the cogency, warrant, and good sense of the categories child abuse, child neglect, and child protection. The validity and incorrigibility of child abuse as a category describing the 'real' world is taken for granted. Social workers do not doubt that child abuse and child neglect exist out there in the real world. They do not doubt that child neglect and child abuse are quite properly matters requiring some form of skilled social work intervention.[2]

As a day-to-day work process, social work relies on documents such as texts, policy manuals, directives, and periodicals. The production of documents and the interpretative work that employs those documents, presupposes the participation of members who are qualified to produce and to recover their good sense. A document's good sense as a well-written text and as a useful guide is dependent on the hermeneutics founded in competent professional practices. Through documents, social workers insert themselves into the abstracted and impersonal social relations of what Smith has called a 'documentary reality' (1974).

Social workers' fact-making practices are rooted in texts and textual forms of order. Their production of factual claims is both shaped by documents and intends documents. The production of facts produces a documentary form of order that appears to be independent of the actual investigative and naming work. For example, the notations in the running record that a child's 'occiput was flattened,' the child suffers a 'developmental delay,' and the child is 'underweight,' appear as facts independent of the work process where a social worker looked at the child's head, shook a rattle in front of the child, and placed the child on a bathroom scale. As facts social workers' claims about clients are tied back to universal and abstracted professional discourse that reveals what the facts mean. For example, the facts cited above can be read through articles, books, and reports, to reconstruct the obvious problem of child neglect and to infer that the parent is neglectful. Once the meaning behind the facts is revealed, clients' daily lives become visible as organizationally actionable (Green, 1983: 14). Social workers employ such categories to order social problems, to construct theoretical relations between problems, and to develop causal explanations and intervention techniques that aim to modify existing causal sequences.

Through their documentary practices – that is, reading and writing – social workers construct an institutional reality. The referents or signposts of this institutional reality are reflexively identified and navigated by a professional consciousness. The reflexive relation between an institutional reality and professional consciousness means that the forms of thinking and working professionally are bound to the social relations essential for building and sustaining an institutional apparatus. Professional consciousness emerges through the intellectual practices required to do organizational work. The semblances of homogeneity that mark its production, and ultimately its reification as professional knowledge, are rooted in the mundane socially organized methods used by actual practitioners to make sense, sustain the warrant of claims, and distinguish proper understandings from improper understandings. Documentary production provides a basis for the practical expression and reification of a universalized professional consciousness. A documentary reality provides a space where the impersonal, general, and situationally transcendent standpoint of the profession and the organization can be substituted for the lived standpoints of those who are subject to and subject themselves to its determinations.

SCRIBBLING OVER THE LINES: DOING INSCRIPTION

As social workers see and act in specific settings, the details they record as relevant and worth reporting speak to their participation in a textually mediated discourse. Social workers know how to inscribe everyday or mundane occasions as proper instances into organizational categories. Such inscriptive work quiets the tumultuous noise of drunken shouting between husband and wife. It cools out a child's hot tears. It manages the welts from a beating. Simply put, it modulates the noise, multiple dimensions, and uncertainties of an immediately experienced reality. It substitutes the regulated tonal symmetries provided through professional categories and texts for the noise of daily life.

Social workers' inscriptive practices are effected primarily through documentary production. Thus, a social worker will make sense of a face-to-face conversation with a client by inscribing particular details into record. The details and the record follow established protocols for documentary production, such as length of entry, focus on clients, attention to mandated concerns – child protection – as well as professional language and attitude towards clients. What may have been an hour-long interview – social workers do not normally have conversations – becomes compressed as an entry in a running record into a few lines, such as 'Crystal and mother into office. They were both quite unresponsive and uncooperative. They continue to refuse to address the problems in their relationship. Both hide behind defense of sarcasm, memory loss, and ingenuous grins. Mother insists that Crystal will have an abortion. She is to see Dr P on March 15. Mother feels that he will support the plan to abort this pregnancy. They were warned that unless they make a more significant effort to work on their relationship that I would terminate the Short Term Care Agreement.' In this example, the complex interplay between actors, who said what, the tones of voice used, the content, the emotional energy of exchanges, and the relationship with the social worker, are reduced to a few sentences that reflect the agency standpoint and agency concerns, namely: Should the short-term care agreement be renewed?

In face-to-face interactions with clients, social workers use agency forms to solicit case particulars and sift information through known indicators and concerns to determine the action to follow regarding care. The agency forms available to social workers allow them to inscribe particulars into the structures of an organizational order, such as a report to the court, a temporary custody agreement, or an application for income assistance.

To make proper professional accounts, social workers do inscriptive work 'in which events in the ordinary world are re-conceptualized and entered into documentary reality' (G. Smith, 1990: 267). Social workers in the field engage in inscriptive work when they proceed from, for example, a 1:00 a.m. call from the RCMP, drive to an apartment on 5 Cobalt Street, conduct investigative work, scribble notations in a work log, enter facts on an intake report – such as, no parent present, empty vodka bottle on table, no food in cupboards, scabs on youngest child's face, smell of urine, children placed in car – to produce, thereby, a professional finding of child neglect that can be presented in a report to the court. Social workers in their day-to-day practice encounter a series of situations that at first sight defy categorization as a case of this or that: Is this really an abused child? Can I make a case for neglect in court? Are there missing facts that might explain the situation? The social worker's inscriptions, noted in daily logs, jotted in running records, and typed in formal documents, provide a discursively organized constellation for rendering visible practice on behalf of an organization.

This inscriptive work, performed from within an institutionalized standpoint and grounded in the social relations of power and control, is ideological, in the sense developed by Dorothy Smith (1990). She expands the notion of ideology Marx developed in 1845 in his work *The German Ideology* (Marx and Engels, 1976). She addresses ideology, neither as a set of ideas – correct or incorrect – nor as a characteristic of all knowledge, but as a socially organized practice.[3]

Like all practice, ideological practices arise within determinate social relations and settings. Unlike our routine and regularized practices of daily life, ideological practices arise from and intend organizational forms for transcending the vicissitudes of daily life.

Ideological practices are embedded in the work processes of organizational actors for constructing the organizational standpoint for ruling and regulating other people's lives. Ideological practices are tied fundamentally to organizational forms of action. To grasp the distinction between mundane or routine practices and ideological practice I offer the following example. When the phone rings at home, and I answer to hear my brother's voice, I engage in a conversation that seeks to find out what he and other members of his family are 'up to,' hence what is 'new in his life.' As we talk I ask: How is Alexandra (his infant daughter) doing? How is Caroline (his wife) adjusting to being at home caring for the baby? What plans do you have for your birthday? Have you seen mom and dad recently? My talk with my brother dances back and forth through the fabric of our lives. Our talk is a moment of 'doing' family, being brothers, keeping in touch, sharing experiences, and sometimes getting support. Certainly, our talk is a practice. Its ability to be constituted as a telephone conversation relies upon a complex web of artful sense-making moves such as pacing, questioning, responding, use of silence, and selection of topics. As the phone conversation unfolds, it is directed at the fabric of our daily lives, our pasts, and our futures together. As the call unfolds we also realize that 'we must keep it short' or else face an exorbitant phone bill. When the call is over, it is registered in our memory as another moment of our particular lives.

From the standpoint of the telephone company, however, our phone conversation is a transaction for which we as consumers must pay. The phone company is not concerned with details of our talk, nor with the work that our talk performs. Rather, our call is another business transaction, another entry, among millions for which a charge is laid. Our talk represents the purchase of their service. For telephone company employees and managers, our talk is a matter whose length in minutes is recorded on a computer and which is to be billed to my brother's telephone number. Our talk is important to the phone company only as a consumer transaction, as a profit-making exchange, and as a statistic to guide decisions about billing rates, marketing strategies, and advertising campaigns. Our talk, when understood from the standpoint of workers within the organization, is transformed into 'fact' – namely, a long distance call between Ottawa and Vancouver conducted from 11:05 to 11:27. What the call means for organizational purposes is dramatically different from what the call meant for my brother and me.

Imagine that the next day I am back at work and the phone rings, but this time it is a client calling. I begin by jotting down the date and time of the call, and the caller's name in my black log. I record the general direction of the conversation in the log, and I make note of requests for service or any statements that might indicate that there is a need for my intervention, for example, 'I hit Billy with a belt last night.' If there are concerns, I will ask further questions to determine if there is a need for service. I may even give directions about policy, services, and procedures for resolving problems. The phone conversation conducted at work is itself a piece of a work process. My practice on the phone is organized by my work. My practice is shaped by the agency mandate, my job description, and my professional knowledge. My work of recording the phone conversation intends an anticipated possibility of needing documentation of the talk for organizational purposes. The simple talk on the phone may result in an investigation, an apprehension, or it may even be entered as evidence in a criminal proceeding. The conversation with my brother, however, is located within a far different practical universe, and it relies upon quite different social practices and social organizations.

Smith argues that ideological practices begin by disattending (Polanyi, 1967), or glossing, the concrete or actual relations and structures of lived experience. Thus, specific occasions of seeing, experiencing, and talking about, which are rooted in concrete social settings, are detached or taken up outside of people's lives and social contexts (Smith, 1990: 43). These fragments, particulars, or facts are glued back together into some pattern using 'mystical connections' derived from an institutionally grounded social discourse (Marx and Engels, 1976: 62; Smith, 1990: 49). 'Mystical connections' arise when social workers reorganize the particular facts of the matter at hand according to the theories, frames, and models of an institutional discourse. Institutionalized discourse subjects people and the stories they tell of their daily lives to the scrutiny and relevances of its terms, its relevances, its problematics, and its regimes of power. People who are appropriated as the objects of discourse become clients. As clients, they are cases. They are a child abuse case or a child neglect case. As such, they need institutional direction and management. How people know themselves and, most importantly, the social relations where they have come to know themselves are dissolved and reconstituted through ideological methods.

INSTITUTIONAL PRACTICE AND IDEOLOGY

Ideological practices and the professional discourse that ideological practices build are understandable only as grounded in an institutional apparatus. Smith defines 'institution' as follows:

I am using the terms 'institutional' and 'institution' to identify a complex of relations forming part of the ruling apparatus, organized around a distinctive function – education, health care, law, etc. In contrast to such concepts as bureaucracy, 'institution' does not identify a determinate form of social organization, but rather the intersection and coordination of more than one relational mode of the ruling apparatus. Characteristically, state agencies are tied in with professional forms of organization, and both are interpenetrated by relations of discourse of more than one order. We might imagine institutions as nodes or knots in the relations of the ruling apparatus to class, coordinating multiple strands of action into a functional complex. Integral to the coordinating process are ideologies systematically developed to provide categories and concepts expressing the relation of local courses of action to the institutional function and providing a currency or currencies enabling interchange between different specialized parts of the complex. (1987: 160)

Social workers use ideological practice to produce specialized professional discourse for managing and coordinating work among themselves and other organizational professionals and for connecting their work to that of psychologists, psychiatrists, nurses, teachers, police, and occupational therapists.

As noted above, when a social worker arrives at the client's doorstep, what she sees, not what the client sees, and what she inscribes in her log as the facts of the case, not what the client believes or says, become the particulars of a proper organizational account. The client's beliefs and comments may be recorded, but social workers will most likely frame these as exemplars pointing to an underlying category, such as the client's beliefs, the client's story, the client's degree of insight, the client's delusions, or the client's concern or lack of concern for her child. As a social worker inscribes instances from client's lives into her log, and connects the 'manifest' content to 'latent' content and the superficial to the underlying cause (Hoffman, 1992: 12), she demonstrates her competency, legitimizes her exercise of power, and affirms the truths of the organization. The social worker's versions of 'reality;' her textually constructed stories, her ability to link client situations with organizational mandates; and her ability to demonstrate hidden truths combine to affirm the incorrigibility of her accounts and, thereby, to affirm the corrigible nature of client accounts.

Daily life is ever changing, confusing, fluid, and subject to ongoing reinterpretation. This fluid movement of daily life, however, must be frozen. Particular moments become an incident, such as child neglect, child abuse, wife battering, or incest. As a meaningful incident, it can be accounted for in documentary form. The work of documentary production freezes daily life and enters particulars into what Smith has called 'document time' (1974: 260). She says, 'This is that crucial point at which much if not every trace of what has gone into the making of that account is obliterated and what remains is only the text which aims at being read as "what actually happened" ... In reading back therefore the interpretive procedure bypasses the processes which produced the account and lodges directly in the actuality thus constituted' (ibid.). For example, a front-line social worker's investigation of a suspected case of child neglect will produce a series of organizationally relevant particulars. These particulars will be entered into a family assessment report as the facts of the case. Such facts then stand for, or represent, the actuality of the situation itself, independent of the projects of the organization and the constitutive work that produced it. When professionals read the documents and distil the particulars of the case, they can either accept or reject the story and its claims, using professional categories, themes, theories, insights, and connections.[4] By employing such discursive matrices, social workers pose and answer a maze of questions: What information is needed to decide what kind of case this is? What is the truth about the situation at hand? Who can be believed? How can these people's partial, biased, and self-interested stories be sorted out?

Cases at hand, with their chaotic, gory, disgusting, sensuous details, challenge the worker to fit them into legislation, policies, and directives. In a very practical way, social workers bridge local situations with extra-local policies, directives, and protocols. Of necessity this bridging work is effected through ideological practices. Ideological practice is not merely a way of working or a method that social work practitioners can freely choose to employ or not. Rather, when social workers do work on behalf of an organization as professionals – hence, when they speak and write using the discourse of a professional reality – they necessarily work ideologically. Thus, despite whatever insights I might have had about 'ideological practice,' my practice as a social worker doing child protection work was necessarily and inescapably ideological. So long as I entered actual situations into the language of policy, so long as I wrote cases into the record, so long as my practice advanced the organizational inscription of daily life – my work was ideological. The cogency, warrant, and authority of my practice and my very place and status in the organization as a social worker depended on ideological practice.

Ideological practices are situated in the problem of ruling and making sense. Ideological practices emerge from the relations of power, and they are tied to the standpoint of the rulers who seek to monitor, control, and govern the lives of the ruled. Ideological practices imply a social separation and social division between those who are entitled, authorized, and warranted to generate social accounts and those who are subject to the terms of the accounts. Ideological practice presupposes inequalities of power, prestige, and authority. The possibility of these forms of sense making presupposes class, gender, and race inequality. William Ryan, in his book *Blaming the Victim*, provides the following recipe for engaging in ideological practice: 'First, identify a social problem. Second, study those affected by the problem and discover in what ways they are different from the rest of us as a consequence of deprivation and injustice. Third, define the differences as the cause of the social problem itself. Finally, of course, assign a government bureaucrat to invent a humanitarian action program to correct the differences' (Ryan, 1976: 8–9). Key to the sensibility of Ryan's account is an imbalance of power between those who have a problem and those who 'study those affected.' Second, the ideological practices Ryan addresses require an us–them bifurcation. Curiously, such a bifurcation may even be internal: the scientist or even the professional who treats his personal life as epiphenomenal to his scientific work, hence, who experiences his life as 'other' and as outside his observing, measuring, investigating work.

Ideological practice is more than a mere moment of intellectual activity. Understanding ideology demands focusing on actual sensemaking practices as inseparable from an actor's social grounds. Actions are always embedded in or indexical with determinate social relations or forms of life. Therefore, to the extent that meaning can be uncovered, it is only by reading the action back into the contexts of its occurrence. However, having said this, social workers' activities, in the form of their accomplishment, appear non-indexical, and as organized by concerns that extend beyond the present contexts and moments of their performance.

Ideological practices, although having as their effect the production of apparently non-indexical realities, are nevertheless contradicted by the ground, context, and history of their practitioners. Indeed, the failure to recognize the social organization of ideological practice usually results in talk about practices being the same, or isomorphic, or even arrayed along a continuum of similar acts. Such ways of conceptualizing ideological practice gloss the context dependency and artfulness of sense making, by ascribing an 'objectivity' and 'meaning' to an action as independent of context. For example, both I and Luciano Pavarotti might sing 'Ave Maria.' Although we are singing the same song, we are holding different books in our hands, we read the texts differently, we stand in different places, and we produce quite different renditions. In this example the possibility of presuming 'sameness' presupposes the 'text' and the ability of the text to freeze meaning in the dead letters of the page. The text must be read, and here, thankfully, people will forgive my reading and the singing that results because it is drowned out by their own equally horrific voices. Far different expectations greet Pavarotti as he sings on stage before an audience of five thousand people. Unpacking practice demands looking beyond its obvious form. Making sense of practice requires bracketing the objectiveness of action on a common-sense level as visibly obvious. Making sense of practice requires examining the artfulness of performance, the context dependency of meaning, the historicity that opens up the possibility for the practice, and the reverberations for the future.

A social worker's ability to link people's situations to policies and mandated courses of action seems rather straightforward or a matter of common sense. Even to an 'educated' observer, it might seem that all a worker has to do is to find the relevant policy in the correct manual and apply it to the client's situation at hand. The apparent simplicity of the process hides both the complex and the artful character of such matching work. It hides the complex repertoire of ideological practices required to effect the translation between daily life and the texts. Indeed, as we become more experienced as professional workers, we tend to forget that a major problem we faced in our early years was figuring out what was 'real.' We either were not aware that certain problems existed, such as sexual abuse of infants, wife battering, elder abuse, glue sniffing, or else we denied that the problems occurred with regular frequency. An essential piece of being an experienced and mature worker is knowing what problems exist and how to identify them without being fooled by appearances.

The shift from a consciousness of daily life to an institutional consciousness centres around the issues of management and control. This imperative to manage the social worlds of clients extends to the management of workers themselves. Workers must be able to engage in a practice that produces the appearance of transcending its own particular place. The vicissitudes of mundane and situated sense making must be transcended. Standardized forms, protocols, and policies operate to effect this transcendence. The office context is essential for shaping common sense and the boundaries of good work. A competent social worker must be aware of the backlog of clerical work, the amount of time required to type a report to the court, the cabinets where blank forms are held, the amount of information required to produce an acceptable form, the procedures for obtaining and returning files, and so forth.

Social workers begin by acting in a social world, according to a mandate of their employing organization. When they act, they connect their mundane practical activities to a network of organizational and professional relevances. They reframe mundane activities, such as picking up a phone, listening to the caller, and deciding that this is a report of child neglect, so that these activities become visible as part of a work process, namely, intake. What the activity of picking up the phone and talking to a caller means is grounded in the work process. The apparent good sense generated by a social worker talking on the phone to a caller becomes visible within the protocols of policy and organizational operation. Say that in the process of listening to a caller (let us name her Mrs Hope), the social worker hears a story. For Mrs Hope her story is organized according to the relevances of her life. Her story is rooted in problems she has had with her upstairs neighbour in her apartment building. Mrs Hope tells the social worker, 'I have told my neighbour, Betty ... Betty Lively that is, that she's got to stop her kids from running in the halls, you know, but, hmm, it's water off a duck's back. It gives a body such a headache. I think she drinks too, I've seen her take out bottles to the trash and, my word, I've seen into the apartment when she opens her door, land-sakes what a sight. I think she leaves the kids alone too. I have seen her leave, and have heard the wee ones crying at night.'

For Mrs Hope her telephone conversation is an attempt to manage some difficulties of her lived situation by requesting some help from 'the authorities.' To get that help, she makes a series of claims that she believes will prove that a problem exists and that she is herself a reliable and concerned citizen. Her claims are organized by multiple levels of situated experience and history. She may simply desire to sleep at night or to avoid being disturbed by children playing in the halls. She may be calling to affirm deep beliefs about parental responsibilities and a concern that the children may not be properly looked after. She may be calling to rebuke Ms Lively because she is a single mum.

The social worker's job is to sort through the myriad of motivational possibilities that may have led Mrs Hope to make a report. As Mrs Hope talks to the social worker, her claims are incorporated into what probably is for Mrs Hope an alien organizational frame. Within this frame the social worker need not care, and probably does not care, about Mrs Hope's concerns as such. What matters to the worker is whether or not there are reasonable grounds for treating the caller as reputable and, accordingly, for suspecting that Betty Lively neglects her children. From within the organizational standpoint, the worker simply wants to determine whether or not this telephone conversation really is a report of child neglect. She needs to determine that the call is not something else, such as an attack for revenge, an angry response to a conflict between neighbours, or a delusion.

What 'actually' makes a call a report of neglect is usually treated as a matter of common sense. The social worker assumes that she and her colleagues can all agree on what counts as neglect. For example, 'It's inappropriate to leave young children alone at home unattended.'

The telephone call, which for the caller may have been to 'blow off steam,' 'teach Mrs Lively a thing or two,' 'get some peace and quiet around here,' or 'act as a responsible citizen,' becomes for the social worker, who is located in an organizational standpoint, a piece of a work process. What was for Mrs Hope a conversation is for the social worker a moment of 'doing intake.' The social worker systematically structures the call as an intake investigation. What counts as a proper intake harkens back to professional training, texts, and discourse, and, most importantly, to the organizationally vested power to name or define situations. The social worker interacts with Mrs Hope in a manner that elicits particulars which intend an account of

a report of a child in need of protection. She asks the questions necessary to assess the degree of risk to the child, directs the conversation
away from the caller's concerns – especially when the caller's concerns are not understood as relevant to the organizational matter at
hand – and tries to get at the facts of the situation.

Despite the matrix of organizational power that sanctions front-line
social work, the practical imperative to transform calls into an interview can nevertheless be frustrating for social workers. This frustration becomes particularly acute when a social worker encounters
talkative callers, such as Mrs Hope, who have little appreciation of
the organization's mandate. Such callers' talk is problematic because
it is oblivious to the social workers' concerns. Such callers seem
insensitive to the social workers' efforts to direct the interview. Some
callers' accounts when first heard appear to be hopelessly muddy,
muddled, and filled with irrelevant and extraneous details.

The child abuse schema allows the social worker to select only
those particulars that can be used to constitute a report. Those
callers who violate the rules of proper reportage create problems for
social workers. Garfinkel observes, 'Persons take for granted that
what is said will be made out according to methods that the parties
use to make out what they are saying for its clear, consistent, coherent, understandable, or planful character, i.e., as subject to some
rule's jurisdiction – in a word, as rational ... 'Shared agreement'
refers to various social methods for accomplishing the member's
recognition that something was said-according-to-a rule' (Garfinkel,
1967: 30). When callers fail to respond to the social worker's questions and prattle on about their own concerns, they cause the worker
both to waste valuable working time and to struggle to recover some
discursively rooted sense from the account. To recover discursive
sense, social workers must invoke complex procedures to transcend
the indexicality of the report. They sort through excess and irrelevant
information to distil those particulars that are discursively relevant.
Social workers, like the coroners Atkinson studied, employ 'members'
methods for repairing indexical particulars' (Atkinson, 1978: 183).
The transparently indexical nature of a caller's report, that is, the
obviousness of the caller's anger, the rambling talk, the attention to
irrelevant detail produces a problem for the front-line social worker.
The social worker must transform the caller's rambling, incoherent,
disorganized, and hesitating talk into an account both coherent and
linked to the work at hand.

As noted above, social work is fundamentally a bridging and colonizing enterprise between the realities of people's daily lives and an institutional reality. First, social workers inscribe bridges in texts. These textual bridges open points of entry into people's lived realities providing frames, concepts, and categories. Once the shores of daily life are bridged, specific topographical features and particulars can be mapped out using a grid of organizational relevances and concerns. Social workers use these maps of the territories of daily life to guide the work of invasion, domestication, and colonization.

Through their intervention, work social workers teach clients how to think their own lives in discursively organized terms as marked by specific 'problems.' People come to see themselves as particular types of cases. Former psychiatric patients describe themselves as schizophrenic,[5] manic, depressive, anorexic, bulimic. A man confesses to his worker that he is a child abuser and an alcoholic. A woman describes herself as a victim of wife abuse. A mother, such as Elizabeth Camden, confesses to being a child abuser.

Through their practice, social workers help people to think through and, thereby, to see their own lives employing the conceptual currency of a professional discourse. The consequence, as we saw at the beginning in Camden's work, is that people subject to social work also learn how to think through their lives employing the terms of an institutional reality.

3

Constructing a Professional Standpoint

This book began by mapping the disjuncture between my experiences as a member of the working class and as a professional social worker. As a manual labourer, I obeyed and served others, minded my place, and worked physically. As a professional, I ordered and directed others, assumed responsibility, and worked mentally. To become a professional, I had to learn how to create my place within a professional standpoint, and it is this problem of finding my place that provides the central question of this chapter. How do people produce the specific professional consciousness required to manage their place and their work as social workers within an institutional apparatus?

I came from another place, another class, and another reality, which made being a social worker difficult. As the child of a self-defined 'working class' home I found it difficult being professional. From my standpoint, I found it difficult believing that social service organizations were about helping, fairness, equity, equality, and human dignity. Having stood in line for unemployment insurance, having entered a welfare office needing money, having the problems of making 'ends meet' on pogie, I could not accept professional versions of organizational beneficence. Nor could I accept the clinical reduction of social problems to issues of personality or individual maladjustment.

Perhaps most vexsome, however, was the difficulty I encountered when having to assume the standpoint of expert in my day-to-day social work. As the young man who had grown up labouring for others, I was not accustomed to being in control of my work situation or managing and supervising others. Whether as a retail clerk, a janitor, a hammer-mill operator, a shipper/receiver, or a labourer, my working experiences comprised countless moments of being told what to do, when to do it, and how to do it. Even as a child in school with other boys and girls, I had learned to assume a place and an attitude of inferiority. I had learned myself and my family, as 'my father is only a janitor,' 'my mother only completed grade eight,' 'my mum is just a cook.'

Once I began working, I quickly learned that to keep my employment, and to earn a living, I had to acquiesce to the orders and the commands of others. My place in the world was not to account for, order, or make sense, but rather to accommodate myself to the accounts, order, and sense making of others. Becoming a social worker demanded that I take up the place and the powers of social work. This meant entering myself into the reality and standpoint of social work powers and authority.

ENTERING POSITIONS OF POWER

As a new social worker, I suddenly found myself in what I had always understood to be the position of the boss. I was forced to occupy not only another position, but rather, the position of the other. The ways that social workers approach the world, order daily life, make sense, and communicate these sensible features to each other were visible to me as alien class practices. For me, social workers lived in a world different from my own. The good sense of social workers' language and the professional reality this language expresses was alien and in conflict with my own experience. Social workers use grammar, language, and conceptual practices that were radically different from those which I used as a member of the working class.

To survive as a professional candidate in the school of social work, I had to learn, along with fellow students, not only a new language, but a grammar of expression and a professional form of disembodied presence marked by containment, control, and managed emotionality. This professional imperative to produce emotional composure, rationality, and regulated expression seemed not only alien but antithetical to the passion and outrage that I felt were essential to political activity from the standpoint of the working class. Learning to do social work required taking up an alien class standpoint and alien ways of being that meant suppressing my own knowledge, insights, and class practices.

Again and again, I was told that my understandings of the world were not compatible with the understandings represented in the school of social work. If I outlined that a client's problems were the effects of social factors, such as unemployment, poor housing, exploitative landlords, racial harassment, or unsupportive social workers, I was understood as rationalizing the client's failure to cope.[1] By addressing matters of oppression, injustice, and inequality, I revealed either a refusal or an inability to think properly. For example, in a paper on social work practices, I took up the situation of a client who was in prison as a result of a minor theft. I connected the problem of class oppression and alienation to the client's 'sense of having suffered an injustice.' I added, 'Social workers usually label this projection, denial, or defense mechanism,' and I quoted a young prison inmate as follows: 'I took a twenty dollar statue. They give me a year. They help me lose my job. They help me lose my house. They took my wife away from me. Where's the reasoning? Where's the justice? Where's the ... (pause) I'm supposed to sit here and take this? Understand? Rationalize? Then they'll let me out on the street, saying you can handle it. You can take it. You've got big shoulders.'

My instructor's response to this quote was to insert the young man's words into a social work problematic. First, she asked, 'Are these statements true, literally?' Ironically her query demonstrated exactly the professional moves I had identified as being used to discredit client accounts, namely labelling a client's sense, 'projection, denial, or defense mechanism.' By asking if the client's statements were 'literally true,' she demonstrated a professional scepticism and disbelief in the client's story. Once my instructor bracketed the client's claims, she positioned herself inside a discourse in which the real meaning behind the client's story could be discovered. In a marginal comment she developed the following analysis: 'It seems to me that rather than expressing his frustration with "class oppression," Larry is asking to be placed in a protected supportive environment where he might *learn the skills* of independent self directed social living which he has apparently been unable to learn satisfactorily in his life so far. His crimes seem small and even somewhat innocuous as you describe them – but he does seem to have developed a pattern of lethargy[2] and a-social attributes in his life so far which he himself seems to see as being dysfunctional.'

For me it was unthinkable and ludicrous to suggest that this man – by getting drunk, smashing a window, grabbing a twenty-dollar statue, and getting caught by the police – was 'asking to be placed in a protected supportive environment.' Like the welfare workers Zimmerman studied (1976), my adviser, nevertheless, demonstrated her professional competence by adopting an 'investigative stance' (1976: 332), marked by scepticism. Additionally, once having suspended the cogency of the client's story, she provided a professional account which 'really' explained the client's claims.

When I agreed with this client's understandings that the justice system was oppressive, that social workers did not understand clients' lives, and that a social work focus on client change was inadequate, my supervisor responded that I was mistaken and that I was not being properly professional. By accepting the cogency of a client's story, I was acknowledging a heresy within a professional discourse, namely the possibility that neither social workers nor their agencies help clients. Surely, the client must be mistaken.

Despite the conflicts and difficulties I faced in becoming a social worker, once hired I was compelled to enter and sort through the lives of my clients, as if I were an expert, as if my knowledge was better than the clients', as if I were in control, and as if I had the power to determine events in clients' lives. I had to produce stories about their situations that would be visible as professionally sensible, cogent, and proper. To have professional credibility, my stories had to endure against the opposition of client stories, the critical scrutiny of other professionals, and the legal review of lawyers and judges in court. My responsibility to produce authoritative accounts of other people's lives placed me in what felt like an alien position of power. I did not have to manage such power when I was a grocery clerk, a construction worker, a cook, or even a psychiatric aide. As a member of the working class, I had to listen to those in authority and act according to their dictates and scripts, such as the customer is always right, smile when greeting a customer, and always appear helpful.

I had to learn how to manage institutionalized power in my work with others. Not only did I have the power to create accounts that transcended the clients' but I had, by virtue of my professional membership and employment status as a social worker, the power to intervene in their lives. I could apprehend their children, require that they seek alcohol treatment, refer them to a detoxification program, or even seek a permanent custody order for their children.

When I exercised mandated power as a social worker in a child protection organization, the courses of action I pursued often brought me into direct conflict with clients. As a professional social worker, I knew how to manage such conflicts by invoking professional schemata that either discounted or undermined the credibility of clients' stories. I could discount clients' stories by bringing into question their self-serving motives or their limited understandings of processes and dynamics. I could explain away their explanations as rationalizations, denial, resistance, and projection. I could discount clients' stories by attacking their knowledge as unsystematic, illogical, situated, biased, incomplete, and self-interested. I could claim that my own knowledge, which I had culled from texts, assembled as theory, and expressed as facts, was superior to theirs.

GROUNDING PROFESSIONAL PRACTICE

Certainly, I was not alone in my discomfort with social work. Radical, socialist, and Marxist social workers have long complained about both the ways that social workers identify social problems and the social work interventions that follow. For radical, socialist, and Marxist social workers, the categories and forms of mainstream social work practice are part of an ideology that functions to advance control and legitimation of the capitalist state (Carniol, 1992; Mullaly and Keating, 1991; Banton, Clifford, Frosh, Lousada and Rosenthall, 1985; Bolger, Corrigan, Docking, and Frost, 1981; Gough, 1979). The left critique has tended to focus on the institutional base or organizational structures of social work practice and its connection to capitalist production. This book, although clearly located within a left critique, shifts our focus away from pre-given, existent, or ontological structures. Instead, I focus on day-to-day and practical activities that social workers engage in, as the stuff that creates patterns and forms and action and organization that we call structure. Structures must be explicated as practical accomplishment. This requires examining not only what Garfinkel, Lynch, and Livingston have called the 'in situ apt and familiar efficacy of the day's work' (1981: 133),[3] but the ground or social relations in which social workers' practices are embedded.

Such an approach seeks to transform structure. Structure is no longer treated as a thing, an external entity, or a dense block awaiting penetration by the analyst. Instead, structure becomes visible as a two-fold problem, located in differential moments or rhythms of actual practice. First, structure emerges through actual people's day-to-day and coordinated activities, hence, as tangible detritus or artefacts of practice, that is, primarily as courses of action, both completed and ongoing, and as textual productions. Second, as artefacts of practice, practitioners 'read' structures to shape their ongoing day-to-day practices. Simply put, what people do is oriented to the legacy of past practices and anticipated future outcomes dictated and conditioned by those practices. Structure is that which people, thousands of people, struggle to produce, and reproduce, as they work day after day. Structure is the reification of these activities which they come to call the Ministry of Corrections, the Children's Aid, the Children's Hospital, or the Department of Indian Affairs.

PROFESSIONAL LOCATIONS

The structures identified as central to the profession of social work – skills, knowledge, and values – are themselves artefacts of coordinated work processes. What the profession is, hence, its 'quiddity,' grows out of members' situated and practical work, and from the professional legacy as texts, mores, practices, and culture that structure the work which produces it. As ethnomethodologists might say, social work is created through the reflexivity of social workers' practices.

When I, Gerald de Montigny, arrive at the doorstep and enter a client's apartment, what I see and what I understand to be the conditions of the situation at hand are reported in log notes and running records as what any competent social worker would see and understand. My accounts rely upon a professional and an organizational topography that I and other members inhabit together. We use this topography, orient to its features – understandings, categories, sensible landmarks – to move about and to replicatively find our ways. Inhabiting a professional standpoint presupposes being able to find one's way across a social landscape employing maps generated within a professional discourse.

The concept of the profession itself provides tools for effecting control over a messy and often equivocal lived world, as its discourse is framed by issues of control, management, deliberate action, and planned outcomes. The concept profession must be addressed in a two-fold manner. First, the concept 'the profession of social work'[4] is itself understood as embedded in social relations 'which it names without explicating' (Walker, 1986: 36). Second, by constructing the concept of the social work profession, those who are social workers create discursively organized boundaries for accounts: Is this moment of practice properly social work or is it something else? This has the effect of rendering discrete and in situ practices visible for social workers and others as exemplars of professional work. Social workers' talk about the profession both operates as a piece of organizational work processes and constructs the coherence, visibility, and warrant of activities as professional work performed on behalf of the organization.

PROFESSIONALS VS BUREAUCRATS?

While social workers must manage their work professionally, they must also manage the work of the organizations that employ them. Where I worked, what counted as good professional child protection work generally counted as good organizational work. As front-line workers, we struggled to manage both professional and organizational imperatives. Generally we were successful. Most of us felt that organizational policies and protocols could be reframed positively. For example, even a policy that excluded 'single-parent mothers' from the 'unemployable' category – in effect reducing their welfare benefits – could be professionally justified as preventing 'dependency,' promoting greater 'responsibility,' and providing an incentive for 'self-determination.' Even workers who were unable or unwilling to reframe such policies in a positive way or to imagine some good resulting from a policy were usually able to continue working for the organization by partializing the policy as just 'one piece,' albeit negative, of their work. They could argue that the need to provide good professional social work outweighed the limits imposed by 'a few bad policies.'

When tensions and strains between social workers and their organizations regularly arose, these were usually managed through the use of a repertoire of professional justifications.[5] For example, during a time of service cuts I heard front-line social workers argue, 'Although I still believe in the principles of the profession, at this time some compromise is needed.' 'I will continue to provide the best service possible given present conditions.' 'When times are better we will try to have services restored.' Similarly social workers acting as administrators justified cuts by arguing, 'We are attempting to foster greater self-determination and independence among our clients.' 'Due to funding cuts, and to maintain overall levels of service, it was necessary to eliminate this special program.' Such justifications demonstrate that neither front-line workers nor administrators need eschew the profession to defend their agencies, nor do they need to attack their agencies to be professional. The subtleties and flexibility of professional discourse provide workers with sufficient tools to resolve working problems.

Clearly, front-line practitioners are not only professional social workers; they are employees working for agencies and organizations. As employees they are bound to carry out the legislative mandates, policies, and directives of their organizations. It is this location as organizational employees that has alarmed social work scholars, both on the left and right, and which has led to invoking the problematic of 'bureaucracy.' Traditionally, social work academics on the left and on the right have understood that there is an inherent conflict in this dual location and dual loyalty to the profession and to the organization (Mullaly, 1993: 193; Lipsky, 1980: 201). They have warned against the danger that workers may become bureaucrats, even 'stinking bureaucrats' (Carniol, 1990: 102) rather than acting as proper professionals. In these characterizations of a professional-organizational tension the location of professional practice within bureaucracy is itself understood as problematic. For example, Zastrow states: 'There are basic structural conflicts between helping professionals and the bureaucratic systems in which they work. Helping professionals place a high value on creativeness and changing the system to serve clients. Bureaucracies resist change and are most efficient when no one is "rocking the boat." Helping professionals seek to personalize services by conveying to each client that "you count as a person." Bureaucracies are highly depersonalized, emotionally detached systems which view every employee and every client as being a tiny component of a large system' (Zastrow, 1985: 288). In this version of opposition, the goals[6] of the profession and the goals of the bureaucracies are portrayed as though they were in conflict (Johnson, 1986: 240; Rai, 1983: 55; Dolgoff, 1981: 292; Howe, 1980: 182).

Such construction of opposition between professionals and bureaucracy is extremely functional for managing day-to-day conflicts and tensions in the field. By identifying bureaucrats and the bureaucratic standpoint as depersonalized, impersonal, uncaring, cold, and inflexible, and therefore as antithetical to good social work, front-line social workers are able to construct their own place of independence within the agency. This place is not just defined in opposition to bureaucracy. It is also defined positively as caring, humanizing, warm, personal, empathetic, compassionate, flexible, and enlightened. These positive values, codified as the values of the profession, become a source of empowerment. Borrowing Woolgar and Pawluch's analysis of 'ethnography of argument,' the assumption of separation between the profession and bureaucracy is best understood as an instance of 'boundary work' (1985: 216) that provides distinctions for evaluating moments of practice as properly professional or properly organizational. By constructing the boundaries of the professional, social workers can proclaim their moral superiority, correctness, and goodness. From a strong personal identification with the positive features of the profession, social workers construct an *esprit de corps*.

This sense of belonging and mission is strengthened by occasional adversity, objectionable administrative policies, and the rigors of the work. Success in the face of adversity confirms the moral superiority of professional practice over and against the bureaucracy. Social workers' claims to professional values, skills, and knowledge become symbols and ideals guiding their practice. Guided by a morally superior set of values, social workers argue for agencies that are more compassionate, policies that are more flexible, relations that are more empathetic, and programs that enhance self-determination.

Even scholars who understand that there is an interdependence of professional and bureaucratic forms present this relation as inherently oppositional and as a problem requiring professional resolution. Thus, Compton and Galaway state, 'Social work has been a bureaucratic profession from its very beginning, and social workers employed in agencies are not only professionals but bureaucrats. Thus, while social work has struggled to synthesize bureaucratic and professional norms, it has not always recognized that a profession and a bureaucracy possess a number of norms that are opposed in principle' (1984: 182).

I argue that this presentation of opposition is too simplistic. Rather, the ideology of the profession provides a set of conceptual tools for organizing practice and for managing a situated work process. The art of producing a professional identity allows a person to insert himself or herself into discursively organized and warranted relations of power and authority. Professional values and ethics are invoked to resolve dilemmas and conflicts arising through organizational work. As Larson argues, the moral claims to provide professional service must be understood as located in the tacit separation between professionals who have a 'monopoly of training' and the rest of the population who become 'market consumers' of social work practice (Larson, 1977: 223). Second, social workers' claims that people need help that is caring, enhances self-determination, empowers, and builds mutual respect, becomes an argument for demanding expansion of services and social work practice. The professional morality that calls on social workers to help, nurture, and even empower, provides them with a powerful sense of self-justification and mission.

This sense of self-justification and mission is carried over into the managerial structures of social services agencies and organizations as senior social workers often assume administrative positions. As supervisors of other social workers, they must develop policies that can be justified as congruent with 'the social work profession.' By cuing their policies to professional discourse, social work administrators struggle to create the organization as committed to professional principles of service, helping, and caring. To ensure that policies are adhered to and carried out by front-line workers, administrators match the language of policy to the language of professional concerns. For instance, home visits to welfare recipients, although implemented to curb welfare fraud, can be positively reframed as providing a means for building closer relations between social workers and their clients. Like front-line social workers, most social work administrators selectively use knowledge, gained through their own formal education, to justify their policies and actions.

From the standpoint of clients, however, there is often little question that social workers are bureaucrats. Indeed, even front-line social workers experience the tension between their lived encounters with clients in day-to-day work and the pressing necessity of assuming bureaucratic forms of action (Leonard, 1990: 22). Similarly, as a social worker dispensing social services, including social assistance (welfare), I too have acted as a bureaucrat. The never-ending grind of the work, the line of clients progressing through my office, the evening call-out, and the trauma of crisis situations demanded that I buffer myself from clients' lives. Under such circumstances, survival required regular retreat into the cold comfort and distance afforded by the bureaucratic space. As a skilled professional I was able to manage my place in the bureaucratic space such that clients would not see me as a bureaucrat. As a social worker I was always able to avoid the shouting matches and arguments that frequently erupted between semiskilled financial assistance workers and clients. As a professional, I used my skills to communicate warmth, genuineness, and concern to clients even when I had to apprehend their children. By reassuring a client that I really would like to help, that I would see what I could do, that I wish it were different, I involved the clients in the difficulties of my job (Lipsky, 1980: 64) and thereby elicited their support and sympathy. Professional training enabled me to transform cold procedures, such as completing an agency form into an occasion for communicating genuineness, concern, empathy, caring, and helping. When I told a client, 'I'm sorry, policy does not allow me to provide services to you,' I was able to use my knowledge of other resources to refer the client to another agency that might help. Once an employed man came to our office for financial assistance to send his wife to a distant urban centre for dialysis. Because he was employed and 'earned too much money,' he was ineligible for our services. As a professional, I gave him moral support, encouraged his efforts, and advised that he approach a service club, such as the Lions, who took an interest in helping people in need of medical treatment. As a professional, I was expected to use my skills to help clients re-channel and redirect their frustrations and anger into constructive change.[7]

Professional training allowed for a managed integration of personal characteristics with a professional identity. Professional training provided me with an alternative mask. As a professional, I knew better than to appear as a cold impersonal bureaucrat, even when I retreated into the bureaucratic space. I learned how to use my warmth, humour, empathy, and understanding to administer distant bureaucratic policies. Through professional training, I had learned how to manufacture a professional self that would be congruent with a personal self. Through professional training, I became visible to myself as reflexively construed to match the general expectations of a good social worker. What I understood myself to be – that is, my feelings, thoughts, and actions – I discovered to be congruent with the profession.

Social workers take up the professional–bureaucratic opposition to bind their practice to the organization. For example, a group of dissatisfied social workers may organize a meeting with an administrator to discuss problems with a new adoption policy. As a result of the meeting, differences are aired, each side hears the other, problems are identified, a common commitment to service is reaffirmed, a compromise is reached, social workers are given broader parameters for interpretation, ambiguities are eliminated, and policy is changed. Through such procedures, working problems are continually identified, addressed, and resolved. Social workers by constructing their opposition to bureaucracy, which they characterize as insensitive, cold, impersonal, and so forth, are able to develop positively framed practices. When social workers extol the virtues of their profession while lamenting their place within a bureaucracy, they simultaneously generate strategies that affirm their ability to act like professionals and carry out the organizational work.

By placing their faith in professional practice, social workers sustain the ideals of the profession: 'If only I had more time to do therapy, I could have helped Mr B.' 'Although, people waiting for U.I. are no longer eligible for assistance, I can at least help them connect to other resources.' 'It is difficult to be genuine and empathetic when you have thirty different people pass through your office in a day.' By reframing conflicts inherent in the work which manages, controls and orders the lives of working people, professional social workers can avoid critical analysis and radical action. Their complaints against the bureaucracy buttress and support their ability to continue working within their agencies and organizations. Such complaints can redirect anger and critical activity into organizationally situated and organizationally constructive problem-solving practice.

PRODUCING SUITABLE EMPLOYEES

Professional education and work within a bureaucracy are practically linked through the real movement of living people. Actual individuals proceed through the schools of social work and later into state organizations and agencies. These individual and apparently idiosyncratic movements through universities into social service organizations produce the appearance of discrete social spheres independent of each other. However, it is living people's practical activities that integrate front-line social work, academic work, and administration into the matrices of an institutional apparatus. Through their lived and embodied activities, people concretely tie social work education to the work of the organizations and agencies of a welfare state. For the graduate with a BSW or MSW the prospect of going to work for a governmental social service department or private agency denotes arrival at a critical junction along a professionally constructed career path. If successful and offered a job, the graduate may enter an organization where she can work to build an imagined successful future. As days become years on the job, she builds a reputation of competence, trustworthiness, and respect among colleagues and supervisors. As the years pass, she gains a sense of personal competence and accomplishment. But, before any of these imaginings become a reality, she must first get a job. The student's plans and hopes are chimerae until a job is found. The new graduate, although trained in a school of social work as a generalist practitioner, cannot properly assume her place in a community as a professional until she is hired by a social service agency or organization.

Being employed as a professional, although based on a wage relation shared by other workers, presents several unique features that do not exist for non-professional employees. To unfold these differences, I return to my own experience as a working class teenager employed by Canada Safeway as a grocery clerk. My job was quite simply to carry out the orders of those who had more authority than I. If I was directed to bag groceries, I bagged groceries. If I was directed to stock shelves, I stocked shelves. If I was told to 'take this lady's groceries to her car,' I took her groceries to her car. My store manager expected that I would come to work dressed in dark pants, white shirt, and black bow-tie. He expected that I would work with enthusiasm and energy, that I would be obedient and carry out orders, and that I would be courteous and helpful to customers. Beyond such superficial expectations, the only skills and attitudes I was expected to possess were those that store managers and administrators consider to be part of the realm of common sense. I was expected to have a nice smile for customers, a pleasant tone of voice, self-discipline and a liking for hard work.

As a grocery clerk, I was not bound to any specific code of conduct, nor was I expected to act like a manager in my work. I was not expected to make decisions, but to carry out orders. I was not responsible for managing the store, for increasing profit margins, for increasing volume of sales, or for organizing employee work routines. When I performed specific tasks, like bagging groceries, stocking shelves, or washing out the garbage room, I experienced in a clear and direct sense that these tasks were ordered, planned, and directed by others. Even as I performed the work with greater skill over time and took a certain pride in my skills, so long as supervisors considered that my work was acceptable, I did not have to justify or explain what I did. I did not have to believe in my work, I just had to do it.

As a clerk, I often engaged in repetitive, boring, detailed, and physically exhausting labour. To cope, I produced a fundamental mind–body split in which there was the work to be done by my body and then there was me, who could think, fantasize, daydream, and pursue ribald anti-authoritarian antics with co-workers.[8] I maintained a basic separation between a me who was alive, active, and independent, and the clerk. It was the clerk who listened to orders, maintained an attitude of deference to authority, and did as he was told. Through this split I systematically distanced myself from the work; it was the company's work not my work.

My work as a social worker, however, was quite different from my work as a clerk. As a beginning social worker, I felt uneasy. I recognized that I was expected to act 'like a manager.' I was expected to have a plan. I was to be purposive and clear-headed. Yet, I remained me. I worried about my forgetfulness, lack of confidence, disorganization, and tenuous grasp of reality. However, despite these insecurities, I was expected to be in control. My caseload was to be under control. If things went wrong in the lives of my clients, I felt responsible. As a social worker, I was expected to have clear intervention goals for my cases, to keep my records up to date, to carry out the required number of contacts, and to work to improve the lives of clients. In a curious way, how I was expected to act as a professional was what I had associated with company 'sucks,' 'brown-nosers,' and scabs.

As a social worker, I was expected to not only perform, but to believe in the good sense, cogency, and legitimacy of my work. As a social worker, I was required to believe in the values of the profession or at least to avoid creating a visible separation between my professional self and my 'real' self. I was expected to adhere to a code of personal conduct both when I was at work and when I was off work. Though I was expected to perform work directed by others, I was expected to perform as though I, too, believed in the good sense and warrant of the work. I had to act as if the managerial standpoint that had informed policy was my own. I had to appear to my colleagues and supervisors to be yet another controlled, self-administered, objective, and impartial professional who would preserve the values of the profession.

In my daily work as a social worker, I was not merely doing work for another, instead, I had become another for myself. As a professional other, I displayed my belief in the propriety of this self-alienated professional form of being. I felt unable to challenge openly this self-alienation because the challenge would have been heard by supervisors as expressing my unwillingness to act professionally. If I would have admitted to my poor memory (forgetting appointments, failing to complete forms on time), my disorganization (misplacing files, losing records, double-booking appointments), or my bad attitude (disliking what I saw as the obvious middle class attitudes of co-workers), I would have risked being labelled a poor worker. As a result, I continually struggled to cover up my incompetencies and to construct a facade of professional competence.

Even within a social service office, the work of social workers and clerical staff are quite different. Social workers and clerical staff engage in separate, though related, tasks in an office division of labour that produces the records necessary for effecting a documentary reality. Social workers and clerks enter into fundamentally different relations regarding the document or thing itself.

The office clerk, through her contribution to the document, alienates her labour. The social worker alienates the realities of her very being in the world. For a social worker, the document emerges as the constitutive reality for expressing her organizationally embedded practice. The document signifies the appropriation and reinterpretation of the social worker's situated and embodied activities into a form where these activities become visible as the work of the organization.

Whereas the social worker is responsible for the activities that the document reports, the office clerk is responsible only for the general physical form of the document – the accuracy of the transcript, proper layout, and prompt production. For the clerk, the document is merely a thing in and of itself. Just as I chose to understand that my work as a grocery clerk was alien and distinct from my 'real' self, so too can an office clerk. She may disagree entirely with the assessment of the social worker in the report. She may think that social workers are bleeding-heart liberals. She may even believe that the client does not deserve the service. But the only thing that matters organizationally is that she type the report accurately and quickly.

The contribution of the social worker to the document is of a different order. She produces the document by submitting a handwritten draft of the document with appropriate sections marked and filled in.

It is the social worker who produces the story the document tells, and this is the point of fundamental difference between her position and that of the clerk. The story the document tells is about the social worker's own activities performed somewhere else at another time, worked up to display her competent performance. Thus, she produces the document as that which tells what she has done as a professionally ordered account, located within the professional discourse. Through the textually mediated practices of documentary production, social workers display that they are 'proper' professionals. Their reports match their activities to courses of action using relevant concepts and categories.

Social workers assume ownership of and responsibility for their documents, but they do not own these documents as such. Rather, they own the documentary productions only by virtue of being professional. Although the documents belong to the organization, social workers, as agents of the organization, claim the documents as a sign or display of their professional work. Thus in a court a judge might ask: 'Is the social worker who wrote this assessment here in court today? Would she please take the stand?' This institutionally mediated form of ownership requires that those who occupy professional positions construct action as performed for an employer. They are required and will be held accountable to show the congruence between their acts, the profession, and the organization.[9]

As the office clerk alienates her labour, she is silenced; without a voice. The words in the report are not her words. This is not her report. These people are not her clients. As a clerk, she is merely a skilled set of hands, a filer, an operative whose thoughts and feelings are irrelevant to the work at hand. However, as the social worker alienates *her* labour, and alienates *her* being in the world, she acquires a voice and a being in the world, albeit an institutional and professionally mediated voice and being. This institutional voice and being, though alienated, provides social workers with authority and power that is denied to the clerk. As a professional, the social worker is entitled to tell the stories of her work, display her expertise and wisdom, and claim a place of power within the organization. She has the power and the authority to tell and to appropriate stories as parts of her daily work, her professional wisdom, and her professional growth and development. Only so long as the social worker performs within accepted professional discourse can her speech and actions have professional authority and warrant. If she acts otherwise, her words and actions become visible as idiosyncratic, opinion, conjecture, and bias, and she leaves her place of power and warrant within the profession. She joins the place of powerlessness and vulnerability inhabited by clients and office workers.

BEING A PROFESSIONAL

Being hired as a social worker means 'being a social worker.' Being a social worker is far more inclusive than merely doing social work from 8:30 to 5:30. Being a social worker means performing (Goffman, 1959)[10] as a social worker in the multiple dimensions of one's life. Being a professional requires adopting what Goffman has called a 'rhetoric of training' that marks off the professional as different from the common person. As Goffman says, 'the licensed practitioner is someone who has been reconstituted by his learning experience and is now set apart from other men' (ibid.: 46). To be reconstituted is to be changed into something other than what one was. The proper accomplishment of self as a professional social worker means that those who become social workers have learned how to order and manage their lives. They engage in 'impression management' (Ferguson, 1984: 105), particularly concerning those aspects of themselves which are visible to others, that is, dress, attitude, vocabulary, talk, and record keeping.

Being professional requires social workers to be active within their communities in determinate ways. Social workers demonstrate a commitment to community and a desire to serve by sitting on community boards, leading youth groups, and doing other forms of volunteer work. They construct respectability by trying to conduct personal affairs in an exemplary manner. They try to avoid controversial or untoward actions that might bring opprobrium, such as binge drinking, psychiatric hospitalization, and criminal charges. Being a professional social worker requires not merely the production of oneself but one's family and those in one's life as displaying the proper class standpoint expected of professionals.

It becomes a matter for remark should a social worker be having difficulty with her marriage, a problem with alcohol, sexual relations with clients, a teenage son in jail, or problems managing personal finances. Gossip and other tactics that signify disapproval are used to define the appropriate boundaries of professional behaviour and personal life. Social workers who transgress these boundaries bring their credibility, reputation, and professionalism into question. Co-workers may ignore them, their problems may become the topics of vicious gossip – usually invoked as a discrediting tactic. They may be responded to with condescension, advice giving, or they may even face hostile challenge. Mike Simpkin, in *Trapped within Welfare*, outlines the fate of a colleague who had suffered an admission to a 'mental hospital for agitated depression': 'The misfortune she had suffered was considered to transcend the boundaries of normality. While we were busy persuading our clients that nothing was as bad as it seemed, we were expected to apply a completely different standard to our colleague. By crossing the divide which separated us, she had placed her status in question, deserving no doubt our compassion and understanding, but apparently forfeiting our respect' (1983: 2). Being a social worker is not just a job. It is a way of life.

PROFESSIONALS OR WORKERS?

Understandings of social work produced by scholars have tended to cluster around two opposing positions. First, the liberals in the main-stream understand that being hired is a private relation between an individual professional and an employer. Mainstream scholars advo-cate that workers pursue a professional standpoint to solve the prob-lems of daily work. They promote membership in professional associ-ations, call for professionally regulated registration of social workers, and insist that professional rather than administrative concerns must guide policies and practice (Zastrow, 1985; Compton and Galaway, 1984; Howe, 1980; Siporin 1975; Wasserman, 1971). More leftist authors argue that, although social workers may not yet be properly classified as working class, the changes in the organization of the social welfare state brought about by the election of right-wing gov-ernments are fast reducing social workers to the status of working people (Bolger, Corrigan, Docking, and Frost, 1981: 22; Gough, 1979: 142; LEWRG, 1979:7).[11] They argue that social workers must recog-nize their affinity to workers and join trade unions, become involved in labour struggles, join local political organizations, and support the political struggles of the oppressed (Mullaly and Keating, 1991).

Both the arguments from the right and from the left are inade-quate. First, both arguments fail to address the social implications of becoming a social worker and the implicit entry into social relations of power and inequality occasioned by professional membership. The

right, by focusing on the employment relation as a private transaction between an individual professional and an agency, conceals the
distinct class position social workers assume by virtue of becoming
and being professionals (Simpkin, 1983: 125). The left, by focusing on
the employment relation, as a wage relation fails to recognize the
broader entry of those who become social workers into organizational
forms of life. Being a social worker enters the practitioner into a
series of social positions that involve far more than merely an individual or private relation of exchange. Second, the generalized abilities of those who become social workers to ideologically produce the
social work profession and the terrain of social problems addressed
by their profession establish social workers' collective claims for
certain types of work. The result, as Johnson observes, is that 'a
profession is not an occupation but a means of controlling an occupation' (1972: 45). This observation undercuts both the liberal understandings of the private character of the employer–employee relation
and the leftist arguments that gloss the distinctive professional
character of social work.

Proponents of the thesis that social workers are workers (Bolger et
al. 1981) document several important changes in the organization of
social work production, most notably the process of increasing centralized management control over policy formation and systematic
deskilling of social work tasks (Tudiver, 1979; de Montigny, 1980).
Yet this documented process of change does not mean that social
workers are becoming simply wage labourers; rather, it means that
the social organization of the profession is changing. Social work
continues to be front-line ideological work. Social workers rework
material that they extract from people's lives to fit the concerns of an
institutional reality. Through ideological practice, social workers,
enter and enact an institutional consciousness.

Despite the common link provided by the wage form, professional
employment must not be collapsed into non-professional employment.
For social workers, the wage relation designates much more than
merely an exchange of labour power for money. Indeed, the designa-
tion of the exchange between employer and social worker as a salary
identifies a privileged relation founded on mandated responsibility to
carry out the work. The salary is not just a pay packet, but a relation
of 'symbolic exchange' (Baudrillard, 1975) founded on a relationship
of trust, the granting of authority, and supervisory capacities. The
salary signifies the accomplishment of self as a professional. It sig-

nifies membership of the person as social worker, as a graduate of a particular school of social work, the holder of a BSW or MSW degree.

Being hired and receiving a salary supports the social worker's ability to sustain her position within a world marked by class divisions and separations between employed and unemployed, productive and unproductive, valued and devalued peoples. The steady income provided by the salary provides the worker with a means to be in control of her life, to manage her affairs, and to work towards a future. Being employed as a professional provides a point of entry to meet a community of other professionals, to build friendships, to live in particular neighbourhoods, to develop orderly daily routines, and to participate in community groups and events.

Social workers' position of power derives from the organization of inequality basic to capitalist society. This inequality is expressed and affirmed through professional salaries. In contemporary society, social workers' salaries, like the salaries of other professionals, provide for the performance of proper displays of class situation. Salaries provide for the enactment of the social codes of class separation. The salary allows social workers to build a particular lifestyle. The salary allows social workers to participate within the consumption rituals of a middle class. It provides a means for constructing and displaying the esthetic sensibilities of a member of the professional classes. The salary can be used to purchase the proper clothes, car, apartment or house (in the right neighbourhood), furniture, dinner ware, wine glasses, and other signs of a 'proper' lifestyle. The salary is used to purchase life experiences, hence, to partake of a lifestyle, which might include trips to foreign lands, season tickets to cultural events (the symphony, the ballet, an avant garde playhouse) or membership in clubs.

Although in a capitalist society social workers earn less and enjoy less status than doctors, lawyers, or psychologists, nevertheless, their salaries allow them to emulate, although seldom replicate, the lifestyles of their more affluent professional counterparts. They do exercise considerable institutionally mandated power. Their duties at work place them in a relation of trust as executors of a variety of legislative and policy mandates. It is precisely this relation of trust that requires purchase of their loyalty, fidelity, and allegiance to the profession and to their employers. In a sense, then, the professional's salary signifies a pact between the organization and the individual as a professional agent of the state apparatus.

By asserting that there is a difference between professional and regular employees, I am not arguing for the superiority of the former over the latter, nor do I want to justify the differences of power, status, and privilege that exist between the two types of workers. Although attempts to gloss or dismiss the 'real' differences between regular workers and professionals are often motivated by altruistic and egalitarian political concerns, any strategies for change built on imaginary or idealistic conditions must be doomed to failure. We witness this idealism in the work of Bolger's group. They analyse the effects of a social workers' strike as follows: 'This experience ... stripped away the veils of ideology around such things as 'professional autonomy.' It increased the welfare workers' perception of themselves as workers. It is a difficult and very tight dialectic that we are trying to explain here. First, we are stressing the objective process of proletarianization which turns people into pure members of the labour force ... Secondly, subjectively we are suggesting that this set of experiences has a direct impact upon worker's consciousness' (1981: 71–72). Despite the claim by Bolger et al. to use a tight dialectic, their work remains idealist. Social workers are not workers in the sense implied by Bolger. Indeed, social workers enter into the lives of working class people from a position of authority and power, and this expresses their situation within an institutional state apparatus for governing, ordering, controlling, and accounting for a social order. Social workers are inescapably bound to use ideological methods, to execute courses of action determined by organizations, to produce a professional self, and to act as agents of order. Social workers are intellectuals, in the sense developed by Gramsci (1971), as their work contributes to the ideological reproduction of the forms of order necessary for the continuation of established social relations.

4

Professional Discursive Powers

SEEKING SOCIAL WORK

What is the glue that ties a social worker's practice – whether performed in Vancouver, Winnipeg, Toronto, or Halifax – to social work in general? How is it that we can speak of 'doing social work?' What do we mean when we speak of social work? In the pages that follow, I move to examine the centrality of textual practices for producing a professional location. Textual practices carve out ideological spaces, domains, and symbolic terrains where social workers can generate a professional corpus, identity, and practice. Constructing the profession requires that members both return to a professional history embodied in a textual reality and reconstitute this history through their own textually mediated productions. In texts, whether journal articles, monographs, case reports, case assessments, or course papers, social workers both presume and constitute the ontology of the profession as a domain existing beyond their immediate mundane activities.

For people who call themselves social workers, the presumption of a corpus called social work, is cogent in itself. Thus, it is perfectly sensible for someone, upon being asked, 'What do you do?' to reply, 'Social work.' What this response glosses is the dense weave of socially organized and textually mediated practices that provide for the possibility of this answer. To reference one's being to the symbolic domain of 'the social work profession' is enter into a reification of actual practices. However, such reifications of the profession are an essential element to its constitution: 'Social work in Canada ... has had difficulty in establishing a definition of itself as a professional discipline' (Yelaja, 1985: 2); 'Social work believes that clients have the right to express their own opinions' (Zastrow, 1985: 38); 'Social work continues to search for the acceptance of common concepts and common frames of reference to test hypotheses' (Johnson, 1986: 5). The language of these texts quite simply represents the social work profession as an actor in its own right, and in this sense the profession is a fetish (Marx, 1887).

The fetishization of social work is revealed in the question: 'Is social work a profession?' (Bartlett, 1970: 19; Compton and Galaway, 1984: 33; Johnson, 1986: 23–4; Zastrow, 1985: 8–9). As mainstream texts address the problem of the social work profession, they tend to centre on two major themes. The first is that social work is not yet fully a profession, like law or medicine; the second is that a systematically developed base of abstract conceptual knowledge is needed if social work is to attain full professional status. This sense has lengthy roots, for example, Bartlett writing in 1970 states, 'While social work is generally regarded as having attained professional status, it cannot be regarded yet as a strong profession' (1970: 16). Appealing to authorities she outlines two essential attributes of a profession: '(1) a high degree of generalized and systematic knowledge and (2) orientation to the community interest rather than to individual self-interest (ibid.: 19). Bartlett's formulation continues to appeal to the common-sense experience of the bulk of social workers that they lack the status, prestige, wealth, and power that are granted to other more established professions, notably medicine and law. In this sense, social work is a weak profession. Rather than examining the history and social organization of social workers' situations compared with members of other professions, Bartlett focuses on the problem of developing a 'strong profession,' that is, the development of a systematic, generalized, and abstract 'knowledge base.' Through this invocation of abstract professional knowledge, Bartlett stakes out a terrain of scientific and research techniques (ibid.: 64) which is continued into the present day. Knowledge lifted from the anchors of daily life, practical existence, and experience is considered 'strong.'

The path that Bartlett followed to build a strong professional has become a well-trodden road. Louise Johnson spoke of social work as a 'fairly new' or 'young profession' and called for 'the development of a systematic knowledge base' (1986: 23). Zastrow, after noting that 'social work is a profession of relatively recent origin' (1985: 6), detailed the traditional social work triad: knowledge, skills, and values, and the need for their development. Yelaja asked, 'What, then, marks the distinction between a professional social worker and a concerned member of Canadian society?' He suggested, 'To answer this question, it is necessary to examine the concept of what a profession is' (Yelaja, 1985: 3).[1]

Finally, Compton and Galaway's classic text began by asking, 'What do social workers do? Where and how do they intervene?' (1984: 3). Although their questions raised the possibility of examining 'what (actual) social workers do' in their day-to-day work, this is not how Compton and Galaway chose to answer their question. Instead, they turned to the professional literature. They quoted William Schwartz's generalization (1961) that the social work job assignment is to 'mediate the process through which the individual and ... society reach out for each other' (ibid.). Later they quoted Martin Rein (1970), who believed that 'one of the obstacles to the development of a professional social work creed has been the difficulty in defining the social work profession' (Compton and Galaway, 1984: 4). This led them to examine the work of Werner Boehm, Harriet Bartlett, William Gordon, Alex Gitterman and Carol Germain and so they proceeded throughout the text. While posing the practical and potentially illuminating question, 'What do social workers do?' Compton and Galaway never examined actual work settings of types of social work as practiced by people in the field. Instead, they choose to explore the textual construction of the concepts of the profession.

All of the authors cited above understand that the concept of the profession is a sensible and warranted sphere of enquiry. They assume that there is a social work profession, out there, as a social fact. The form of the question (What do social workers do?) and their answers provide a window for observing how the discursive accounts about the profession are themselves an integral aspect of a professional work process.

DOCUMENTARY PRODUCTION OF PROFESSIONAL REALITY

Performing as a social worker, whether front line or academic, requires producing documents, such as reports to the court, running records, client assessments, journal articles, or monographs. Documents provide a medium for conceptual construction of the profession precisely because they provide a space for sedimented and apparently crystallized meanings. The transitory and elusive utterances of daily life become recoverable, as indices of professional talk within an ongoing hermeneutic of professional inscription (Smith, 1984; Green, 1983; Wheeler, 1976).

The accomplishment of a proper documentary construction and reading is always a 'social occasion' (McHoul, 1982: 4). Documents produced and read professionally become the material from which stories are constructed about which members can agree. The capacity of documents to appear as impersonal and objective makes them extremely effective conveyers of professional power and authority. Textual work, like a galvanizing process, provides social workers with a series of solution(s) into which cases can be dipped. Textual solution(s) transform the rusted, ugly, and unattractive debris of daily life into chromed, gilded, and artful professional creations.

Text also displaces the interactive focus from the storyteller and listener. It obliterates the listener's attention to the voice here and now. It transforms the listener into a reader who engages in the apparently solitary act of recovering a meaning from the words on a page. Furthermore, the isomorphism of the text as a thing in hand, which in its appearance claims identity with the copy in the hands of another, implies a singularity of recoverable meaning. The voice of the storyteller becomes the voice of the text. The text tells the story. The concreteness of a text–a book, or journal taken from a shelf by a hand and read individually–separates that which is said from the person who said or wrote it.

The text is a mask, concealing the embodied speaker who utters this or that claim. Through the text, social workers can promote their claims as though these were the universal wisdom of the profession in general. Thus, Bartlett (1970), Siporin (1975), Pincus and Minahan (1973), and others do not define what counts as social work. Rather, as experts they merely report in an objective and scientific fashion what they have discovered, and of course what they have discovered is what any reasonably competent member of the profession could discover social work to be. They are merely reporting the facts of the matter.

By entering their activities into a professional discourse, social workers legitimize their work. The legitimizing character of professional accounts is revealed in Siporin's discussion of the profession: 'Social Workers are professional helpers designated by society to aid people who are distressed, disadvantaged, disabled, defeated, or dependent. They also are needed to help people lessen their chances of being poor, inept, neglected, abused, divorced, delinquent, criminal, alienated or mad' (Siporin, 1975: 4). This story of social workers' activities is ordered by a warranted set of abstractions – for example, as designated by society, as helping, as aiding, and so forth. Such accounts affirm the goodness, propriety, and warrant of social work. Conflicts between social workers and clients, whether occurring over battles for children, entitlement to services or benefits, or enforcement of legal orders, can be reframed as painful but necessary moments of professional helping.

By invoking the legitimacy provided by extra-local forms of action, such as investigations, warrants, arrests, legal obligation – social workers gloss the coercive character of their day-to-day practices. The language social workers use allows them to appear neutral – for example, 'client systems are linked to resource systems' (Pincus and Minahan, 1973: 18) – even when what they mean is that people are locked up in prisons, confined to mental hospitals, forced onto welfare, and compelled to deal with Children's Aid Societies. Social workers remain 'neutral' as they revoke a client's parole, apprehend children, assess involuntary psychiatric patients, classify or counsel prison inmates, and deny social assistance. Social workers know both through the texts and through their situation within organizations that as professionals they have been 'designated by society' to carry out necessary work. Social workers know that, as professionals, they do not operate on behalf of any specific interest group or specific class. Rather, their practice is informed by professional knowledge, values, and skills (Bartlett, 1970).

TEXTUAL WORK AND DISCOURSE

A central piece of my education in social work, and that of my colleagues, was our exposure, through our classroom lectures, readings, and participation in fieldwork, to texts that addressed the issues, topics, concerns, and boundaries of the profession. Our discussions, writings, and reflections constituted practical experimentation with professional categories, theories, and frames. As students, we engaged in ongoing experimentation or playing to see and think through the situations at hand as we imagined idealized professional social workers would.[2] The work assigned in field placements, the supervision developed to monitor our progress, and the demand to produce written assignments were designed to ensure that we refined our ability to interpolate our activities into a professional horizon.

To gain social work skills for producing proper accounts, we attended lectures, discussed cases, read texts and journals, wrote papers, filed reports, and built collegial relations with fellow students, faculty, and social workers in field settings. In our day-to-day schoolwork our activities revolved around documents; both those produced by others and those which we produced. Passing in the school required that we prove that we were able to integrate the ensemble of understandings, frames, and common sense, which I have called professional discourse, into our verbal and documentary productions.

To produce competently crafted professional documents we engaged in dialogue with texts, periodicals, policy manuals, and legislation. We displayed our dialogue with the texts through citations, references, quotations, and adoption of themes and problematics. We constructed documents that conformed to the established protocols of academic production. Our documents displayed social work theorizing, employed specialized (impersonal) grammar, focused on social work topics, and provided appropriate bibliographic citations. Over time, we mastered practices for situating our lives, our work, our thinking, and ourselves inside a professional reality.

In field placements, our experiences became data to be inserted into, ordered, and accounted for through textual productions. A drive to an apartment building and a meeting with a woman and her child became a home visit. Details from the home visit were entered into the agency record as proof of service. The entry in the running record became part of the case file, and so on. Through process recordings, journals, reports, and files, we made our practice visible for supervisors.[3] Our progress, our commitment, skill, facility with theory, problem-solving abilities, and intervention skills were monitored through textual productions.

As student social workers, we soon learned that not only were the lives of clients subject to the terms of professional sense, but so too were our own lives. Our experiences, our history, our emotions, our very selves became material to be entered and worked up inside the frames of an extended professional discourse.[4] By participating in professional discourse, we became its objects. We were defined in its terms. Once entered into the social relations of professional discourse, we became social work practitioners, action systems, participants in societal resource systems, problem solvers, intervenors with client systems, and identifiers of 'target systems' (Pincus and Minahan, 1973). Our accounts constructed an abstracted place in the profession as a universal (non-indexical) standpoint within the generalized forms of an institutional reality.

The messy day-to-day work at hand was systematically taken up through the categories and frames of proper social work, that is, through systems theory, the ecological approach, network analysis, family theories, and personality theories. To use Piagetian language, we were like children who 'assimilated' a professional reality by playing at being social workers. We toyed with the theories, models, and frames we encountered in the literature as descriptors of our own lives. Even the ordinary event of suffering a headache – perhaps experienced after a lecture on systems theory – could be (playfully) understood as a manifestation of 'system disequilibrium.' We learned to make sense of our own fatigue at the end of the day not as a result of our concrete life situations – such as a 6:00 a.m. alarm, a mis-placed pair of pants, a long drive through traffic, a stream of clients through our office, the frustrations of attempting to manage an un-manageable case – but as expressing 'the second law of thermo-dynamics' or the 'principle of entropy.'[5] We were systems that had 'run out of energy.'

Professional sense precluded using natural language to talk about or explain the mundane organization of our lives. Both my own and clients' common-sense stock of understandings about our lives were understood as anecdotal, unsystematic, and contaminated. To sustain our place as social workers in professional discourse, we produced ideological accounts of our own and other people's life situations. Matters at hand provided particulars that we matched to conceptual frames, theories, and models. Our challenge was to make over lived realities; both our own and the clients.'

Occasionally problems arose that we could not adequately think through and resolve in a proper professional manner. These were the times when we recognized our lack of experience in an area, our lack of knowledge, or our biases and prejudices (for example, dealing with sexual abusers). When faced with a tough problem, we might turn initially to our professional colleagues in the hope that they might suggest an answer or that through discussion we might better grasp the problem. Although this first step often proved to be successful, there were times when our colleagues were not familiar with a problem or when we felt uncomfortable about asking them; then we might turn to the literature. Even then, we might not find articles or texts written on the matter. For example, in the 1970s when social workers first began to identify 'sexual abuse cases,' very little literature was available to sort it through. Workers were left without clear direction. Should the child be believed? Was the child's story merely a manifestation of an Oedipal fantasy? Should the child be left in the home? Should the matter be addressed openly or would this only further traumatize the child? In the ensuing decade social workers staked out a territory, pushed back the lacunae, and dispelled ambiguity, to develop a series of professionally acceptable responses. They have established a domain of understandings and practices that are laid out in an impressive literature on the problems of sexual abuse, incest, and family violence. Through the development of a literature that presents opposing positions and arguments on problems, questions which plague practitioners are answered and universal standards and protocols are established for managing cases.

By routinely turning to the legislation, policy manuals, journals, monographs, and other texts, social workers reveal their commitment to learning and to improving their practice in specific problem areas, for example, sexual abuse, domestic violence, or alcoholism. Indeed, it is a claim of pride that 'whenever I have a problem case I turn to the journals or go to the library.' Social workers depend on texts to serve as sources of information and guides for practice. The value of turning to texts for ongoing professional development is repeatedly affirmed by social work educators, directors, and supervisors. During our case conferences and supervision meetings, we were repeatedly urged by our district supervisor to 'keep up with the literature' and to 'check resources in the library' whenever we encountered a problem.

DISCOURSE: JARGON OR SOCIAL ORGANIZATION?

Contemporary advanced capitalist society is marked by a proliferation of professional groups – physicians, psychiatrists, lawyers, psychologists, nurses, physiotherapists, engineers, and social workers. Each of these professional groups has developed specialized language for marking out a terrain for its practice. For those outside the institutionalized work sites of professionals, such language sounds peculiar, distinct, and at times impenetrable. Simply put, professional language sounds like jargon (Larson, 1977: 228; Lee, 1980).

For working class people, social workers' specialized talk may be interrupted by requests for explanation, queries (for example, 'what do you mean'), confused silence, or various devices to mask ignorance (for example, nodding in feigned agreement, responding with yes or no answers, or uttering vague or monosyllabic replies). It is precisely, however, this confusing and obfuscatory character of specialized talk and writing that competent members so easily appear to transcend. They understand what each other is saying. Through their talk, members accomplish their participation as insiders aware of the boundaries and the good sense of each other's utterances. Specialized talk is a sign of membership in a discourse. Social workers may also signify joint membership by smiling knowingly, nodding with agreement and responding with their own verbal elaborations that can be heard to match the flow, concerns, and relevances of the other. Social workers interactively constitute and acknowledge each other's situation within a mutually shared professional terrain.

The peculiarities of social work language become obvious for laypeople who hear social workers talk. For example, social workers applying a systems approach to families may talk about a family's problems with boundary maintenance, equilibrium, communication loops, and so forth. Similarly, social workers operating within an ecological approach may address environmentally induced stress, by explicitly referencing the work by Carel Germain (1991), outline what the principle concerns in this case are – how does Mr K perceive stress, how does he cope, what kinds of interchange does he have with his environment, and so forth. Additionally, social workers in specialized settings such as prisons and psychiatric hospitals will adopt the languages of other professionals, for example, using medical and psychiatric terms contained in the *Diagnostic and Statistical Manual* (DSM) IV of the American Psychiatric Association. Skilful use of such terms is essential for sustaining efficient work relations as members need only refer to specific categories, for example, schizophrenia, bipolar disorder, or affective disorder, to obtain a quickly accessible working understanding of cases at hand. Because a client is diagnosed as schizophrenic, for instance, the social worker already anticipates and expects a process of discovery in which the client presents delusional ideation, loosening of associations, flattening of affect, mental deterioration, or hallucinations.

Although the peculiarities of specialized language or jargon are interesting in themselves, the notion of discourse I develop in this chapter moves beyond merely attending to spoken or written words. All language is, at the moments of its utterance and hearing, inextricably embedded in the relevances of the speaker's and listener's determinate social ground. However, as language it also expresses social relations that transcend and go beyond the immediate situation. As language, speech acts articulate and coordinate any immediate present with other moments, other spaces, and other speech acts. Professional discourse is ideologically constructed, and therefore speakers in such discourse, unlike speakers in ordinary language, construct the appearance that their speech acts and understandings are not indexical or tied to determinate lived and shared personal domains.

The use of specialized language produces a standpoint, a form of consciousness, and a reality for members inside an institutional nexus. As people engage in socially organized talk about the world using specific words and concepts, they come to 'think' about the world (Volosinov, 1973: 19;[6] Kress and Hodge, 1979: 5). The understanding of discourse I develop in this chapter points to far more than just specialized language practices. Discourse is about socially organized grounds or forms of life in which speakers and writers live. It is about the imbrication of textual practices disarticulated from time and space with embodied practices embedded in local settings and lived time. It is about the artful transcendence of ambiguity and confusion through a controlled construction and recovery of a commonly shared institutional reality. It is about the ways that people produce extended social relations marked by identity, membership, and power. It is in the living, material practices of discourse that social workers construct a distinct identity as professionals and as authoritative and powerful. It is within the matrices of discursive power that social workers and other professionals differentiate insiders from outsiders.

Indeed, the negative connotations of jargon arise from the outsider's critique of certain speakers and their language and the anxiety posed by fundamental imbalances of power. Attention to jargon denotes a protest against a social separation made visible through language practices. It denotes claims to superior knowledge and expertise expressed in language. Jargon denotes the outsider's attempt to dismiss the specialized language practices as esoteric, embellished, inflated, and unnecessary. As I have argued, such specialized language is not at all accidental, not merely a matter of choice, and it is not just designed to obscure and confuse. Rather, specialized language is essential for the exercise of institutionalized forms of power and authority.

Social workers' specialized language is rooted in the social relations of a class society, as it is one tool for constructing the differentiation from clients and a sense of professional distinctiveness. It legitimizes social workers' authority and allows them to effect a privileged purchase of reality. The place to begin enquiry is not with specialized language as such, but with the social relations of institutional power. To be a social worker demands being able to produce a consciousness properly constitutive of a shared professional reality. Wittgenstein states, 'To imagine a language means to imagine a form of life' (1958: 11). He elaborates: 'The term 'language-game' is meant to bring into prominence the fact that the speaking of language is part of an activity, or a form of life.' (ibid.). Language games require that members, situated in actual social forms of life, invoke and employ both explicit and tacit practices to construct the good sense of their interpretations and their talk. These sense-making practices are bound to a place and to the specialized activities of that place. The notion of a language game (Wittgenstein, 1958; Bologh, 1979) highlights the reflexive relations between mundane practice and the institutional accounts of practice as candidate correct (Pollner, 1974) types. For example, when I drive along the highway to an outlying community to keep a 2:00 p.m. appointment, my activities will be documented in the running record as a 'home visit.' Such textual absorptions of actual located and temporally bounded activities serve to transform my activities into exemplars of proper institutional categories.

DOCUMENTARY DISCOURSE

Through the practical exercise of professional discourse, social workers link their activities to those of other professionals located in diverse organizational settings. Equally important, however, they link and coordinate presently unfolding activities to the activities of workers in the past and to anticipated activities of workers in the future. Through discursive activity, social workers mediate the prior moments of institutionally grounded production, which appear as dead entities, for example, bound policy manuals, old client files, or wrinkled operational directives, to the ongoing production of a presently lived meaningful reality. By talking with senior workers, new workers learn the history of their organization, they get a sense of past working conditions, past cases, and past applications of policy. By reading introduction brochures for new employees, scanning legislation manuals containing old acts, or reading annual reports from past years, social workers construct their location within a tradition and within an organization that extends beyond their immediate times and places. Every time a social worker takes up a case on her caseload, she searches for an existing file. As she familiarizes herself with a case, by reading through the records on file, she encounters the work performed by colleagues in her office, by workers in other district offices, and frequently by workers long since departed from the organization.

While the institutional location of social workers structures the unfolding nature of their practice reciprocally, their discursive practices themselves produce documents through which the institution can be discovered. The organization's past is encountered through documents as an existent and accomplished reality that bears the authority of past mandated courses of action, legal decisions, court orders, and assessments. These artefacts of past practice duly recorded and documented in running records, court orders, and certificates on file, are data for working up assessments of present client functioning and appropriate interventions. Such records brought forward from the past allow social workers to meet clients as already discursively organized. The client is a textually mediated case marked by a continuity between the past and present. By reading a file a social worker may observe: Mrs Jones's children, Billy, Debbie, and Wanda, were first apprehended in 19xx. Debbie Jones died in 19xx as a result of an infection, which the court felt was possibly the result of lack of medical attention. Mrs Jones attended a drug and alcohol rehabilitation centre in 19xx. Mr Jones was tried and convicted for sexual assault against Wanda in 19xx and sentenced to eight months in prison.

It is through textually mediated social work practice that the case becomes visible. Records from the past warrant cogent interpretations for presently observed behaviours and circumstances. Documents provide a medium for producing the temporal structures of an institutional reality in which time is linear, ordered, and administered – what Kovel calls bound time (1981). Linear time extends backwards through dated case histories, completed courses of action, file records, and aggregated policy manuals. As social workers produce the good sense and warrant of cases, they lay down a documentary record, which will itself become a piece of an aggregate. Their record is solidified into the layers of paper on file.

Documentary production emerges from institutionally grounded social relations. It is distinct and separate from natural language, that is, oral folktales, mythology, and day-to-day conversation. Natural language remains tied to the social relations of daily life, while documentary production is governed by the extra-local, the discursive, and the rules of textuality. The paramountcy of documentary production in an institutional reality has important effects. Kress and Hodge note, 'Quite unconsciously, a community which is defined by its mastery of the written medium disvalues the resources of oral and gestural language, and hence the culture of its users' (1979: 10). The implication is that the culture of daily life, and accordingly the worlds where people live, eat, work, sleep, love, and raise children, are devalued as contaminated until appropriated and transposed into decontaminated textual forms of institutional documents.

The hegemony of textual expression silences working people's talk, tonal modulations, gestures, visual symbols, and use of their bodies in space. Additionally, the imperatives and forms of life that inform natural language – such as the practical activities of playing with the children, cleaning house, making meals, doing laundry, shopping for groceries, loving the husband, or earning a wage – differ from those that inform an institutionally grounded discourse. Lee addresses the negative language used by professionals to describe the poor and he criticizes the oft-used description that poor families are 'disorganized.' He counters that 'middle class eyes do not easily see and comprehend the nature of the organization they behold' (1980: 582).

INTELLECTUAL DIVISIONS OF LABOUR

If the state apparatus is explicated as a web of social relations (Smith, 1987), rather than as a thing-like structure, the various moments of social workers' activities, that is, front-line practice, research, scholarship, record keeping, administration, and so forth, come into focus as integrated practices in an institutional division of labour. The process of bringing the madly equivocal and confusing swirls of daily lives under the smoothly regulated signs of professional discourse demands manifold forms of work conducted across multiple sites.

From out of the realities of people's lives, their acts of drinking alcohol to excess, beating and hitting spouses and children, and applying for welfare, social workers produce the problems that their work addresses: alcohol abuse, child abuse or neglect, domestic violence, and unemployment. Through day-to-day work, front-line social workers translate mundane occasions into those organizational categories that warrant professional action. The problem categories social workers use to sort through situations at hand must work within organizations. Even as new problems are identified, they too are taken up within the extended division of labour essential in a ruling apparatus. Professional discovery works up new problems, new categories, and new services to be explored, theorized, and administered by royal commissions, social workers, nurses, police, courts, program planners, and senior bureaucrats. The processes of generating cogent meanings for organizationally rooted categories – such as the battered wife, family violence, incest, sexual abuse – extend beyond the province of social work.

The work of the committee to study sexual offences against children and youth provides an example of the process of professional appropriation of social problems. The report *Sexual Offences Against Children* (1984), also known as the Badgley Report, involved members from a range of helping professions, including lawyers, psychiatrists, social workers, and nurses. Their work staked out a territory, documented that sexual abuse of children actually occurs, and then proposed institutional remedies for the problem, such as to change the laws, provide new services, and create coordinating offices.

Despite the clear organizational need to understand and thereby manage problems, front line social workers generally lack the authority and the mandate to conduct research. Research is not part of their job description. In addition, most front line workers have been taught that proper research is impartial, develops abstract hypotheses, is based on broad samples, and is replicative. Accordingly, they know that they lack the position – spatially and organizationally – and the time and the expertise to conduct proper research. Because proper research requires a standpoint of distance from problems, social workers appreciate that their situation at the front-line vitiates their ability to make cogent theoretical claims. The continuous demand to address the day-to-day world of casework leaves them little time to sit back or to distance themselves from the work. Finally, as hourly workers, there are neither the budget allocations nor the time allocations needed to plan or execute research.[7] The intensity of their mandated work virtually precludes conducting comparative provincial or national analyses of specific problems.

Social work academics working in universities, however, are not bound by such restrictive job descriptions, nor by the horizon of the front line, nor by the intensity of front line practice. Indeed, academic social workers, unlike front-line social workers, are not only encouraged but often required to conduct research. Career advancement, professional status, and basic security within the university demand that academics engage in scholarly production. Most often this is understood as conducting research and publishing reports. For academics 'publish or perish' becomes a constant goad to develop expertise in specific problem areas. The display of expertise is produced through publication in scholarly journals, collected works, or monographs, and by presentation of papers at professional conferences.

To produce expertise, successful academic social workers incessantly seek out new research projects. To develop research projects, academics may interview agency contacts to identify problems or to discuss joint applications for research funding. Through a collaborative effort, a grant proposal might result and funding may be received from places like the Social Sciences and Humanities Research Council, the Secretary of State, the Department of Health and Welfare,[8] or some other body. Academics compete in the hope of winning a sizable and prestigious research grant that will allow them to do innovative research, develop new approaches to problems, publish papers about their results, write authoritative texts, and gain recognition as experts in the field. Expertise is academic currency for becoming widely known, being granted distinguished professorships, and winning professional recognition and honour. In addition to the imperatives of a career, academics are able to examine the puzzles and challenges posed by social problems. By developing new conceptualizations of problems, discovering new categories, and initiating new treatment strategies, academics affirm their power. They construct their own sense of competence and mastery of their craft.

Social worker academics attempt to develop methods and conceptual structures that can be taken up by front-line workers to sort through the problem situations at hand. Academics struggle to ensure that education in social work is relevant and meaningful for practitioners. It is a truism that research and front-line work must be linked.[9] Reciprocally, administrators and front-line practitioners are faced with a ceaseless litany of problems. From their professional training, they usually believe that solutions to their problems may be found through research. For example, Awasis, a Manitoba Native child welfare agency formed in 1983, contracted with the University of Manitoba School of Social Work in 1987 to complete an evaluation study conducted by Hudson and Taylor-Henley. Similarly, Eric Sigurdson and Grant Reid, also with the University of Manitoba, completed the *External Review into Matters Relating to the System of Dealing with Child Abuse in Winnipeg* (1987).

Front-line social workers and agency administrators are usually quite willing to enlist the assistance of academic social workers. Additionally, through consultatory work, contracts, workshops, and field supervision, academic social workers construct a working network of professional contacts within the agencies.

Over the past two decades, social work researchers, along with other helping professionals, notably psychiatrists, radiologists, pediatricians, and psychologists, have coined new vocabularies for framing and making sense of 'social problems.' A number of previously undiscovered social problems have surfaced. Professionals have claimed sexual abuse of children, domestic violence, the battered-baby syndrome, failure-to-thrive infants, bulimia and anorexia, borderline personalities, youth unemployment, learned helplessness, burnout, and multiple personality disorder as areas requiring their intervention (Walker, 1986; Deglau, 1985; Pfohl, 1977). The efforts of an expanding cadre of helpers have developed increasingly elaborate understandings of problems and appropriate interventions.

Through participation in a professional discourse that generates categories, topics, and concerns, researchers and practitioners join together to identify, sort, arrange, and order a lived world such that it becomes a suitable locus for organizationally grounded activity. The methods, concepts, theories, and analyses developed by researchers are employed by front-line workers in their day-to-day work to construct interpretations of their clients' lives that are cogent, warrantable, and properly situated within the profession. Research provides the conceptual currency social workers need to effect an ideological purchase on their clients' lived realities.

As social workers take up the conceptual and formal systems developed by researchers and apply them to their work, the difficulties they encounter become material for further research. For example, a social worker working with sexual offenders may employ Summit and Kryso's schema (1978) to understand cases at hand, that is, is this 'incidental sexual contact,' 'ideological sexual contact,' 'psychotic intrusion,' 'rustic environment,' 'true endogamous incest,' 'misogynous incest,' 'imperious incest,' 'pedophiliac incest,' 'child rape,' or 'perverse incest?' From the standpoint of the front-line worker, the case may not simply fit any single category or it may fit more than one category. Such mundane working problems become material for which researchers develop and refine increasingly elaborate or even fundamentally different taxonomic systems.

By reading texts and making reports, social workers encounter and take up the frames, categories, insights, and horizons of the research. The next chapter demonstrates that both front-line social workers and researchers strive to employ sense-making techniques which construct their practices as isomorphic forms, that is, as scientific or as problem-solving social work. Both front-line social workers and researchers construct a discursive stance within and towards the encountered world. This is a stance in which the understandings, knowledge, insights, accounts, and integrity of the clients or subjects of the research are displaced in favour of professional understandings.[10] Front-line social workers and researchers unite to connect the lived world to the structures of an institutional apparatus.

Proper social workers would not deny that child abuse and neglect, domestic violence, sexual abuse, alcoholism, or mental illness, actually exist. Nor would they deny that these problems should be studied, measured, assessed, and treated. Though there may be heated debate over how to properly define child abuse, how to treat child abusers, how to help the abusive family, and so forth, there is no debate about the existence of child abuse, per se. Yet, because a central component of front-line social work is administering, managing, ordering, governing, and controlling people, social workers routinely experience points where the good sense of their interpretations of the phenomenon under study rupture and break down.

Front-line social workers are by definition required to encounter people face to face. The social worker is required to develop an assessment of the case that identifies matters of fact, develops relations between these facts, and arrives at a social diagnosis, problem assessment, and treatment plan. Order must be imposed upon the situation at hand so that it is intelligible and reportable, within documents, and before colleagues as a properly worked-up case.

Such face-to-face encounters are replete with ambiguity, indeterminacy, equivocation, and partiality. Cases frequently present conflicting pieces of information, odd bits that cannot be fit in, and gut feelings that something else is going on. The worlds of day-to-day life continually threaten the cogency of social workers' categories and the professional enterprise of managing daily life itself. There is a disjuncture between the world as lived and experienced and the ways in which that world can be known institutionally. There is a disjuncture between the relations of daily life and the categories that name those relations.

Participation in discursively organized activities structures the imaginative possibilities of what can count as acceptable practice for resolving the crises of day-to-day social work. This is not to claim that social workers, are simple automatons over-determined (Althusser, 1977) by the structures of an institutional apparatus. Rather, participation in an institutionally embedded discourse means that social workers enter themselves, by virtue of their practical activities, into social relations of a determinate character and thereby participate in the epistemic horizon of the profession. For front-line workers, addressing clients' crises through discourse may create internal conflict and value dilemmas. However, it must also be recognized that, from the standpoint of social workers, the disciplined or artful use of discourse is the source of creativity, mastery, competence, self-expression, and energy. Foucault observes: 'What makes power hold good, what makes it accepted, is simply the fact that it doesn't only weigh on us as a force that says no, but that it traverses and produces things, it induces pleasure, forms knowledge, produces discourse' (1980: 119). Although helping clients is assumed to be a painful process, because clients are resistant, ill informed, uneducated, unmotivated, and so forth, there are those moments for social workers and clients alike of joy, triumph, and success. Certainly, at times it seems that whatever the social worker attempts to do to help often fails, as the client is still drinking, the children are neglected again, the husband has beat his wife again, the single mum is evicted from another apartment, and the boy is still having school troubles. Even in the face of such trials, social workers by remaining in discourse are able to recover from failure and affirm the value of their work.

DISCOURSE AND PROFESSIONAL BOUNDARIES

If a social worker rigorously addresses the fundamentals of her profession, she risks bringing into question her membership as a professional. As a student social worker, I was allowed to ask: What does it mean to help? Is helping compatible with social workers' function as state agents? How can helping proceed when social workers subject clients to involuntary and compulsory service (for example, incarceration and involuntary hospitalization)? Is helping possible within agencies and organizations that allow neither social workers nor clients control over policy? Why is it that social work often seems unable to solve social problems despite the proliferation of scientific research, specialized treatment facilities, and expertise? Why despite all my efforts do my clients still feel such pain and suffering? Why is there never enough money available to develop proper services for people? Why is it that once programs are created clients are generally uninterested in participating? As I moved closer to graduation, however, such questions were less tolerated by professors.

Supervisors and colleagues assume that because students are learning and because they are not yet professionals, they do not know that such questions are misdirected, misinformed, and not professional. Furthermore, it is understood that there will be a faculty member or a field supervisor available to redirect their questions and thereby help them work through these value dilemmas. In the working flow of staff meetings, case conferences, workshops, investigations, apprehensions, and so forth, social workers cannot be situated simultaneously in professional discourse and in a phenomenological discourse that brackets or brings into question the discourse they perform. Social workers whether writing a report to the court or investigating a report of neglect must situate themselves within the discourse. They must perform within the natural attitude of the discourse. The concerns of the discourse are their concerns. Their performance relies on accepting the inscrutable, incorrigible, iterative, literal, and unquestionable boundaries of professional work. A child protection worker cannot simultaneously perform her work and bring into question or bracket child abuse as a real-world event.

The relations of social work discourse provide for safe ways of addressing crises and conflicts. Social workers can address the problems of daily life as though they exist out there; hence, they project the products of their own work as features of the social environment.

They ask: What can I do to help? What do I need to know to understand alcoholism? What are the dynamics of domestic violence? What is the etiology of child neglect? What is the prognosis for correcting poor empathetic ability?

Within the extended social relations marked as discourse, a series of external targets emerge. Corrective action is directed to these targets, whether clients, colleagues, researchers, directors, or government officials. Thus, front-line social workers recover their discursive situation when they lament: 'If only the research was better, I might be able to help this client.' 'If only someone had studied this problem more carefully, a solution might emerge.' 'If only I had more time to do family therapy, I might have been able to help the family avoid this crisis.' 'If only there were better information and resources available, she might not have killed herself.' Such lamentations construct an epistemic domain that can and should be addressed and regulated within the regimes of discursive social work knowledge.

As social workers construct their places inside discursive realities, they create a currency, issued in language, concepts, and methods. They use this currency to purchase recognition and acknowledgment of each other as like-minded, sensible, knowledgable, and proper professionals. Through professional work, social workers generate comradeship, collegiality, friendship, and community. By accomplishing solidarity as a community of professionals, they simultaneously construct a separation from others.

Social workers' talk, writing, and intervention activities distinguish them from a legion of other helpers, for example, psychotherapists, psychiatrists, psychologists, nurses, and occupational therapists. Social workers thus distinguish themselves from psychologists who focus on personality, psychiatrists who see people's problems as illness, and nurses who work inside a medical model, by laying some sort of claim to the social. As social workers, they know that their concern with social factors, whether expressed as social systems, ecologically induced stressors, network functioning, or even structural social work marks them off as a unique profession.

Being a professional means inhabiting a world with a socially organized epistemic horizon and discursive structures. Smith states, 'to be recognized as a proper participant, the member must produce work that conforms to appropriate styles and terminologies, makes the appropriate deferences, and is locatable by these and other devices in the traditions, factions, and schools whose themes it elaborates, whose interpretive procedures it intends and by whose criteria it is to be evaluated' (1987: 61). Social workers have to think about the world using the categories, concepts, methods, and standpoint of professional discourse. This means both accepting and producing as warranted and sensible talk about parental pathology, social work helping, the need for intervention, and social work values.

5

Ad Hoc Science:
Constructing Child Abuse

That children are 'abused,' 'neglected,' and 'sexually assaulted' and that such children need protection is a matter of common sense for social workers. Actual children are beaten, starved, and abused; however, as I argue in this chapter, what counts, and what is counted as child abuse and neglect arises from methods for making sense which are inextricably linked to an institutional apparatus. Untoward occasions of hitting, slapping, punching, or stabbing between parents and children are worked up – and become visible – through the work of social workers, psychologists, pediatricians, public health nurses, and teachers, not just as remarkable but as properly warranting their interventions.

For social workers doing child protection work, the problems of child neglect and abuse appear to be only too real. These problems exist in society and are 'out there' awaiting study and analysis like other 'facts' in the real world. Competent social workers know that each possible case of injury to a child must be followed by a complex series of questions and investigations to determine: What is the probable source of this injury? Does the parents' story make sense? Do people's stories contradict each other? What problems emerge in an assessment of this child or parent or family? How do I find out what is going on? Who can I believe? Do I have a role to play in this case? How shall I treat the victim(s)? What treatment or services do these people need? What are the dangers or degree of risk? Will this intervention work? What is the prognosis? As such questions are posed, and then answered, a professionally defined object emerges as clearly defined and as subject to professional interventions.

The parent's angry push, the child's fall, the shattered wrist, and the screams of pain, once understood as 'abuse, effect a disconnection between the actual event and a professional work process for taking up such events as categories of an organizational reality. Events, once they are understood as abuse, become pieces of broader 'social problems that can in turn be subjected to generalized techniques of social work intervention. In the problem-solving discourse of social workers, both the problems themselves and even the specialized techniques developed for their resolution come to have an existent or ontological character. This process of appropriating the realities of daily life through professional work is captured in Smith's discussion of the battered wife:

The Battered Wife ... illustrates a method of using language which makes a little bundle, a little package out of instances in the lived world ... I might go around in my professional capacity as a sociologist and do studies of the Battered Wife. I would go out into the world and find samples. It would be like a botanical enterprise ... We take this – what shall I call it – a something? – we lift this entity which we have called the Battered Wife out of actual lived experience and the social relations which organize and articulate it. We section the lived world to produce this entity. We divorce it from everything which might tell us about the real situation in which people live and in which women experience violence in the home – among other places ... It is a typical use of the oppressor's language to talk about the Battered Wife as if she existed prior to actual women's experiences of physical abuse in varying relational contexts. What an odd focus is produced. The entity that is brought into being in this way doesn't exist. (Smith, 1979: 15)

In the problem-solving and scientific work of social workers and other professionals, moments of people's lives are sliced off from the relations and ground of their occurrence to become identified as discrete and 'problems' having an independent existence and ontology apart from people's daily lives.

SCIENTIFIC CONSTRUCTION

What gives social workers' accounts of child abuse their good sense and cogency? Clearly, sensible accounts rely on social workers' skilled use of practices closely associated with scientific methods. Through the application of logical argument, causal explanation, operational definitions, application of scales, invocation of statistical correlations, and theoretical formulation of problems, social workers attempt to construct skilful and knowledgable accounts of client situations. Good social work, whether textual or verbal, reveals the artful use of scientific devices and techniques. Additionally, proper scientific technique not only gives warrant to texts and talk, but generates the forms of consciousness required to sustain specific and particular activities as a cognate member of the class of activities that are properly social work.

Although there has been some critical work in social work and therapy, notably by McNamee and Gergen (1992), Oliver (1990), Parton (1985) and Phillipson (1982), employing phenomenological and constructivist approaches, positivist social science theorizing continues to be invoked as the dominant paradigm. Social workers' claims to using positivist science and positivist methods are characterized by the portrayal of their discovery work as routine, systematized, replicative, and orderly.

In addition to the invocation of science, the sense making social workers do must invoke the imperatives of the organization, hence, it must be in accordance with the rules governing organizational action. However, the work that produces correspondence between daily life and universalized policies and protocols relies on positivist methods for generating the sensible properties of specific occasions as cognate members of universalized sets, theories, and frameworks. Social workers fancy themselves employing methods of science to translate and interpret what they actually do as moments of a practical scientific discovery, such as an investigation, an interview, collection of the facts, review of past files, or creation of an assessment.

Front-line social workers understand that their work is guided by logic, objectivity, systematic investigation, reasonable explanation, and facts. When required to account for their practice or when required to justify a decision, social workers frame their accounts such that they demonstrate a similarity with or invoke the language forms of scientific explanation. Their activities are systematically reframed such that what they actually do is accessible and becomes visible, accountable, and reportable as a mundane science,[1] hence, as practical moments of problem-solving work.

From social workers' standpoint inside the epistemology and reality of the organization, all 'phenomena' must be understandable, and accountable, and therefore subject to the rules of objective observation. For front-line practitioners objectivity emerges through the production of a correspondence between any putative 'phenomenon' and a series of ritually inscribed descriptive statements constituting the 'facts' of the matter. Just as within positivist science, where the 'fact,' its discovery, and identification are accounted for as arising independently of the work of observation, so too must 'facts' be understood as arising independently of the work of social workers. For example, a front-line worker's report of a case of child neglect cannot portray the incident of neglect as contingent on the work of observation nor as contingent on the policies and mandate of the organization. Rather, the case of neglect, comprised of specific incidents, factually recorded, must be construed as a real-world event, existing independently of the work of its discovery. It must be an actual case of neglect.

SCIENTIFIC STANDPOINT

What are the implications for researchers and front-line social workers who account for their work using the rhetoric of scientific method? First, they assume that there is a scientific practice that provides a self-corrective process. They assume that there can be a scientific practice that is non-indexical, systematic, and transcendent of existing times, situations, and social relations. They assume that it is possible to adhere to this practice to construct rational, logical, and systematic knowledge. By entering their work into a discourse of positivist science, social workers' stories about cases are construed to be guided by relevances that transcend the personal, the situated, and the equivocal. To be seen as warranted practitioners of scientific discourse, social workers must create an epistemological standpoint fundamentally apart from their daily lives. To do their science, social workers must be organizationally situated in the social relations of power and authority which provide the attitude of confidence necessary to claim that the work was carried out using careful investigation, detailed consideration of case facts, theoretical skill, and knowledgable interventions in the case. Through their science talk, social workers lay in place a standpoint that empowers their apparent transcendence of the vulnerability and partiality of their own concrete existence in the world. Such professional stories, framed as instances of objective and scientific work, also have the effect of erasing from view the background social relations of power, control, and authority that inform social work.

When social workers make sense of their practice by employing the logic and codes of positivist science, they affirm their authority as members of a profession. The authority they command emanates from their claims that the knowledge they possess is not particular, local, or temporally bound, but that it is professional knowledge derived from universalized policies, theories, and objective measures. The claim to be participants inside the forms of universalized knowledge allows social workers to claim an epistemological superiority over those whose knowledge is bound to a particular place and standpoint. To produce a warranted claim for scientific practice, front-line workers account for their activities so that they are visible to colleagues and other professionals as meeting the methods and ideals of science.

Second, the categories and concepts of social workers' professional discourse are understood to represent 'real' phenomena. The categories and concepts speak in a professionally common-sense way to the facts of the world, that is, child abuse and neglect, domestic violence, spousal assault, and so forth (Aronson, 1984: 3). Social workers understand that their categories and concepts extend beyond discourse, and beyond talk, to reach into a world that can been seen, accounted for, and reported independently of their work.

Categories and concepts provide front-line social workers with working guides to be cited and recited when applied to cases at hand. Categories and concepts provide an intellectual currency to effect purchase of specific features and characteristics of individual cases. Consider the following example: A social worker works with Mrs Frame, a 'battered wife' who has just returned to live with her husband. Her return follows yet another hospitalization resulting from injuries sustained from an 'abusive episode.' The social worker uses Seligman's theory of learned helplessness (1975) to explain why Mrs Frame has returned to the home. The social worker understands that her return, although lamentable, is understandable and makes sense. The worker explains that Mrs Frame has lost control over her situation and has resigned herself to accept her husband's abuse. Her depression, her inability to care properly for her children, her flattened affect, and her sense of resignation are all indicators of the syndrome called learned helplessness.[2] The category learned helplessness is discovered and operationalized through a series of indicators that themselves suggest possible intervention. Through the practical applications of concepts, categories, and theories, front-line workers construct a professionally defined province of real-world events amenable to their interventions.

CONSTRUCTING CAUSAL ACCOUNTS

The requirement that social workers do something, that they take some corrective action, that they intervene, and that they solve the problem, presupposes the identification of some cause of the situation at hand. Social workers must explain why Mrs Barry left her children alone in the apartment at 11:00 p.m.; why Mr Valmet struck his daughter Jackie; or why Jane was sexually assaulted by her father. Causal accounts link social workers' interventions to the situations they encounter: for example, because Mrs B is depressed she neglects her child; therefore, as a social worker I must treat her depression.

Causal accounts render the relations of the world visible in organizationally cogent, determinate, and manageable ways. Displaying cause sustains the appearance that a social worker's daily work is conducted as proper, unbiased, impersonal, and legitimate. Cause is a work imperative. Cause is a code for generating accounts of cases at hand, such that untoward situations are identified as requiring some intervention. When social workers generate causal accounts, they enter their work, and themselves, into a 'scientific' logic where every instance of an event (y, or dependent variable) must be preceded by another event (x, or independent variable). Although social workers are educated to appreciate that causal relations can never be proven conclusively, for the practical managerial purposes at hand, they talk in a way which assumes causal relations.

Practically, social scientists and social workers realize the problems with talking about cause, therefore, when they employ causal explanations, they usually provide a series of cautions and qualifications. Cause is proposed provisionally as probable. Polansky, Chalmers, Buttenwieser, and Williams, in *Damaged Parents: An Anatomy of Child Neglect*, comment on a statistically significant association between two variables that supports their hypothesis: 'One cannot, of course, conclude from an association that there is a cause-and-effect relationship present, but the findings are certainly consistent with this hypothesis, which has been validated in many other studies' (1981: 134). These authors realize that they cannot logically assume a cause-and-effect relation from a statistical correlation. However, they argue that they can proceed, and, indeed, it is this necessity to proceed, hence, to get on with the work at hand, which requires calling on evidence to claim that a causal relation actually exists. These authors' pragmatic resolution of the paradox of positivist logic is neither unique nor uncommon. It is a necessary device for sustaining the ability to proceed with the work at hand. Why this should be the case is revealed by Aronson: 'An event has a cause when there is something someone can do about it, either to make the event happen or to keep it from happening. Any given individual will define the cause of an event as that means by which he or she can intervene in the outcome' (1984: 22).

Cause is an integral conceptual device for sustaining the legitimacy of social work accounts and social work itself. Cause allows problems to be connected to available means for their resolution. The work that identifies the cause of child neglect in this case simultaneously creates an entry point for social work interventions. Social workers know that because Mrs Dillon drinks she neglects her daughter Amy. Mrs Dillon's alcoholism 'causes' neglect. If she stops drinking, a factor in the pattern of neglect is removed, therefore, she should be referred to an alcohol treatment centre.

Showing cause structures practice. Practitioners display causal relations by using common-sense steps, formulas, codes, and taken-for-granted methods for investigation. The textual devices that are employed by academic social workers to display causal relations are also used as guides and points of reference for front-line social workers who have to execute organizational courses of action. For example, I encounter Bill, a thirteen-year-old boy, who is skipping school, acting out when in class, and is suspected of glue sniffing. What I do relies upon my ability to generate some causal account of these behaviours. I ask, is there psychological abuse in Bill's home? Has Bill been traumatized by parental separation? Is his problem the result of a transfer to a new school? What are his relations with peers like? Are parental role models adequate? However, how I practically craft an account that convincingly demonstrates a causal relation is itself problematic. Garfinkel outlines:

In the course of an interview an investigator is likely to find himself addressing a series of present situations whose future states that a contemplated course of treatment will produce are characteristically vague or even unknown. With overwhelming frequency these as of here-and-now possible future states are only sketchily specifiable prior to undertaking the action that is intended to realize them. There is a necessary distinction between a 'possible future state of affairs' and a 'how to bring it about future from present state of affairs as an actual point of departure.' The 'possible future state of affairs' may be very clear indeed. But such a future is not the matter of interest. Instead we are concerned with the 'how to bring it about from a here-and-now future.' It is this state – for convenience, call it an 'operational future' – that is characteristically vague or unknown. (1967: 97)

The construction of specific 'causal' accounts legitimates my practice so long as future interventions and their results sustain the cogency of my initial formulations. Thus, if I determine that Bill is sniffing glue because of his physically abusive father, I may decide to apprehend Bill, and place him in a 'nurturing' foster home. If Bill stops sniffing, then my causal analysis will have been sustained as a cogent formulation of the problem. However, if Bill continues to sniff, I am faced with the problem Garfinkel addresses as 'what to do in case of ...' In such an instance I need to salvage, modify, or discard my causal explanation of Bill's behaviour. Practically, this is not very difficult, for I need only invoke an elaborative device, which adds other levels of analysis and inserts additional factors for consideration. So, when I begin work on the case, the abusive and unhappy home environment is the primary intervention target. It is identified as the cause of Bill's solvent abuse, however, the persistence of solvent abuse, despite intervention efforts, requires a more elaborate explanation. I could argue that the solvent abuse has become an addiction itself; that Bill has learned a dysfunctional coping strategy that he has transferred over into his new environment to manage separation loss; Bill is still suffering the trauma of physical abuse and turns to solvents to assuage his hurt, and so on. My ability to create causal accounts as guides for my practice which can be retroactively modified, revised, and sustained as cogent, is a competency which is taken for granted and which I and other social workers are expected to possess.

Social workers' production of causal accounts matches the phenomenological boundaries and imperatives of organizationally embedded action. For example, Straus (1980) by demonstrating a causal relation between stress and child abuse, constructs both a horizon and a phenomenological topography for thinking about cases. His work elaborates a domain of discrete social problems that can be categorically addressed through specific policies and programs for their amelioration, for example, stress reduction workshops, parent effectiveness training, or infant stimulation programs. However, while cause provides practitioners authority and legitimizes their practice, artfully crafted causal accounts also anticipate unexpected results by admitting to the provisional nature of findings. The provisional nature of findings displays a social worker's skilful anticipation and recognition of real-world equivocality and uncertainty. This recognition provides workers with an out or escape should their claims be challenged or disproved.

Identified uncertainties and equivocalities provide material for further professional enquiry. For example, contrary to his hypothesis, Straus discovered that 'most of the parents in this sample who experienced a high degree of stress did not abuse a child' (1980: 94). This challenge to his causal hypothesis is a problem and therefore requires further investigation and research: 'A critical question is brought to light by this fact. What accounts for the fact that some people respond to stress by violence, whereas others do not?' (Straus, 1980: 95).

What emerge as relevant concerns for research and front-line social workers, hence, what emerges for Straus as a matter worth reporting, commenting on, and sorting through, is structured by the problematic of explanatory adequacy. The 'real world' as encountered does not perfectly correspond to hypotheses and theories. Research maps out relations in the field, drawing lines of correspondence, connections, bridges, barriers, and separations between categories such as poverty (wealth) and neglect, bonding (bonding failure) and failure to thrive, healthy personality (dysfunctional personality) and abuse, nurturing (neglecting) culture and parenting. Social workers, both theorists and practitioners, like the creators of all maps, anticipate problems of correspondence between symbol and 'reality.' Social workers, like map makers, establish provisos, limits, and qualifiers between their models and reality. Anticipating the identification of a rupture between the model and reality, they bracket the literality of their creations. For example, Polansky et al. acknowledge the 'limitations of this study' (1981: 134), while Straus observes: 'The interpretation of the data, although consistent with, was not proved by the data. Many of the findings are open to other equally plausible interpretations, particulary as to causal direction. The question of causal direction can only be adequately dealt with by a longitudinal study. In the absence of such prospective data, the following conclusions must be regarded only as what the study suggests about the etiology of child abuse' (1980: 100). Similarly, Wright formulates a 'sick but slick syndrome' to describe abusive parents, but when analysing his results, he is forced to admit, 'This study was not structured in such a manner as to make its results definitive' (1982: 137).

Such additions act as disclaimers. They disclaim the researchers' adherence to these formulations as final, ultimate, or conclusive. They construct the appearance that the researcher remains open-minded and willing to consider alternative explanations. This shows that the researcher does not have a personal investment in his find-ings, that he is objective, and that when presented with contradictory data he is prepared modify his position.

Researchers' causal accounts anticipate problems of correspondence, and, accordingly, they seek schemata for embracing and enveloping problems posed by the equivocality of the 'real world.' As noted, they provide a contingent literality, hence, a literality for practical pur-poses, and a literality salvageable by employing an 'et cetera device' (Garfinkel, 1967), such as we see through invocations of mediating and intervening variables. The invocation of mediating and interven-ing variables anticipates challenges by other members of discourse who object, 'yes, but,' 'I know that, but,' 'all things being equal,' and 'however, normally we expect.' Mediating and intervening variables provide for statements of qualified fact, while also allowing for slippage and escape. Thus, a front-line social worker can explore a situation at hand to check 'socialization for violence,' 'legitimacy of family violence,' 'marital satisfaction,' 'socioeconomic status,' 'marital power,' 'social integration,' and so forth, as variables related to domestic violence, but ultimately claim that the cause of the abuse lies with the parent's 'borderline personality.'

CAUSING NEW THINGS: SOCIAL WORK INTERVENTIONS

Front-line social workers rely on causal accounts to make sense of cases at hand. The imperative to discover cause arises from their location in organizational settings. As noted above, organizational actors confront difficult cases where they must do something. What-ever that something is, is governed and structured by organizational protocols, mandates, and policies. The determination of the underly-ing causes of a client's problems is shaped by organizational courses of action available to the social worker. For example, Mrs Brown, who is on welfare, lives in a downtown hotel room with her three children. She is reported, yet again, by the school to the child protection agency. The principal complains that the children 'arrive filthy to school,' 'are infested with lice,' 'show signs of malnourishment,' or 'fall asleep in class.'

The social worker who is familiar with the case knows: Mrs Brown receives her maximum welfare entitlement. Mrs Brown is looking for new housing, but she has been unable to find an apartment, as most landlords will not accept 'an Indian woman with three children.' The social worker recognizes that she does not have enough time to help Mrs Brown find housing and that Mrs Brown will probably be stuck in the hotel for several more months. Resolution of the housing problem requires long-term planning, for example, application for public housing and entry of the client's name onto a lengthy waiting list. Meanwhile, the social worker must demonstrate that something has been done and that she has taken some steps to remedy the immediate problem.

The requirement to do something means that certain problems drop out of sight or are suppressed because they cannot be dealt with by the social worker. Thus, the lack of running water in the room, the location of the washroom down the hall, the problem of sending the children to a hotel washroom unattended, the lack of a playground or space where the children can play, and the lack of money to rent adequate housing – are not issues that the social worker can remedy. Instead, what the social worker can do is to provide 'life skills' counselling to help Mrs Brown appreciate the importance of good personal hygiene. The worker can make a referral to have the public health nurse check the children to ensure that they are deloused. The children can be referred to a downtown child care worker who will take them out for recreation. Mrs Brown can be helped to use her time without the children to pursue some type of personal development.

The creation of a cause-and-effect relation between 'life skills' and 'poor hygiene' allows the social worker to develop specific organizational solutions for resolution of problems. Once the cause-and-effect relation is in place, the worker can spend time working on this case. She can direct agency resources to the case and refer the case on to other services.

Sometimes despite the social worker's best efforts, problems persist. Even when this happens, a skilled social worker can invoke an elaborate theoretical repertoire to account for the persistence of the problem. The social worker may revise the account of the cause-and-effect relation by factoring new elements into the problem equation, for example, the arrival of a new boyfriend, the effects of an eviction, or the loss of a job. She may ascribe blame to the client by referencing a psychological theory, for example, identifying a lack of motivation, a problem with impulse control, or unresolved narcissistic rage. She may invoke sociological insights to complain that the agencies where the client was referred are insensitive to Native client needs, that there are a lack of services on the reserve, or that Native people suffer the effects of discrimination. She may even engage in a critique of her own agency's services, programs, and structures, for example, cutbacks in child care workers, excessive caseloads, or inefficient organizational structures.

Front-line social workers not only take up authoritative research findings, they structure accounts of their practice to reveal the same rigour, exactitude, control for bias, and quest for truth as is characteristic of science. Social workers appreciate that so long as they appear committed to a scientific method, they are buffered from challenge from clients. They may from time to time need to acknowledge that their accounts are provisional, however, so long as they claim to follow scientific methods, they affirm their integrity and virtue as practitioners. Furthermore, despite the escape provided by provisional explanations, in the absence of carefully crafted and warranted challenge, social workers' accounts generally count as the facts of the matter.

DEFINING PROBLEMS

Polansky et al. in *Damaged Parents* begin the second chapter by asking 'How much is enough?,' meaning, 'At what point do we decide that a child's care has become so poor it is neglectful?' (1981: 10). They address as an academic or research problem, a serious matter for front-line workers, namely, how are they to decide if this child is neglected? Researchers want operational definitions of child abuse so that it can be discovered, and so that it be determined to exist. They need an operational definition that allows all professionals concerned with a case to agree that this really is child abuse.

Front-line child protection workers face cases where no clear answers to their questions are available. They confront developmentally delayed children reported by schools. They meet women who live in slum housing. They find alcoholic parents who leave their children unattended. They encounter an unending stream of cases where it is not at all clear, and not very easy to decide, whether or not the children are being abused or neglected. As child protection workers, they must determine the degree of risk and whether or not the child is in need of protection (Sigurdson and Reid, 1990).

The urgent need to make a decision is underscored by the knowledge that some situations can cause the death of a child. The key questions for a child protection worker are: How am I to decide if this is or is not a child who needs protection? What is the risk to the child? Researchers want to help front-line workers answer such questions, and to do so they develop diagnostic tools, instruments, and methods to address the messy situations of practice. Researchers hope that the concepts and tools they produce will be used by practitioners to enhance their diagnostic and predictive abilities (Sigurdson and Reid, 1990; Polansky, Gaudin, and Kilpatrick, 1992: 273; Polansky, et al., 1981: 70). For example, Polansky et al. state: 'We have had numerous requests for copies of the scale (Childhood Level of Living Scale) since it was first published ... mostly colleagues in social work and public health. It is, of course, a rather long scale, and some have wondered how to shorten it to make it more palatable for practitioners to use (1981: 70).

Damaged Parents reviews the problems that arise for social workers wanting a definition of neglect. The authors cite the problem of the child's rights versus the parents' rights, the problem of class bias, the problems of cultural and racial differences between social workers and clients, the legal variations in the definitions of neglect from region to region, and finally the problems of the rights of families against state intrusion (1981: 10–15). Yet, despite these difficulties the authors still manage to advance the following 'definition of neglect': 'Child neglect may be defined as a condition in which a caretaker responsible for the child either deliberately or by extraordinary inattentiveness permits the child to experience avoidable present suffering and/or fails to provide one or more of the ingredients generally deemed essential for developing a person's physical, intellectual, and emotional capacities' (1981: 15). These authors, like social workers in general, employ the discipline of science to construct a conceptual definition of child abuse and neglect.

The legislative requirement that social workers provide protective services for a child 'abused or neglected so that his safety or well-being is endangered' raises the questions: What types of behaviour or action or circumstances can I reasonably see as endangering safety or well-being? Can I collect enough evidence to convince others of the correctness of my decision?[3] In such circumstances, operational definitions[4] are an essential device for practically establishing visible terms, factors, indicators, and situations to which legislatively mandated provision can be applied.

Operational and conceptual definitions are produced by social scientists to render certain features of the world visible in replicative, predictable, and controllable ways. The conventions governing operational and conceptual definitions require that some phenomena be constituted as existent, distinct, and distinguishable from other phenomena. The facticity of an operational definition relies on what Kress and Hodge call a non-transactive style as opposed to a transactive style where 'there is an actor, the verbal process and an affected entity' (1979: 19). In an operational definition, the actor who sees, identifies, and names is substituted for an 'entity directly involved in the process' (ibid.: 19). For example, Murray Straus, in his paper 'Stress and Child Abuse,' defines stress as follows: 'The definition used here treats stress as a function of the interaction of the subjectively defined demands of a situation and the capacity of an individual or group to respond to these demands. Stress exists when the subjectively experienced demands are inconsistent with response capabilities' (1980: 90). For Straus, stress becomes an entity. Stress is treated as real apart from the particular and situated lives of those who are identified as suffering its effects. Here stress exists apart from the identifying work of the social scientist.

Similarly, the authors of *Damaged Parents* create a definition of child abuse and neglect that also employs a non-transactive grammar to create the appearance of objectivity. Their definition begins, 'Child neglect may be defined as a condition ...' This grammar is not accidental. By deleting the actors (social workers) who define the existent character of child abuse, it is revealed to be a real-world condition. The actual socially organized places and spaces where social workers practically define 'child neglect' are deleted in this nominalized grammar. The condition that emerges from actual people's work is cut free from that to emerge as a real-world 'fact' with its own ontology. The work and organizational ground of child abuse operationalizers, definers, and identifiers becomes not only invisible and inaccessible, but irrelevant against the pressing need to take action.

When front-line workers use the nominalized language of researchers, they participate in the social relations claiming authority for science and scientists. Their language practices disarticulate the actual social relations where they produce that which is known. The embodied subjects who actually do the defining, counting, reporting, intervening, and knowing are not only invisible, but, more importantly, the very issue of their visibility and embodied character becomes irrelevant. The proper topics for investigation, study, and analysis are professional theories, models, and facts. These stand as objects in and of themselves.

Academic social workers' texts display the code or language forms constitutive of good scientific talk, that is, conceptual and abstract definitions, which can be used by front-line social workers. These scientifically produced operational definitions can be used to cleave through clients' interpretations and to assert the authority of the front-line social worker. Operational definitions of 'child abuse' and 'child neglect' give child protection workers the appropriative power to count, prescribe, and define the lives of clients.

SCALES

Scales are another important device for accomplishing social work as science.[5] Sigurdson and Reid, in Child Abuse and Neglect: Manitoba Risk Estimation System (1990), provide seven scales for assessing risk: (1) vulnerability; (2) attributes of the current incident; (3) abuse/neglect pattern, prior incidents of abuse or neglect; (4) understanding of the child; (5) personal characteristics – such as ages of participants, substance abuse, psychopathology; (6) family interaction; and (7) relationship to community (1990). Similarly, Straus explored the statistical correlation between 'stress' – measured by an index of eighteen 'stressors' – (1980: 91) and 'child abuse' – measured through a Conflict Tactics Scale – (1980: 93). Polansky and his colleagues in Damaged Parents present a Maternal Characteristics Scale which is linked to the dependent variable, child abuse and neglect (measured through the Childhood Level of Living Scale). Using data generated from these scales, Polansky's group demonstrated a statistical correlation between the two variables to assert that the syndrome is a personality characteristic of neglecting mothers. The authority of scientific method founded in scales, tests, and correlations is expressed in the certainty of their pronouncements, for example, 'The syndrome ... seemed highly significant to child neglect' (1981: 41).

Through such scientific insights, social workers learn to blame the victim (Ryan, 1976) by locating the cause or etiology of syndromes in problems of development or character disorder. The authors of *Damaged Parents* attribute the apathy/futility syndrome to 'infantile personality.'[6] Steele (1980) argues that the problem of parental abuse of children is 'to be understood as a particular constellation of emotional states and specific adaptive responses which have their roots in the earliest months of life' (1980: 50). Spinetta and Rigler, promoting an 'intergenerational cycle of violence,' explain, 'Abusing parents were themselves abused or neglected physically or emotionally as children' (1982: 113). Finally, Klaus and Kennell employ 'bonding' theory to claim that 'early separation may be a significant factor' in child battery (1982: 184).

The obviously pejorative understandings produced by using these scales are concealed through the claims that the scales are objective, rational, and scientific. The Childhood Level of Living Scale measures such things as whether or not mother sets bedtimes, shows good judgment in leaving the children alone, leaves food scraps on the floor, allows the faucets to leak, encourages the child to wash hands, has magazines available, plans overnight vacation trips, and guards language in front of children (1981: 70). Although each of these variables speaks to a class standpoint, the authors of the scale are able to conclude that 'quality of child care is related adversely to poverty, but is separable from it' (ibid.: 80). Similarly, front-line social workers can justify their work by applying particular items from such scales to cases at hand. A social worker might employ the factors outlined in the Maternal Characteristics Scale – such as does mother show interest in others, does she enjoy living, does she show warmth with the social worker, does she take pleasure in her children – to make ad hoc connections to other 'facts.' For example: Mom answered the door wearing an old housecoat. She complains that she is always tired. She has few friends. She tried 'suiciding' two times before by taking pills. Her tone of voice was flat. She avoided eye contact.[7] Clearly, the informed and competent worker will know how to distil certain facts from an occasion to match the items on a scale. By inserting particulars extracted from clients' lives into the relevances of the scale, social workers objectify the evaluative and ad hoc constitutive practices they use to make cases visible as such.

Front-line social workers can cogently and replicatively discover and reproduce concepts such as the 'apathy/futility syndrome' in their work. They work up particulars of a woman's situation into indicators pointing to the presence of a syndrome. Concepts used ideologically practically order situations as actionable and as governable by policy and legislation. Social workers appropriate specific, individual, and idiosyncratic features of people's lives, for example, personal history, personality, family constellation, and family relations to reveal a correspondence with discursively organized theories. Once correspondence is established these particulars are treated as the facts of the case. The facts can in turn be explained through theory, for example enmeshed family relations, diffuse subsystem boundaries, and entropy resulting from system closure. The particulars of a situation are arranged to display the typicality of this case with similar types of cases requiring similar types of intervention.

PRODUCING PROBLEMS AND SUBSUMING CLASS

The line of client after client that moves through a front-line worker's office raises the challenge of explaining why this individual client on welfare drinks, while that client does not; why this client provides a 'decent' home for her children, while that client does not. This endless train of individual clients and cases passing through the life of a social worker redirects our professional gaze away from the social and towards the personal. The social relations where individuals' actions are embedded are dissolved. The attention must be on this person, here, and at this time, with this problem.

Ultimately, what is visible to social workers are discrete problems afflicting individuals. Social workers are required by policy and legislation to work with individuals and families, for these are the only entities to which service can be directed. Accordingly, child abuse and neglect cases are amenable to treatment that addresses individual, personality, and family dynamics. Cases are marked by the signs of disorder, disturbance, imbalance, or pathology. The discovery of pathology demands correction through social work efforts such as intervention into a pathological family system or a therapy for a personality problem. Attention to pathology transforms social phenomena into individual cases marked by syndromes, inadequacies, imbalances, and personal failure (Pfohl, 1977).

Researchers' texts provide working guides for identifying people who suffer from syndromes, disorders, and abnormalities that are understandable and controllable by front-line social workers. For example, Steele suggests that 'abusive, neglecting behaviour is not considered to be purely haphazard or impulsive' (1980: 50). The behaviour or pathology under study is not accidental or random. There must be a logical pattern and causal dynamic to the disorder that can be uncovered by research. Researchers promise to give practitioners methods for discovering and uncovering both the presence and the meanings of syndromes. If child abuse results from personal pathology expressed as a syndrome, then social factors can be dismissed. Social relations need not be seriously considered. In this vein, Van Stolk in her book *The Battered Child in Canada* argues that child abuse and class are not related: 'the literature stresses that child abusers come from all walks of life and all kinds of backgrounds. Child abuse occurs among families living in small towns, metropolitan areas and rural communities; and their housing varies from substandard hovels to high-class suburban homes. It is interesting to note that their houses are usually well kept. The educational achievements of child abusers range from partial grade school education all the way to post-doctoral degrees' (Van Stolk, 1978: 7). Having so forcefully argued against the class / child abuse relation, Van Stolk is obliged to produce an alternative explanatory account of child abuse. Her account must conform to the canons for doing positivist science, as well as having utility for front-line social workers as they struggle to make sense of their caseloads. Van Stolk's solution to the problem of class is to admit that although unemployment, marital status, race, religion, and alcoholism appear to be significant causal determinants of child abuse, the problem is actually far more complex. She invokes an 'et cetera' device to qualify the obvious or common-sense first-hand recognition that social factors might cause child abuse and neglect, but she adds that there is no one single causal explanation and observes: 'The overall phenomenon of the physical abuse of children is multi-dimensional. It results from the stress of social and economic factors as well as from factors stemming from emotional problems' (Van Stolk, 1978: 11). The claim that child abuse is multidimensional allows Van Stolk, and social work practitioners following her, to recognize the child abuse / class relation, yet deny its overall relevance for making sense of cases.

The claim that the etiology of a problem is multidimensional establishes a site on which theorists and practitioners alike can display the thoroughness of their investigative work. Thus, Barth and Blythe show their competence through their thorough examination of the factors that relate to child abuse; these include poverty, life change events, transience, and subcultural traits (1983). Similarly, the authors of *Damaged Parents* show that they are not to be deceived by the 'obvious' or simple connection between poor people and people reported to child welfare agencies. First, they reason that poverty does not cause child abuse, as many people who are poor do not abuse their children. Second, they propose that the cause of child abuse must be searched for in other directions, for example, character disorders, apathy/futility syndromes, and infantilism (Polansky et al., 1981: 25). The focus on the multidimensional aspects of the problem allows social workers to continue to recognize the social and economic contexts of the majority of their clients, while simultaneously it accounts for the problem as situated in personal and idiosyncratic factors.

Van Stolk cannot prove that poverty causes neglect or abuse, therefore, she invokes common-sense insights from casework. This common sense, as noted above, is built on an accretion of individual cases. The focus on individual cases leads social work practitioners and theoreticians to subsume social ground as merely sociological factors, which may or may not have relevance for consideration of the case at hand. The individual case becomes the centre, while the social ground, if considered at all, is transformed into elements, factors, and variables, which are treated only as providing background information about the case. Steele in an article titled 'Psychodynamic Factors in Child Abuse' outlines the importance of social factors, but is compelled to ask: 'We must realize that awareness of the importance of such social factors in situations of abuse does not answer what we consider more basic questions: Why, under circumstances of stress, do some persons respond with abusive behaviours, while others do not? Why do the majority of people in a low-socioeconomic group treat their offspring with adequate kindness, consideration, and love without abuse, even in critical times?' (1980: 51).

Additionally Carlson states, 'Since not all poor families resort to violence, poverty undoubtedly does not cause spouse abuse' (1984:

577). Similarly, Kempe and Kempe, in their monograph *Child Abuse*, argue: 'The enervating effect of continuous poverty and the helpless frustration of social discrimination undeniably contribute to life-long patterns of failure. The interrelationship of these factors with abuse, and even more with neglect is close, but the cure does not lie simply in offering money and social opportunity. The interplay between these factors is such that one might as reasonably say that the effects of a brutalizing or emotionally deprived childhood lead to a disordered life pattern, and then to economic and social disadvantage. The problem of social ills may owe as much to individual and family pathology as to the broad social framework in which the family has its place' (1978: 23).

The transformation of social ground into discrete factors related to an individual case is reflected in organizational policy and procedures manuals, as can be seen in the departmental child abuse/neglect protocol manual that stated: 'Child abuse is a problem that cannot be determined by a colour, race, age, religion or social strata. It is a problem that often self perpetuates. Abusive behaviour is usually an outlet for stress and can be induced by social or economic factors, the problem of single parenthood, illness, drug addiction, alcoholism, marital discord, or a myriad of other emotional stimuli' (author's name confidential). This protocol manual exemplifies social work procedures for transforming social ground into factors subordinate to a case structure. Child abuse is understood as a problem that cannot be adequately accounted for through consideration and analysis of social variables. Instead, it is understood as a self-perpetuating problem with a life of its own. Because it is a growing and living thing with a specific character, or etiology, the social work practice that addresses this problem is understood to be neutral and apolitical (Bernardes, 1985).

To question the existential assumptions informing the problem would reveal that one was not a proper social worker, was unworthy of professional trust, and unworthy of confidence, and, therefore, that one was incompetent, subversive, and dangerous. When radical or progressive social workers address people's lives in a way that involves class, oppression of women, exploitation, or ideology, they need to take care to avoid being heard to violate the common-sense boundaries and definitions of problems. The corollary is that proper social work talk is not political, feminist, activist, revolutionary, but rather professional, objective, impartial, and unbiased. However, social workers recognize that most of those with whom they normally work are poor, disadvantaged, and vulnerable people. They also recognize that not all of these people are guilty of child neglect or abuse. Additionally, many social workers argue that poor people are subject to continual scrutiny by police, welfare officers, public housing officials, day-care providers, and school nurses, and, therefore, it only appears that rates of child neglect and abuse are higher among these people. Social workers counter, 'If we had access to better-off families we would probably find similar rates of neglect and abuse.' Van Stolk recognizes that the majority of child protection clients are poor people, and throughout her text she returns to talk about 'the poor,' despite her claim that 'child abusers come from all walks of life.'

Gil, in *Violence Against Children*, which Van Stolk references, employs the same formula and recipes as Van Stolk for thinking about child abuse. Gil's work is based on a national survey of child abuse conducted by the Children's Bureau of the United States Department of Health, Education, and Welfare. The data were compiled through Central State Registries for child abuse across the United States, Puerto Rico, and the Virgin Islands (Gil, 1970: 73). Using incidents of reported abuse, judged against a pre-established 'conceptual definition of physical child abuse' (1970: 76), Gil addresses what he has determined to be the five dimensions of child abuse: (1) a culturally determined attitude of permissiveness towards the use of a measure of physical force; (2) child-rearing traditions and practices of different social classes and ethnic and nationality groups; (3) chance environmental circumstances; (4) environmental stress factors; and (5) deviance in the physical, social, intellectual, and emotional functioning of caretakers (ibid.: 135–6). Gil provides social workers with a detailed example of how to think through these five dimensions and apply them to cases at hand.

Furthermore, a large majority of families involved in these reported incidents of abuse belonged to socioeconomically deprived segments of the population whose income and educational and occupational status were very low. Moreover, families from ethnic minority groups were over represented in the sample and study cohorts. Environmental chance factors were often found to have been decisive in transforming acceptable disciplinary measures into incidents of physical abuse resulting in injury, and a vast array of environmental stress situations were precipitating elements in a large proportion of the incidents. Finally, a higher than normal proportion of abused children, their abusers, and their families revealed a wide range of deviance and pathology in areas of physical, intellectual and emotional functioning. (ibid.: 136–7).

The dimensions Gil outlines promise to be useful for front-line social workers. Once, when doing intake, I received a phone call from Violet Brown, who complained that Hector, her daughter Brenda's common-law husband, mistreated Rose, Brenda's four-year-old daughter. Violet also worried that Hector might be sexually abusing Rose. I noted that the family was Native and that Violet lived on a reserve. Violet reported that she 'looks after the kid a lot' and that she has 'cared for Rose for all of her life.' Gil's warning about culturally determined attitudes alerted me to appreciate that I was working with a Native client and that Natives did have unique child-rearing traditions and practices. As a worker familiar with Native culture, I appreciated that the care of a child by a grandparent was a common arrangement. Attention to environmental chance factors allowed me to appreciate the economics of reserve communities and the lack of paid employment. Because of these economics, young mothers often had to leave the reserve to seek work in the city. To find work, they would leave their children behind with grandparents or other relatives, and this would create environmental stress factors; simply put, problems would arise when the parent returned. Children would act out, and the mother would get frustrated trying to cope with the child's acting-out behaviour. Some grandmothers would grow very close to the children and resent the return of the children's mother. In such situations, the children felt torn, and family jealousies arose. A report to welfare would result. The final element on Gil's list that needed to be considered was whether there was deviance with regard to the physical, social, intellectual and emotional functioning of caretakers. In this case, I recognized that there were factors that might support the grandmother's concerns. First, I knew that there was a man in the home who was not the father of the child. This increased the risk to the child. I knew that incest rates are higher in 'blended families' than in natural families. Second, the different paternity of the children in the home could create rivalry, jealousy, stress, and strain. I needed to determine if the man's natural children were being favoured over his step children.

When I interviewed Brenda, I wanted to determine her capacity to be a parent. My readings on sexual abuse suggested that mothers of victims were often passive, presented flattened affect, were detached from their children, and were unable to protect them. Through my interview, I wanted to get a sense of who she was. How assertive was she? How articulate was she? Was she dull or bright? How involved was she with her children? Did her needs for male companionship outweigh her sense of maternal protection? When I interviewed Brenda, she denied the possibility that Hector would abuse her children, yet she also seemed able to recognize abuse if it occurred. I noted in my log that Brenda presented as a 'bright, articulate woman who was beginning a day-care worker program through the community college.' I also noted, 'She seemed aware of the issue of child abuse.' Next, I called the band social worker to determine the degree of community integration. The band social worker provided a glowing description of Brenda and also observed, 'Most people on reserve think Hector is okay.' Through my enquiries I attempted to construct an account that would either fit or not fit a discursively organized picture of a typical case of child abuse.

Initially, I and other workers remained sceptical regarding the report of abuse, and our assessment was that the report was a result of the grandmother's jealousy, anger, and insecurity. Two months later, however, Brenda approached our office to accuse Hector of abusing her children. My log records a lengthy interview in which Brenda related several 'disturbing' incidents where she witnessed her children engaged in 'inappropriate' sex play, that is, laying in bed pretending to be 'mummy and daddy,' her four-year-old daughter sitting on the couch spreading her legs and saying to another child 'Look, Billy, look.' With the new information, the initial formulations had to be revised. But the revision did not extend to a re-evaluation of the theoretical and conceptual substructures that organized my accounts. I did not question the correctness, validity, or relevance of the theoretical formulations which had guided my enquiries. On the contrary, the theoretical formulations remained incorrigible. What was brought into question was my investigative work itself, for I had to ask myself: What had I failed to notice? How could I have interviewed the child differently? How could the case have been managed differently? By providing a story of my management of the case which demonstrated that I had done all that could reasonably be expected, and by outlining the barriers to information, I salvaged my practice, and attributed the 'failure' to identify sexual abuse to the nature of the 'case' itself.

BOUNDARY WORK

Gil's writing is at times insightful, particularly when he suggests that 'violence against children ... may be a functional aspect of socialization in a highly competitive and often violent society, ... that puts a premium on the uninhibited pursuit of self-interest' (1970: 142). Gil arrived at this insight by recognizing that child abuse may be related to the forms of social life that he observes in the world about him. Even this admission becomes heretical for Spinetta and Rigler; Gil's rather temperate observations become a source of irritation deserving their censure and attack, and they state: 'If there really does exist as strong a link as Gil suggests between poverty and physical abuse of children, why is it that all poor parents do not batter their children, while some well-to-do parents engage in child abuse? Eliminating environmental stress factors and bettering the level of society at all stages may reduce a myriad of social ills and may even prove effective, indirectly, in reducing the amount of child abuse. But there still remains the problem, insoluble at the demographic level, of why some parents abuse their children, while others under the same stress factors do not' (1980: 118).

Spinetta and Rigler's critique must be appreciated as an instance of control and boundary definition. Their account aims to manage warranted understandings and professional common sense. Their critique aims not only to discredit Gil's consideration of poverty, but to establish through scientific argument a terrain of proper objects for research.

Social workers recognize the preponderance of 'poor' and 'minority' people among the reported cases of child abuse, yet their methods preclude recognizing that the phenomenon they observe may be an artefact of their own institutionally grounded practices. They begin inside institutional processes for working up diverse and multiform incidents – yelling, screaming, insulting, threatening, hitting, punching, screaming, gagging, tying – as typical and generalizable phenomena called abuse. Their focus on the abuse itself, rather than the social organization of incidents and accounts, leads them to hopelessly idealistic proposals and solutions. Gil suggests that 'the underlying value system' be changed (1970: 141). Yet can we reasonably understand yelling, screaming, insulting, and beating, as being the result of a value conflict? Despite the inescapable class location from which social work theorizing proceeds, and despite the 'classifying' (Noble,

1979) character of social work practice, social workers are discouraged in the texts from addressing class. Indeed, good professional work requires that practitioners appear to transcend class.

Mainstream social workers recognize that there are serious differences between the rates of reported abuse among working class families and among middle class families. Furthermore, proper professional practice precludes analysis of class as a social relation. As a result, social workers treat class as a thing. The literature abounds with examples and strategies for transforming social relations into static things to be appropriated as proper objects for social work analysis. Class as thing becomes social economic status (SES). Social economic status becomes yet another factor or variable used to account for pathology, deviance, and disorder. Even poverty, which has sense only as a social relation, is transformed, so that some people become 'the poor.' The poor are then described as having specific characteristics that set them apart from other people (Ryan, 1976).

Gil proposes four ways in which poverty appears to be related to 'the phenomenon of physical abuse': (1) culturally the approval of physical force is stronger among 'the socially deprived strata than among the middle class'; (2) the poor are less inhibited in expressing and discharging 'aggressive and violent feelings' than the middle class; (3) the poor suffer from more serious 'environmental stress and strain' than the middle class; and (4) the poor have 'fewer opportunities than the non-poor' to escape 'child rearing responsibilities' (1970: 144). Gil shows workers how to think through poverty as a thing. He provides social workers with yet another recipe for cooking up an explanation for this case at hand. A social worker reading Gil can look at Mrs X, and say, 'Yes, I see it, Mrs. X is poor. In poor families children are often controlled with coercion and force. She has told me that her dad used to give her beatings. I guess she learned that to control her kids she had to use force. Once she started hitting, her anger carried her away, until she lost control.'

Peter Silverman, the author of *Who Speaks for the Children* (1978), also works up class relations into forms actionable by social workers. By asking how is it that the poor comprise the most reported group, yet, poverty cannot be seen to cause child abuse, Silverman develops an analysis that opens a space for social work practice. He outlines: 'Abusers come from all walks of life. Many experts argue that neither ethnic groups nor economic class determine who become abusers; that the main factor is the way in which the parent was reared. An abuser is a person responding to his or her own maltreatment as a child, to feelings of low self-esteem and self worth, to improper maturation and socialization. Although these feelings may be aggravated and perpetuated by overcrowding, unemployment or poverty, the abuser is basically responding to his or her inability to cope with emotional stress. In general abusers tend to be dependent and narcissistic.' (1978: 41–42). Even in this passage, there is an obvious tension, and, despite his claim that 'abusers come from all walks of life,' Silverman is unable to silence or erase the effects of class. The problems of managing class vitiate social workers' claims that their practice is not political. Later in Silverman's text the tension between class and individual pathology emerges yet again: 'Listen to any Canadian professional talk about the causes of child abuse and you will hear: environmental stresses caused by poverty or poor housing, personality difficulties, marital and child parent and child parent conflicts, immature parents who are unable to meet the emotional needs of their children, families who are isolated, families who are poor, families who have a parent who was abused when he or she was a child' (ibid.: 51). Silverman's work is marked by the difficulty that faces social workers who find themselves caught between the reality of daily life in capitalist society – which has class as its fundamental social organization – and an institutional reality – which transforms class relations into neutralized and objective individual and family problems warranting professional intervention.

THE POLITICS OF SCIENCE

Social workers' practice is political. Their place inside the institutional apparatus of the capitalist state is political. Their methods of working are political. Managing class conflict is political. Social workers' use of power is political as it enacts organizationally determined courses of action, names reality, and manages their own and clients' lives. Social work power, expressed in the codes of science, ideologically appropriates a lived world and sets the boundaries for professionally appropriate action. As front-line social workers use problem-solving methods, they are enmeshed in a political standpoint.

The authors I have reviewed in this chapter are not exceptional, other than with respect to the general esteem in which they are held. Indeed, the problem-solving methods they use to examine child abuse and child neglect are understood to be the common-sense bedrock of the profession. Mainstream problem solving constricts the phenomeno-logical horizon to focus on pathological personality and individual problems. It is not accidental that Steele addresses deficient empathy, Polansky et al. outline the dynamics of the apathy/futility syndrome, and Kempe and Kempe explore medical models for treatment. Their texts provide social workers with formulas, guides, rules of thumb, and outlines for thinking and doing day-to-day social work practice with individuals and families. They provide tools for bringing individ-ual after individual into focus as a particular type of case. Within the case structure the daily lives of clients are largely invisible.

Social work is bound to a horizon of individual and family cases, as it is bound to a horizon of legislation, policies, directives, and organiz-ational mandates. Social workers' practical activities systematically disarticulate people from their social ground. People become visible and actionable as individuals suffering from specific problems. Once a person has been institutionally scoured of his or her social ground, the social worker can select bits and pieces of social life, reframed as mediating factors, ecological influences, and social variables, and rewrite these into the case assessment. Grandparents become possible 'resources.' Neighbours become 'friendship networks.' Aunts become a 'support system.' Systems theory, the ecological approach, and network analysis are tools that help social workers reframe, reorder, and reattach selected pieces of the individual's social world into a case narrative.

In this chapter, I have argued that what counts as social problems taken up by researchers and front-line practitioners must be under-stood as indexicals of institutionalized work processes. By the time that social workers graduate from schools of social work, they usually have learned that child abuse and neglect are not caused by class or poverty. In a way they are correct: Given the rules of the positivist paradigm, and the rules of scientific falsification, any identifiable phenomenon cannot be conclusively proven to have been caused by any other phenomenon. Social workers' location in an institutional apparatus binds them to problem-solving and scientific language games. They search incessantly for factors that really cause child abuse and neglect. These factors are almost invariably centred in and belong to the core objects of their organizational work, namely indi-viduals, families, or small groups.

Skilled social workers can sustain the cogency of problem-solving work despite disjunctures with the everyday realities of clients' lives. When anomalies arise what social workers doubt is their own ability to accomplish the ideal of positivist science. From their standpoint, inside the work of child protection, social workers lack the space to bracket the ideals of positivist science or problem-solving processes themselves (Schutz, 1973). As a result, their actual practices and those of clients are systematically subordinated to the terms of an ideal, the scientific and problem-solving method. Front-line social workers need not be intimately familiar with the precise rituals, manipulations, and requirements for effecting rigorous positivist research. By beginning inside the discursively organized concepts and categories which are elaborated, systematized, and codified by researchers, front-line social workers accept the epistemological reality of science. By beginning inside concepts and categories produced through science work, front-line social workers are compelled to think through situations at hand using methods that claim isomorphism with science. By beginning inside putatively scientific methods, social workers construct an institutionalized professional form of consciousness itself.

6

Producing Good Sense

A thin dusting of snow had fallen half an hour earlier. The grey light of pre-dawn made the tracks on the white ground look like dirty images in a grainy black and white photo. Yet, they were moose tracks and they were fresh. The moose had moved up the trail. Was it going to the lake? How big was the animal? Was it male or female? What could be divined from the two crescent shapes, each about four inches long and spaced slightly apart? Behind each set of prints was a faint brush of dirt. What did this mean? How was this animal moving? Was he meandering slowly? Was he moving at a steady gait? Was he running? How long before I arrived had he passed? What did the tracks mean? If only I knew how to read the tracks? How could I ever learn to read them?

As a front-line social worker, I have driven to a succession of apartments, flats, and houses to find children at home without parents, children crying, children with scars from old injuries, beer bottles strewn about kitchen tables, and wine bottles on floors, the stench of urine and feces permeating rooms, piles of dirty dishes in kitchens, and beds with sheets turned brown with filth. Doing child protection work required hunting for the places where I would find these signs. Once I tracked down the signs, they had to be collected. I entered them into my logs and running records. I told stories about the beasts running through people's lives.

I had to follow these tracks of day-to-day life to create social work accounts. I had to learn how to read these signs and others to tell stories about neglect and abuse. I and other social workers collected these signs to make cases. Our collections of signs from daily life became the base for legitimizing our interventions into clients' lives.

Signs become the facts of the case. Professionally inscribed facts are guides for social workers' interventions. Such facts help a worker decide whether to return the children to the parent(s) or whether to appear before the court to request an order for custody. Before a social worker can make decisions on such important matters, she or he must do considerable background work, involving investigation, consultation, assessment, consideration of alternatives, and referral to other resources.

As social workers enter the lives of clients, as a matter of routine they raise questions informed by the need to manage and control the case. What is the degree of risk? Is this an isolated incident? What supports can be put into the family? What can be done to prevent a recurrence of incidents of abuse or neglect? Does the parent really want this child? Can we effect enough change in x months to make the home safe for the child's return?

Day-to-day encounters with clients rarely provide clear answers to social workers' questions. Even when clients do not lie, withhold information, distort the 'facts,' minimize effects, or harbour delusional beliefs, making sense of the everyday worlds of people's lives remains a daunting task. Social workers must transform the equivocal, indeterminate, and mysterious spaces of day-to-day life into manageable and managed accounts.

MANAGING EQUIVOCAL DOMAINS

What happens when stories told by a mother, father, and child conflict? How can a social worker recover some sense from the conflict? To begin with, the social worker must proceed as though there were one 'true' story and one 'commonly shared world' (Pollner, 1974). However, social workers also recognize that the power to tell stories about that world is not equally shared between themselves and their clients. Social workers recognize that by virtue of their education, their position inside organizations, and their place outside the immediacy of clients' lives, they are able to craft authoritative accounts. Social workers have a power to tell stories about their clients and to act on the basis of those stories: A social worker is mandated through child welfare legislation, for example, to investigate a case of sexual abuse. To fulfil her mandate, she must construct an account of the 'facts' that transcends and manages the competing versions of 'what actually happened.' The worker decides, 'mother is in denial,' 'father is minimizing his actions,' and 'the child is probably telling the truth, because children don't usually lie about sexual abuse.' What emerges is an assessment that the child has been sexually abused and that temporary custody is necessary to protect the child.

The demand to transform equivocal matters into veridical accounts is a strain for social workers. Veridical accounts demand the assumption of a single real world in which there are specific facts that are discoverable and discovered. Indeed, the focus on facts generates an imperialism of the real. The certainty of a real world demands professional knowledge, control, and management. Conflicting accounts are put out of play, or bracketed, as social workers struggle to produce a single viable account of what actually happened.

Social workers must assume there is, and indeed must be, a single and commonly shared world. This assumption of a real world allows social workers to manage conflicting accounts of lived experiences as just stories. Social workers manage clients' stories as contaminated by bias, self-interest, delusions, lies, deception, or rationalization. The stories clients tell about day-to-day lives, and the events in them, are understood to be inferior to professional and organizational accounts. Thus, when Wanda, a thirteen-year-old girl, appeared at my office with dark blue bruises beneath her eyes, and a marked bend in her nose, I knew that her nose was broken. When she said, 'Dad was drunk last night, and punched me in the face because I got home at 3:00 a.m.,' I knew that this was an allegation of abuse. Later, I met with Wanda's father and he said, 'Wanda came home drunk last night, and began shoving my wife about. When I stepped in to stop her, I accidentally pushed her in the face.' The mother's story seemed to support her husband's. She told me, 'Wanda was pretty belligerent last night. I tried to sit her down to talk to her. She refused, and tried to get up. We began shoving each other. Herb got angry, jumped up, and pushed her away from me. I guess his fist hit her in the nose.'

Despite these competing versions about 'what really happened,' my job was to craft a single version of the events. First, it was clear that Wanda's nose was broken. Second, all accounts agreed that some contact between Wanda and her father's hand was responsible for the injury. Third, however, it was unclear whether this was purposeful, as Wanda suggested, or accidental, as father and mother suggested.

Certainly, at no point did I doubt that Wanda's nose was broken and that 'something must have happened to break it.' Indeed, the intervention that followed was an almost single-minded pursuit to determine what really happened and to craft a single sensible story based on observations of family members. The account I finally produced effectively managed these conflicting accounts as partial stories, told by different family members. These stories were themselves enveloped by my own story, or assessment, of what actually happened.

Social workers are obliged to admit that errors are a possibility and that unforseen elements may demand revising an account. Front-line practice is continually buffeted by surprises. A client revises her story. Undisclosed facts are revealed. New information 'sheds a new light on the case.' Furthermore, as the case moves forward problems, processes, and issues begin to congeal or take form under the heat of the investigative gaze. What may have begun as a vague 'gut feeling' becomes a personality conflict or value conflict between the client and the social worker. This conflict is then used to make sense of the 'lack of trust' and the client's 'refusal to disclose.' Indeed, under special circumstances the social worker can admit to having his or her problems with a case. He may cite value dilemmas and personal conflicts generated by working with certain types of clients – notably sexual offenders. He may plead a lack of expertise in the area. He may even raise unresolved issues from his own past which may make working on the case personally difficult.

Clearly, under such special circumstances, a social worker may employ professional discourse to identify problems and to bracket the putative veridicality of their accounts. By turning the professional gaze onto their own sense making, and their own accounts, skilled social workers can demonstrate their ability to be self-critical, self-reflective, honest, open to criticism, and determined to work through their own personal issues. Some standard responses might be to reassign the case, to get a second opinion, or to work through the difficulty under supervision.

THE SINGLE VOICE OF PROFESSIONAL ACCOUNTS

By the time the date of the hearing arrives the social worker must be able to appear before the court ready to deliver a professional assessment of the case and a series of recommendations. A professional presentation demands that evidence be presented at the hearing. The evidence must stand as a coherent account of a problem, a pattern, a situation, and a case. Whatever agonizing questions, laborious searches, or disquieting doubts the social worker may have suffered, if expressed at all, become secondary to the presentation of the 'facts' in court. Even when social workers express doubts about a situation, and admit to the possibility of being mistaken, by speaking such doubts they demonstrate that they are being fair. By opening a space for an alternative version, they nevertheless do assume that something actually happened. For example, when I took the stand in court to present evidence on the case of fifteen-month-old Bobby, I informed the judge, 'A physical examination of the child at the hospital revealed a round red scar just above his pubic area. The doctor and nurse thought it could be a mark from a cigarette burn or from a serious diaper rash. Dad denies that it is a cigarette burn.' In this testimony, I presented the simple fact: 'there was a round red scar.' However, by providing two competing versions of the scar's origin, I created a frame for two accounts – with two very different moral evaluations – and two very different organizational responses.

The problem of competing versions about 'what actually happened' demands that social workers try to contain confusion, doubt, and the possibility of inaction. By focusing on the facts, social workers carve out a space where action can proceed. Hence, in the example just cited, the simple fact of the scar can be read as problematic. Even if it is the result of severe diaper rash, this may point to lack of adequate parental attention.

When a social worker proceeds directly from the call, to the apprehension, to the report to the court, and finally to the hearing, the linearity of the work process itself silences the basic equivocality of discovery. The confusion of day-to-day sense making, the dead ends, the wrong versions, and the misunderstandings, are glossed through the presentation of a singular veridical account.

To do an investigation social workers must render particular occasions into cogent accounts. They must produce the facts of the matter. Thus, Turner and Shields advise: 'It is most important that the social worker use plain and simple language and avoid professional jargon or ambiguous terms which cloud the specific meaning of the evidence. He[1] must adhere to the professional standards of objectivity in his testimony. Evidence submitted must be derived from a thorough investigation of all potential sources of information. He must try to avoid value judgments and generalizations and be able to distinguish actual observations and facts from opinion' (1985: 121). Despite Turner and Shields's apparently simple recommendation that social workers present the facts in an objective manner, during the investigation the facts change. Doing an investigation produces successive organizations and layerings of facts. As the investigation proceeds, what were once relevant facts, hence, the facts at the centre of the work, become irrelevant, or tangential to a new centre. When I was doing intake, I once received a phone call from a person who claimed, 'There's an awful smell coming from the apartment next door. There's a little kid in there, and I don't think it's very healthy.' I found a closed file on the family and discovered that they had been reported to the agency a year before. The file indicated that workers at the child's day-care centre had had some concerns about the child's failure to meet 'developmental milestones.' The social worker at the time noted, 'There are some general concerns about parenting.' The file reported that mum, a 'chronic schizophrenic' and her three-year-old son lived with mum's ailing father. The grandfather, who had been a logger, had suffered a crippling heart attack a year and a half before. Other than a referral to a 'parents and tots' group, no further action was taken at that time, and the file was closed.

With the new report I reactivated the file. My first concern was to determine if there was an unusual smell. Next, I needed to find its source, and, finally, I needed to investigate if there was a connection between the smell and adequate care for the child. The first visit to the home revealed that the child's bedwetting and the accumulation of urine in the mattress was the source of the smell. The focus of my intervention was to teach the grandfather, who was identified as the 'primary caregiver,' some 'parenting skills' for managing bedwetting and for controlling the smell of urine, such as restrict the child's intake of fluids before bedtime, use diapers, get the child up from sleep to 'go pee,' and launder soiled sheets.

At first the case was treated as a minor problem with 'life and parenting skills.' Through contact over several months, however, the severity of mum's mental condition, her refusal to take medication, and the strong possibility that the grandfather might die from a heart attack, led me to explore mum's 'past level of functioning' (DSM IV, 1994). I wanted to determine whether mum might be able to care for herself and her child on her own. At this point my focus shifted to helping mum to accept medication and mental health resources, to assessing her ability to care for herself and her child, and to developing a plan to help mum move towards independent living with her child.

To answer the question, 'Could mum be helped to cope on her own?' I contacted other professionals at mental health, public health nursing, and homemakers. At this point, grandfather, despite his weak heart was understood as a 'positive element in the family system.' My interviews with the man revealed his interest in the child, his concern for his daughter, and his efforts to compensate for mum's illness by taking the child out for walks and for drives about town. To complete my assessment, I requested information about mum's psychiatric history from the hospital. Mum reluctantly signed the 'release of information forms,' and I sent these to the hospital. Three weeks later, I had a telephone interview with a nurse in the hospital records department.

The review of the hospital file revealed that upon last admission mum had presented as extremely 'bizarre' and 'floridly psychotic.' She was 'aggressive' and 'ranted about her father fucking her.' The file noted, 'Her language is extremely sexualized. Nursing records noted, 'Once the patient was stabilized on CPZ [chlorpromazine] her delusions disappeared.' Mum denied incest. After the telephone conversation with the nurse, my focus shifted. This new information led me to be concerned about sexual abuse. Was the trauma of sexual abuse the precipitator in mum's mental illness? Certainly, sexual abuse would make sense of mum's very infantile and childlike manner. I wondered, 'What meaning did mum's ranting in the hospital really have?'

A week later, I conducted an interview with the grandfather. I steeled my courage and asked him straight out, 'Have you ever had sexual relations with your daughter?' To my absolute surprise, the man, without any sense of shame, or sense of wrong, replied, 'Yes.' Once again, I needed to reframe the focus of the case. What began as a routine case of a parent needing some 'life skills' was transformed through sustained intervention work into a serious case involving an exceedingly 'pathological family system' and the identification of a 'child at extreme risk.' I worried, 'If this man has sex with his own daughter, what would prevent him from having sex with his grandchild?'

Once the father confessed to 'incestuous relations' with his daughter, this became a fact on file. This fact became the conceptual organizing centre for stringing together other facts, such as his daughter's mental illness, his decision to stay home, and his inadequate care for the grandchild. Particulars were retroactively transformed to reveal the severity of the problem, such that the file became a veridical record documenting a 'history of concern,' the identification of 'inadequate parenting,' 'past reports of neglect,' and 'pathological family relations.' The particulars of the file were reframed, such that facts emerged as indicators of serious 'neglect' and 'disturbance.'

The incest frame provided for the mobilization of grave concern and justifiable alarm that could legitimize demands for custody of the child. Additionally, the identification of incest connected the case to provisions of the Canadian Criminal Code, that is, part IV dealing with 'sexual offence, public morals and disorderly conduct.' The Criminal Code outlines, 'Everyone who commits incest is guilty of an indictable offence and is liable to imprisonment for fourteen years' (Canada, *Criminal Code*, 1989: 81). My knowledge of the offence, the threat of punishment, and the likelihood of apprehension provided me with considerable power over the lives of the people in this family.

POWER AND COMMON SENSE

What counts as good sense for social workers indexes a complex conceptual background. When a social worker meets a person who is an 'alcoholic,' a rather common situation in front line practice, both the identification and the sense or meaning of that identification references a background of competing theoretical understandings. Some social workers may embrace the 'Twelve steps of A.A.', some a variant of Jellinek's typologies (1960), and others a stage model of addictions, such as proposed by Prochaska, DiClemente, and Norcross (1992). Regardless of which approaches we use, the simple identification of alcoholism identifies a condition or syndrome amenable to social work intervention.

Particular signs from the person's life are connected to abstracted formulas to produce a professional analysis of the case and its problems. The odour of alcohol on the client's body, the detection of fine tremors, the client's admitting to blackouts, the presenting problem of marital difficulties, all become signs of alcoholism. Particulars are combined into a sensible matrix to act as indicators of alcoholism. Once combined, these may suggest an acute toxic reaction, chronic physiological damage, or deterioration of social functioning caused by excessive alcohol consumption. In short, because the client is poisoning himself and destroying his body and his life, he has an 'alcohol problem.' He is an 'alcoholic.' Once the problem is identified, social workers are entitled to direct efforts to the case to help the client resolve the problem and to help the client develop new ways of living.

Social workers search case situations looking for clues, evidence, or signs that can be connected to specific professional categories. They may employ a series of common-sense understandings or rules of thumb to manage decisions about a case, such as, 'No-one can stop an alcoholic drinking but himself. Alcoholics minimize their drinking. Alcoholics deny they have a problem. If a spouse complains about a partner's drinking, then there is an alcohol problem in the family.' If alcoholism is suspected, the social worker searches through the lives of clients for visual and verbal clues that the person might be an alcoholic.

Through interviews conducted over days, weeks, or even months, social workers pull client presentations and utterances into professional frames and theories, to tell a story about alcoholism. Thus, the client who claims, 'I can stop drinking whenever I feel like it' is heard as 'being in denial.' Denial itself is professionally understood as signifying that there is in 'fact' a problem – a Catch-22 articulating the social worker's power to define case reality.

As suggested above, there will be disagreements between social workers. One social worker may place greater faith in one adage over another. Different social workers may adhere to conflicting schools of thought or theories. Through case conferences, staff meetings, and workshops, social workers try to develop a good sense shared by all competent members. Social workers use such gatherings to establish commonly accepted and universally held schemata for making sense of various problems: during the late 1970s and early 1980s a cadre of sexual abuse experts conducted workshops across the United States and Canada (for example, Rolland Summit, Linda Halliday, Florence Rush). Social workers were advised to discard Freud's seduction theory. They were told that understanding a child's allegations of sexual abuse as fantasy is wrong. They were told that children's claims about sexual abuse are to be taken literally. Furthermore, it was argued that sexual abuse should not be left unaddressed and that fears of reawakening the child's trauma are misplaced. Social workers were urged to recognize that sexual abuse is extremely harmful and that victims require treatment to work through the trauma. Simply put, through workshops and seminars the old common sense about sexual abuse was displaced by a new common sense.

Following participation in sexual abuse workshops, social workers in our office learned to employ a series of rules of thumb for addressing a report of sexual abuse by a child. First, 'You begin by believing the child, and you let the child know that you believe her.' Second, 'You give the child support, and let her know that she has done well to report.' Third, 'You confront the mother with the information, tell her that you believe the child, and attempt to enlist her as an ally, against the offender.' Finally, 'You confront the father on safe territory (the office) and you tell him that you believe the child. You request that he leave the house.' When dealing with the father you can expect, 'He will deny the charge; he will accuse his daughter of being seductive (a valuable clue),' or, 'He will attempt to reframe the problem so it appears innocent. The offender might claim, 'We were only wrestling. I wash the girls to keep them clean. I teach my children to not be ashamed of their bodies.' Through the discussions and debates following workshops, social workers in our office continually modified old understandings and developed new sets of adages, beliefs, frames, and schemata.

VOICES FROM OUTSIDE

What counts or gets defined as the dominant categories of social work, whether alcoholism, child neglect, family violence, or sexual abuse, is structured by institutional work processes. Against the authority of professional and organizational categories, women, working people, Aboriginal peoples, and immigrants have reflected on their lives and have struggled to voice their realities. They have struggled to find a language to express their lives against a language that has worked to silence their realities. They have struggled to find spaces for expressing their lives – women's groups, healing circles, community meetings – inside a world where the space for addressing problems is organizational, professional, and institutional. Initially, people whose experiences were silenced tried to take up and use an existing language and its epistemic horizons to think through their experiences. Women who were being beaten by their spouses struggled to figure out how to address their experience. Did they call themselves 'battered wives'? They were not all wives. Were they

'battered women'? However, they were not just 'battered.' Furthermore, what exactly counted as 'battered'?[2]

By illuminating the multiple dimensions of female oppression,
women have compelled social workers, and other professionals, to
address the lived experiences of women and children in families.
However, women's experiences get institutionally appropriated as yet
another area for scholarly study, research, textual production, and
career advancement. Once worked up ideologically, women's lives are
discursively transformed into sites of yet another mental illness,
syndrome, pathology, and deviance (Walker, 1981). The living voice
of protest is institutionally transformed into the objective clinical
voice prescribing individual treatment, containment, and therapy.
Sexual attacks on children, whether perpetrated in the porno-
grapher's studio or in the private home become visible only as institutionally bounded by legal–juridical categories.

Like battered women, Native people have also struggled to voice
the sources of their oppression. In Manitoba generations of Native
children were removed routinely from their homes and placed for
adoption in the United States. It was not until Indian leaders began
to come together to form organizations and to give voice to their
experiences that this was identified as a problem. Only after Aboriginal people identified the problem and mobilized protest did the
provincial government respond: It appointed the Kimelman Commission in 1982. Judge Kimelman's work reframed the problem into
language and terms actionable by the law, agencies and organizations, through the authoritative provision of a series of recommendations, for example, a 'moratorium would be placed on the out-of-
province placement of all aboriginal children' (1983: 2) and the 'development of the Indian child welfare agencies ... under the tripartite
agreement' (1983: 8). Once people give voice to experiences from their
lives, whether women, Aboriginal people, immigrants, or disabled
people, these people become subject to elaborate conceptual devices
for effecting institutional management of their problems.

Even as people express their experiences, front-line social workers
and other professionals begin to incorporate the language of daily life
into the professional lexicon and professionalized accounts. New
information becomes integrated into existing adages, sayings, and
common wisdom. Voices from poor people, thus, led social workers to
propose, 'Neglecting parents are likely themselves victims of neglect.
Neglecting parents themselves need to be nurtured.' Voices from

survivors of sexual abuse led social workers to assert, 'Incest victims feel ambivalence towards the offender. Victims must be informed that they are not to blame.' Voices from Aboriginal people led social workers to propose, 'Indian kids are best left on the reserve where they have a sense of belonging. We should try to place Indian kids in Indian homes.' Such formulas allow social workers to manage cases at hand, while also suggesting preferred intervention strategies.

Through the regular invocation of set formulas, or adages, social workers justify and craft their practice. By 'not blaming the victim,' they can communicate warmth, nurturing, understanding, and acceptance even to those who are most socially stigmatized and despised. Reciprocally, they can account for their interventions by using these frames to show how they act on common sense and are competent, caring, and professional.

When social workers face situations that cannot easily be subsumed within existing repertoires or that resist intervention efforts, the cry is for more knowledge. The plea for knowledge expresses the need for practical mastery of cases. To meet our professional needs for mastery, we may turn to journal articles or authoritative monographs on alcoholism. We search to understand the syndrome. We hope to identify the dynamics. We want to develop a plan and a controlled intervention. Indeed, continuing education and the invocation of lifelong learning are fundamentally rooted in the problem of managing day-to-day experience.

Day-to-day practice remains a confusing terrain of pain and chaos, yet, inside the organization, the social worker must appear to be in control. The imperative for control, planning, and management, leads social workers in the quest for new knowledge. The valuation of lifelong learning fuels academic production. Social workers purchase or borrow new texts, visit academic libraries, subscribe to key journals, attend workshops, and return to university for upgrading. To maintain a sense of themselves as competent professionals, capable of engaging in professional practice, social workers regularly rejuvenate their sense of competence and mastery through immersion in learning activities.

THE RELATION AS AN ORDERING DEVICE

The challenge of sorting out 'fact' from 'fiction' and developing an account of 'what actually happened' has led social workers to develop an elaborate discourse on the social work relationship. The social work relationship is a critical set of strategies for managing practice at the front line. It is generated by the problematic of gathering information that social workers can claim to be true, factual, accurate, and honest. Social workers assume that obtaining true, factual, accurate, and honest information relies on trusting, empathic, understanding, and non-judgmental relations with clients. The professional discourse on social work 'relationship building' (Brill, 1985; Carkhuff, 1983; Benjamin, 1981; Kadushin, 1972; Biestek, 1957) glosses the power imbalances between social workers and clients. Beneath the day-to-day problems of fear, misunderstanding, dishonesty, and concealment that social workers encounter when working with clients is their power. The conflicts posed by the problem of managing clients and the need to assert professional power leads social workers to value 'relationship building skills.' Thus, Shulman has written: 'All new relationships, particularly those with people in authority, begin somewhat tentatively. Clients perceive workers as symbols of authority[3] with power to influence them. Clients often bring with them a fund of past experiences with professionals or stereotypes of helping professionals passed on to them by friends or family. So the first sessions are partly an effort to explore the realities of the situation. Encounters with people in authority usually involve risks, and clients will be careful to test the new situation before they expose themselves to these risks' (1992: 80).

Shulman's presentation of the problem and his resolution prove to be instructive. First, he envelops the specific problems posed by the relationship between social workers and their clients inside a generalized formula of 'all new relationships.' This absorption of the specific social worker / client relation into a generalized form allows him to bypass specific dynamics of power, management, authority, and control. Instead of examining the organizational ground that brings social workers and clients together, Shulman can move to look at some abstract principles and qualities of relations in general. By focusing on relations in general Shulman produces an abstract and professional discourse on relations. He skirts the concrete social organization of actual social workers' power. Second, by addressing the ways that 'clients perceive workers,' he frames client understandings as partial, situated, and thereby subject to error. Shulman's own narrative brackets client's perceptions, while tacitly claiming to speak from a place inside generalized professional knowledge based on the practices of science. Shulman uses the voice of professional knowledge to create a space between his narrative and the vicissitudes of clients' perceptions. He represents client perceptions as structured by 'past experiences with professionals or stereotypes.' The generally pejorative sense of 'stereotypes' discredits the perception and implies that it may be inaccurate and misinformed. Shulman, although raising the problem of authority, frames it as a problem of perception, understanding, and information.

Skilled social workers, using techniques similar to Shulman's, anticipate and manage hostile client reactions. They know how to counter clients' reactions through skilful use of self. They build relations with clients that correct misperceptions by 'clarifying purpose, clarifying role, and reaching for client feedback' (1992: 86).

The professional social work discourse on relationships occludes, yet provides for, the perpetuation of the social organization of power and authority. Even as social workers construct relations of trust with clients, they teeter on the edge of organizational betrayal. The client who confesses, 'Jamie's tooth really broke because I threw her off the couch,' risks having her child apprehended. The client who confesses, 'Jack gives me $200 every month for support under the table,' risks being reported to welfare 'fraud investigators.' The client who confesses, 'I got drunk on Saturday night and masturbated with my son,' risks being charged with sexual assault. As social workers build relations with clients, there is always a recognition that a client might reveal information that demands that the social worker act in a way that goes against the client's interests.

The decisions a social worker makes about a case and the quality of relationships with a client – their intensity, depth, warmth, caring, or hostility – are also conditioned by the practical exigencies of day-to-day work. If a social worker has apprehended half a dozen children over a weekend, he or she may decide to take a greater risk than usual by not proceeding to a hearing or by returning the children to the parents. Social workers who apprehend 'too many' children run the risk of becoming too busy to manage their caseload, losing face-to-face contact with clients, getting bogged down in paperwork, and having a supervisor question their practice. If a social worker apprehends 'too many' children, her supervisor might worry that she is being too eager, that she is imposing her own values on clients, or that she may be prejudiced against people who become clients.

When I worked at the front line, I separated what seemed to be an unending stream of children from their parents. Although I believed that my actions were necessary, often I was struck by the grim recognition that I caused considerable suffering and pain in the lives of my clients. While I attempted to cultivate caring, honest, empathic, face-to-face relations with my clients, I recognized that my power over their lives caused them to feel fear, mistrust, and anger. Despite my own desire to avoid making negative judgments about clients, I faced the hard case 'facts.' I was horrified by the infant's flattened skull, the sexual abuse of a three-year-old, the stench of urine, the filth covering a child's bed, and the scars and injuries that marked children's bodies. As a professional, I could empathize with the parents' difficulties, but I also recognized the pain, hurt, and suffering experienced by their children.

Beneath my own confusion and conflicted loyalties, I sensed another reality behind the case facts. I could see that my clients lived in grinding poverty. They were trying to raise children in awful housing. They could not afford to buy proper food. They went without recreation. There were few opportunities for safe and healthy respite from child care. They suffered social stigma, prejudice, and racism as welfare clients, Native Indians, and single parents. As a professional, I recognized that my professional powers and organizational mandate did not allow for preventive intervention. As Wharf has observed, 'Child welfare in Canada consists of a set of poorly funded residual programs designed to assist only when families cannot cope' (1993: 211). How social workers can see their cases, how they can act, and the services they are able to provide is structured by the relative expansion or contraction of their organizations and the social service apparatus as a whole.

Behind the facts requiring apprehension, I recognized the 'reality' of children's and parents' experiences. I removed children from their parents and placed them in the homes of strangers. These children suffered.[5] They cried because they missed their parents, their brothers and sisters, their friends, and their familiar surroundings. As Falconer and Swift note, 'Even a small child grieves for the loss of an adult he is attached to and will usually feel that he is 'bad' and to blame for being removed' (1983: 139). Their parents suffered too. They cried because their babies had been taken away, because they felt lonely, and because they were afraid that their children would never be returned to them. Where social workers act more like police than professional helpers, building relations of trust, caring, mutuality, and respect is difficult, if not impossible.

COERCIVE AUTHORITY

Social workers may personally dislike apprehending children, but as professionals they accept the duty to protect children from abuse and neglect. This may mean removing children from their parents. When I did child protection work I was impressed by the compassion of my colleagues, by their caring and commitment both towards children and parents. Despite our best personal intentions, we were obliged to follow policy, legislation, and organizational directives that many of us experienced as vitiating our capacities for compassion. We were compelled to act in ways that many clients experienced as coercive, punitive, and threatening.

Although we almost always apprehended children only to provide immediate protection for them, we also recognized that it placed both the parents and the children under our power. Once a child was apprehended, we could demand change from the parent. We could demand that the parent stop drinking, find new housing, attend a Systematic Training for Effective Parenting (STEP) (Dinkmeyer and McKay, 1976) program, agree to work with a family support worker, and receive mental health counselling. Social workers by apprehending children hold parents at ransom.

The price for returning a child to a parent is defined by the social worker. Where I worked, social workers clearly understood that apprehension is a coercive tool. During office talks, staff meetings, and case conferences, I heard social workers say, 'The loss of the children has given the parent the motivation to change. The apprehension has taught the parent a good lesson. The apprehension finally seems to have thrown a good scare into her.' Social workers used apprehension as a key tool to enforce demands for client change.

The coercive use of apprehension can be positively reframed. We can invoke the texts, such as Shulman's, to argue that we are merely 'making a demand for work' (1992: 94).[6] However, to respond to our 'demands for work' clients may still deceive. Their compliance may be artificial. Laird warns, 'Referred families often feel coerced into a treatment plan that seems to have little meaning or relevance for their lives' (1985: 361). Social workers appreciate that, in the end, our power to demand change through the final option of apprehension is lamentable, but necessary, to reach resistant or irresponsible clients.

The adversarial relationship between social workers and parents was expressed every day where I worked. Colleagues spoke of 'teaching the parents a lesson' of 'winning in court,' of 'getting the goods on them' and 'catching them this time.' Certainly, as social workers, we are well aware of clients' reactions to our power. All of us meet with verbal abuse from clients. We face their fear of our power, whether expressed as anger, withdrawal, depression, or alcohol abuse. I once worked with a woman who became increasingly despondent after I apprehended her children. She began to drink even more excessively than when I had first apprehended her children. During one interview I tried to 'impress on her' the real danger that I would not return her children to her unless she stopped drinking. She exploded with, 'If you want my fucking kids so bad, you keep them.'[7]

Unfortunately, social work practice texts either avoid addressing the coercive and manipulative nature of professional power, or when they do address social worker's power they fail to analyse the social organization or mechanics (Foucault, 1980) of that power. Baily and Baily, in *Child Welfare Practice*, urge social workers to employ a practice that aids parents through 'coaching, persuasion, encouragement, information, role modelling, and instruction.' they warn social workers that 'attitudes of retaliation and rejection have no place in the practice and repertoires of child welfare staff' (1983: 4–5). They add that practitioners must create doubt in the parents' mind about their parenting without 'criticizing or shaming the parent' (ibid.).

Similarly, Kadushin, and Martin recognize that child protection practice may be coercive. They cite Stein, who suggests that the 'best interests of the child' may be 'used to punish parents for behavior that the community finds distasteful' (1982: 64, cited in Kadushin and Martin, 1988: 107). However, even in this formulation Kadushin and Martin have already bypassed professional and institutional power by invoking the 'community.' It is this idealized, romantic, cohesive, and supportive community that acts. Later in the same text, Kadushin and Martin argue that 'the demonstration of community power and concern, expressed in the act of intervention, may itself induce change' (ibid: 269). Their account glosses the social organization of power and the struggles against power that mark the boundaries of a capitalist state. They locate social workers' authority and mandate inside an idealized community.

The relations of coercion, force, conflict, and power are embedded in child protection legislation and the legally mandated apparatus that has been created to enforce that legislation. Child protection is organized as an adversarial work process that pits social workers against parents. Social workers have the power to determine if a child is neglected or abused. Together with lawyers and the judge, they determine what is 'in the best interests of the child.' Social workers have the power to remove children from parents, either temporarily or permanently. Mandatory supervision allows them to enter homes routinely and to evaluate the quality of parents' care for their children, and court orders can be issued demanding that parents provide support payments for children in care.

ALTERNATIVES TO APPREHENSION

Social work practitioners and educators recognize that apprehension should be a 'last resort' and that to prevent apprehension, programs and services need to be provided to families. Wharf outlines: 'provincial ministries in Canada have developed an array of programmes ranging from day care, homemaker services, voluntary agreements between parents and the ministry for short periods of care in times of stress, family counselling, and intensive child care programmes for children in their own homes. These programmes gradually evolved in child welfare agencies following years of experience with well-meaning attempts to provide substitute care for neglected and abused children' (1985: 204–5). However, as options for preventive service disappear through cutbacks, as more services are income and needs tested, as child-care workers are cut, and as contracts are shortened, as family support workers are fired, and as caseloads increase, the only tool remaining for social workers to protect children is apprehension.

The assessments a worker makes about a case are structured by the background of available services. When a wide range of services are available, the assessment may shift, and strategies for case management may be innovative, flexible, and professionally congruent. When services disappear, alternatives for practice are constricted. For example, when a child is sexually abused, if there is insufficient evidence to make a case in court, but if the mother believes the child, and if the offender is unwilling to leave, the mother and the child may be trapped in the home and have nowhere else to go. However, if there is a women's shelter, transition housing, co-op housing, and good public housing, a woman and her child may have more choice. If there are retraining programs, funding for education and child care, a woman may be able to break her economic dependence on the offender. If there are support groups, counselling services, and even treatment programs for offenders, 'healthy' change might be achieved in people's lives. Simply put, if social workers have access to resources for clients, then the options for their practice expand.

Even if the mother refuses to leave her husband, but believes her child, a social worker may be able to provide resources to ensure the protection of the child in the home.[8] To keep the child in the home, the social worker must have access to child-care workers, trained family support workers, counselling services, and sufficient time to do regular follow-up. Additionally, if specialized treatment programs are available, rather than incarceration in a prison, even the offender might be convinced that an open confession may be preferable to denial. However, because existing services and resources for child victims, their mothers, and offenders are limited, the options available to a social worker involved in such cases are often restricted to punitive measures. Children are apprehended and criminal charges are laid against the offenders to ensure their removal. Both the apprehension of a child and the involuntary removal of an offender require the production of hard factual evidence that can be presented to court. Sexual abuse cases, however, like all child abuse cases, pose serious problems concerning evidence. The offence usually occurs in the privacy of the family home, where there are seldom witnesses and where the child victim is usually the only person able to provide testimony. Offenders almost always deny that an offence occurred. Mothers often do not know (or claim to not have known) that the child is being abused. The child victims themselves may withdraw their allegations because they do not want their fathers sent to jail.

Even when prosecution is successful, there is usually at least a year between the time when the sexual abuse is first disclosed and a sentence is passed. Social workers, who must be alert to potential dangers to a child, yet, who have no mechanisms for protecting the child while it is in the family home, may threaten permanent custody to force a mother to choose between living with her husband or losing her children. The use of apprehension to coerce women to choose their children over the offender becomes necessary because of the lack of treatment alternatives.

The social worker's duty is to protect the child, and protection is defined within the narrow frame of parental failure, physical abuse, sexual abuse, or neglect. The need for statutory protection centres on a differentiation between children and adults – an identification that is established through reference to chronological age and date of birth as matters of record. Although children are considered to need protection in child welfare legislation, such provisions are not extended to adults. Furthermore, adults are identified as the culprits in the process. Once children are apprehended, considerable money is spent to provide them with adequate accommodation in group homes, residential treatment centres, and special needs foster homes. However, once children are discharged from care, they are returned to parents who may continue to live in substandard housing and on inadequate welfare checks. Wharf argues: 'Children of poor families are provided with adequate support only when they are removed from their families and placed in substitute care. The cost of maintaining a child in even the most basic form of foster care far exceeds the cost of supporting a parent and a child together' (1985: 295).

Despite the apparently innocent yet profound truism 'that poverty is primarily an absence of money' (Ryan, 1976: 6), the individual structure of the case directs the social worker's attention to specific instances of parental failure. The organizational structure of child welfare, with its mandated focus on individuals, focuses the worker's attention on the case. If the parent is poor and lacks the resources to care adequately for the child, according to an imprecise standard, it is the parent's failure. Poverty that results in failure to care for a child becomes a matter of individual culpability. Social workers protect children from harmful effects of parental failure. Organizationally, no attention is directed to considering that the parents themselves need to be protected from racist and slum landlords, from exploitative employers, from inadequate educational systems, and, yes, even from state welfare agencies. Within the existing horizon of the institutional apparatus, innovative and creative practice is reduced to social workers' desires, longings, and imagined tomorrows.

The possibility of imagining child welfare as a sensible and cogent field of action presupposes the fragmentation of daily life into administratively controllable segments. From inside organizations, child neglect and abuse are visible as distinct social problems separate from, although related to, other distinct social problems. Discrete social problems are managed by an organizational apparatus, which includes such entities as a welfare office, a child protection agency, an unemployment office, a mental health office, an addictions' centre, a housing office, a provincial rent control office, a human rights commissioner, an ombudsman's office, and a workers' compensation board.

Social workers themselves are trapped inside organizations which demand that they apprehend children, proceed to court, and request temporary and permanent court orders. Their function as child protection police does not match their idealized versions of professional helping. In their day-to-day work at the front line, social workers interact with clients in ways that are threatening, coercive, regulatory, and punitive. To recover a sense of professional congruence and integrity, social workers must develop elaborate justifications and rationalizations to account for their actions. They must reframe their control and management of clients' lives as determined by common sense, reality, and need. They might argue, 'The reality is that you can't leave a two-year-old alone at home. Common sense says that a child should not be covered in shit. I had to apprehend.' By framing action as necessary, social workers legitimize their work. They would argue that in this case it is necessary to apprehend a child, proceed to court, move for permanent orders, demand treatment, and recommend incarceration of the offender.

Workers also argue that their actions have therapeutic effects. The threat that parents will lose their children, for example, is employed to generate a life crisis. Workers note that the crisis may or does lead the parents to re-evaluate their parenting, behaviours, relations, and responsibilities. Workers try to convince clients to change to reduce danger to their children. The professional adage, 'Healthy change is often precipitated by crisis,' legitimizes their intrusions into clients' lives. This adage allows social workers to believe that they can influence clients to change. It affirms the capacity of the social worker to shape and control the client's motivation to work on a problem. It presumes that with the 'right motivation' problems can be resolved. However, from the client's standpoint, the problem may have nothing to do with motivation, parenting abilities, caring, or personality.

The social worker has the power to define both the problem and its solutions. Often what the client believes hardly matters. For the social worker, the problem must be rooted in individual, family, and private domains. Despite the relatively recent attention social workers have given to ecological approaches (Auerswald, 1968;

Germain, 1981; Germain and Gitterman, 1986; Allan-Meares and Lane, 1987, Saleebey, 1992) and network analysis (Attneave, 1976; Anderson, 1982; Saulnier, 1982; Specht, 1986), the organizational demand is to address individual cases. Each case must be assessed to determine individual motivations, abilities, personalities and dispositions, family dynamics, communication patterns, and structures.

Front-line social workers legitimize their practice by generating accounts that demonstrate their attempts to order, plan, and structure interventions. Effective helping is understood to depend on the development of realistic plans, coherent order, and sound case management. Unfortunately, even here social workers feel caught. Their ideals are betrayed by concrete work demands. Social workers seldom have the time to plan. For example, a social worker might develop a plan to help 'mother resolve ambivalence regarding her parental role.' Intensive family counselling might be proposed. However, the same worker who is supposed to do this 'intensive family counselling' also faces the demands of managing two hundred other cases. The social worker might wonder, 'Am I doing enough? Am I responsible for the lack of progress on the case? Would improving my case management skills help? What can I do to be a better counsellor?' The practical organization of the day frustrates the intention of doing good, managed, purposeful, and directed social work.

Social workers also understand that, as they dash from crisis to crisis, they do not have the time to build idealized relations of trust, honesty, and respect with their clients.[9] In our office, we would burst onto one crisis situation after another. We would grab the 'quick fix.' We protected children by apprehension. We 'covered our ass.' We produced a documentary trail to show that we had done the work. We proceeded, in this way, day after day.

Our practice was not good social work. It did not conform to the idealizations in the texts. Yet, we did our best inside the reality of the organization. It is this reality that must serve as the beginning for enquiry – and not the idealized fantasies of social work educators about what good social work should look like.

7

Producing Reports

An excerpt from a social worker's log reads:

I received a phone call from the RCMP detachment at 4:00 a.m. requesting my presence at #303, 5219 Longbranch to meet Cst Jones. I arrived at 4:30 a.m.

The Cst reported that a couple, Elmer and Cynthia Burbot, were having a party that evening with about twelve other people. About 2:30 Elmer demanded that everyone leave, but most guests were reluctant to move. Elmer became very upset and began to break the apartment windows and to threaten everyone. Cynthia and some guests moved upstairs to the apartment of her sister, Bernice. Meanwhile, someone phoned the police, who arrested Elmer for disturbing the peace at 3:15 a.m. Cynthia and the others decided to head downtown. Before leaving Cynthia asked Bernice to look after her three kids. Bernice refused, but Cynthia left anyhow. Bernice called the RCMP at 3:45 a.m.

Cst Jones found Cynthia and her friends walking down Otter Road towards the Northern Inn. Cynthia told him that she was not going to return to the apartment. Cst Jones told her that child welfare would be contacted to look after her kids.

I interviewed the Cst and Bernice in her apartment, and before apprehending the three children I went upstairs to the Burbots' apartment. I observed that all the windows had been broken, there were five empty cases of beer on the kitchen table, at least two dozen empty beer bottles were strewn across the floor. I left a note for Cynthia informing her that her children were apprehended. I returned with the RCMP to the lock-up to inform Elmer of what had transpired.

The social worker's action on this early morning began when she received a call from the RCMP. The call initiated an immediate response that resulted in the apprehension of three children. For the social worker, even though the call was 'obviously' a report about children who needed protection this judgment nevertheless relied for its formulation on the performance of complex organizational and professional background work. The social worker's background work for constructing the call as a report needs to be explicated to understand the child protection process that follows. For a social worker, receiving a call that purports to report a child in need of protection is only the first step in the complex process called child protection work.

In this chapter, I tease out the practical construction of reports from the raw material provided in calls by focusing on the differential treatment social workers give to calls from private individuals and calls from professionals and other organizational officials. The differential treatment given to private and professional calls speaks to differences in the forms of order, social relations, and realities – both everyday and institutional.

The recovery of a report from a call is a primary moment that structures and determines the child protection work to follow. This work only proceeds after calls purporting to be about abused and neglected children are constructed as acceptable reports. The sensibility of a report arises in an organizational work process for linking local occurrences to extra-local organizational forms of order.

Producing a report requires that social workers follow courses of action, rules for production of documents, and interpretative practices for construing life-world events as 'candidate' instances (Pollner, 1974) of the category report. A 'candidate' instance, that is, a call, a phone conversation, or a remark in a street, will be construed, documented, and framed as a report. The apparent simplicity that this is a report belies the complex organization of its genesis. The simple fact of the report arises from the work of social workers inside an extensive division of labour, organizational mandates, and professional sense making.

Social workers receive many calls that purport to report child abuse or child neglect. Each of these calls must be carefully checked and assessed to determine whether or not it will be taken up as a report. From the time a call is received, the social worker engages in an assessment and evaluation process. The social worker will elicit particulars from the caller, match information provided against professional understandings, and develop some warrantable version of what the call is about. In day-to-day work, social workers address the puzzles posed by callers: Is this really a neglected or abused child? Does this child need social work protection? Can this caller be believed? Why is this person making the call? To answer these questions, social workers assemble particulars that act as 'candidate correct solutions' (Pollner, 1974) to such puzzles. Particulars once assembled into a cohesive account or picture are designed to solve the puzzle.

Even when a call does not seem to be a proper report, a social worker is obliged, nevertheless, to make the problematic character of the call visible. When a social worker chooses to not treat a call as a report, this requires creating a detailed record to justify the decision. Experienced practitioners recognize that, even when a caller's motives are questionable, there is still a chance that a child may be neglected or abused. Even when a social worker strongly doubts the veracity of the caller's claims, she or he will still conduct a home visit with the accused parents and child, lay the charge out before them, and then create a documentary record that demonstrates that the charge has been properly explored. Only after such work has been done can the social worker claim that the report was unfounded.

The call to the social worker is the first stage of child protection work. For front-line practitioners, the reception, investigation, processing, and production of reports are part of doing intake. Social workers in their everyday talk, whether conducted in people's offices, team meetings, or just over coffee, speak of reports as if they are taken-for-granted and common-sense pieces of work. One social worker might inform another that while on standby, 'I received three reports,' 'I got another report about Mrs Carlson,' 'Damn-it, I still have to submit my investigation on the Drymouth case.' For social workers, there clearly is good sense in the talk about reports. Mundane shop talk about reports relies on an organizational background for good sense. The organizational background conditions and structures the language, categories, terms, relevant concerns, and shared meanings held by social workers.

Receipt of a report sets in motion a predefined organizational course of action that is enacted inside deadlines set by legislation and policy manuals. What comes to count as a report is realized against a background of pressing work demands, other cases, clients waiting in the reception area, telephone callers on hold, and reports needing to be written. When social workers construct reports, their work is located in a stream of ongoing work demands and priorities. Should the social worker determine that this call is in 'fact' a report of child abuse or neglect, the amount of work required escalates. The case must be entered into detailed and complex courses of action for managing reports. If this call is sustainable as a report, it will require interviews, investigation, assessment, counselling, liaison, and recording.

When cases are multiplied ten-fold, so, too, is the work. Escalating workloads create problems for social workers. They are unable to keep pace with work demands, they miss deadlines, cancel appointments, and forget to process documents. Mounting work pressures may compel them to treat instances that are properly treatable as reports in any number of other ways, for example, a request for information, a request for income assistance, a crank call, or as a vicious complaint. Situations that only marginally conform to schemata for counting reports may be dealt with on an ad hoc and informal basis. In such situations the worker will not document the call as a report, but will, based on a professional evaluation, decide to proceed informally. The worker might take the risk[1] of just noting the call in a log and in the running records, while providing a rationale for not following it up. Thus, a repeat caller to an office may be disregarded if an investigation has already taken place which has confirmed that abuse has not occurred and if it has been revealed that the caller's motives or mental state are suspect.

When a report is received, there are a matrix of organizational procedures, structures of authority, and professional expectations that social workers must obey. Social workers craft a practice that seems to move methodically through predefined steps. Through prospective and retrospective constructions, social workers produce accounts of their activities that display their work as matching legislation and organizational policy. For a social worker's practice to be recognized by colleagues as professional and properly organizational, his or her accounts of practice must reveal an adherence to protocols and courses of action as outlined in policy manuals, operational directives, and legislation.

WHAT COUNTS AS A REPORT?

What counts as a report is understandable only by explicating the work of those who count, or judge, what a report is and can be. The front-line social workers who produce reports are governed by legislation, policies, directives, and guidelines that are developed and handed down to them by senior administrators, planners, and supervisors. As policies change what is produced as a report also changes.

Beginning in the 1960s, provinces across Canada began to introduce legislation establishing compulsory reporting of suspected cases of child abuse and neglect, for example, Ontario in 1965 (Falconer and Swift, 1983: 13), British Columbia in 1966 (Department of Social Welfare, Annual Report, 1968: 18), and Alberta in 1974 (Van Stolk, 1978: 63). Reporting laws were accompanied by the creation of child abuse and neglect registries in British Columbia, Alberta, Manitoba, Nova Scotia, and Ontario. In addition to the requirement to report, some provinces made failure to report an offence. The Yukon Territories even specified a penalty for failure to report (Van Stolk, 1978: 64). In British Columbia, the Family and Child Services Act (1980) states:

Duty to Report
9.(1) A person who has reasonable grounds to believe that a child is in need of protection shall forthwith report the circumstances to the superintendent or a person designated by the superintendent to receive such reports. (2) The duty under subsection (1) overrides a claim of confidentiality or privilege by a person following any occupation or profession, except a claim founded on a solicitor and client relationship. (3) No action lies against a person making a report under this section unless he makes it maliciously or without reasonable grounds for his belief. (4) A person who contravenes subsection (1) commits an offence.

Such legislative enactments enlist all members of the public, all professions, and all institutional personnel – except solicitors acting for a client – into the child protection enterprise.

A legislative enactment, however, does not guarantee or assure compliance. On the one hand, many professionals affected by the legislation may remain ignorant of their duty to report; on the other, they may, because of their professional belief in the sacredness of confidentiality, choose to disregard the law.

For child protection workers, the ignorance of other professionals had to be redressed through education. The need to educate other professionals demanded the development of ongoing staff training and community development workshops. Social workers for Native bands, public health nurses, hospital emergency nurses, mental health counsellors, police, and school counsellors, all were the targets of such educational workshops.

The legislative enactment of reporting laws was promoted by child protection experts across North America throughout the 1960s and 1970s (Radbill, 1980; Van Stolk, 1978). Once the social problem of abused and neglected children was named, promoted, and legislated as deserving professional attention, a cadre of experts in the field was enlisted to create an apparatus to address the problem.

In Canada the authority for child abuse and neglect reporting laws rests with provincial governments. Once constituted as the law, child protection is embodied in documents as legislation and policy. Through social workers' day-to-day work, duty to report laws have become almost common knowledge among a professional helping community. When social workers demand that other professionals recognize and obey reporting laws, they simultaneously enhance their visibility among professionals and advance their own professional status. By making child protection a visible and important issue, social workers advance the warrant and propriety of the specialized practice required to protect children. Authority for child protection services rests almost exclusively with social workers. They establish their hegemony over the field of child protection practice and develop an exclusive expertise to protect children.

An effect of social workers' promotion of the laws regarding the reporting of child abuse and neglect is that they receive an increased number of calls (Trocme, 1991: 76) that report some instance of child abuse or neglect. As the number of calls increases, social workers manage increased demands on their time by refining their skills for sifting genuine reports from those which are not. Not every call can be treated as a real report. As Maidman outlines:

In addition to valid reports, three types of questionable reports have been identified:

Summer complaints: those made in summer when open doors and windows make it easier to overhear events in neighbours' homes.

Spite complaints: reports by relatives, neighbours, or spouses as ways of seeking revenge.

Crisis complaints: sudden increase in reports subsequent to a newspaper report of a child's injury or death due to maltreatment. (1984: 20)

Despite a caller's wish to have her or his complaint treated seriously and immediately, the social worker may not respond to the client in such a fashion. By examining the problems that arise for social workers as they handle different types of calls, the tacit background which informs the production of a report emerges.

CONSTRUCTING REPORTS FROM PRIVATE CALLS

Social workers often receive calls that purport to be about a child in need of protection and that, during the course of the conversation or upon later investigation, turn out to be about something else. For a social worker to treat a call as a 'proper' report requires accepting that the caller's expressed concern for the child or the children is genuine. Social workers decide whether a call is 'proper' or not by examining both the caller's social location – that is, is this a private caller or a professional calling from her or his office? – and the caller's talk. A 'proper' call displays the caller's altruism, objectivity, caring, and honesty. Such motivational schemata allow social workers to differentiate proper from improper calls.

Social workers treat private calls as a loose assemblage of claims waiting to be verified as genuine. A private caller's claim to report a child in need of protection is bracketed. The claim is not taken up on the caller's terms. Conversely, calls from schools, public health officials, hospitals, public housing workers, mental health workers, and doctors, are automatically regarded as genuine reports of a child in need of protection. Even if an investigation subsequently reveals that the child is in fact not in need of protection, the integrity of the report as such is sustained. Social workers assume that professional callers are motivated by a universalized set of ethical and values imperatives.

When social workers encounter people who present private or individual needs and interests, they must struggle to maintain a professional standpoint marked by neutrality and objectivity. Social workers understand that the private needs, motives, and intentions of a caller may be incompatible with the universal mandates and policies of the organization. Professional social work practice must be crafted to reveal good professional judgment, impartiality, objectivity, dedication, and a general knowledge of the problem. Private calls are, by definition, suspect. The caller's ostensible purpose for making the call, that is, to report a child in need of protection, is placed in doubt or bracketed. The call can be treated as genuine only after an investigation which discovers and assembles the evidence that supports and displays the caller's genuine concern.

Unlike professional calls, which are bound to the logic, relevances, and imperatives of an institutionalized discourse, private calls are bound to a domain of personal interest and daily life. Private callers are contaminated by a place in a lived world outside the organization. Their utterances and claims need to be scoured of an indexicality in daily life. Only after being scoured of this contamination can private callers' claims be considered as facts.

Following Harold Garfinkel, I argue that what counts as a report is 'progressively realized and realizable' (Garfinkel, 1967: 41) inside a series of organizational processes and work practices. A report is not simply a call about child abuse or neglect, but it is an artefact of a work process. An experienced social worker knows how to listen and by listening to produce an account of the caller's intentions, a sense of what might actually have happened, the degree of risk to a child, and a plan of action to investigate a report. Social workers attend to, and thereby interpret, vocal tones, inflection, language, accent, degree of emotion, connotative structures, and words, to progressively create the call as a report. A caller's talk is interactively realized in the work process of a telephone interview. As the talk of caller and social worker is enacted, the social worker inscribes the conversation into professional frames for the discovery of meaning and sense. In the telephone interview, the social worker will attend to the time of the call, the congruity between claims, the kinds of adjectives employed – for example dirty, drunken, lazy – and the cogency of claims weighed against professional knowledge of patterns, disorders, syndromes, and expected types of behaviour.

A caller's genuineness does not simply exist. It has to be professionally constructed. The social worker must listen to the caller to determine if the caller's purpose is really to report a child in need of protection. If the social worker decides that the private call is genuine, she must develop a series of justifications. Examples of justifications might be: The caller doesn't seem to have a grudge. Why would she lie? The caller sounded genuinely concerned and worried about the children. The caller has tried to help on her own, but to no avail. The caller is just a concerned neighbour who has raised three children of her own.

From the moment that a private call is received, a social worker recognizes that the caller might have a personal interest in the outcome of an investigation. The caller's concern about the welfare, health, and safety of a child are suspended, or bracketed. Zimmerman calls this professional move to bracket a caller's story, taking an 'investigative stance.' The investigative stance treats the caller's story as 'no more than a loosely organized and unprocessed collection of claims lacking evidential value as such' (1976: 324).

The social worker cannot accept the caller's claims of concern for a child at face value. Before the call can be treated as a report, the social worker must check out the caller's story against a background of other possible frames. A social worker must invoke a series of explanatory frames to explore whether these might better explain the interests, motives, and desires of a particular caller. For example, is the caller an angry friend or relative who has had a fight with the person being reported? Is the call an attempt to embarrass someone or to seek revenge? Is the caller an ex-husband seeking to discredit the parenting of his wife to advance his own child custody claims? Is the caller a racist landlord wanting to harass a Native tenant? Such frames emerge through work experience in a child protection office.

Consider the following log entry recording a report from a husband. Although the background concerns that guided my questions were readily understood and recoverable from a professional standpoint, for the caller these remained unspoken and thereby unknown. As noted above, my work was guided by an investigative stance that sought to discover the 'real' reasons for the call.

Husband: She left me a week ago, she moved out all her furniture. Last night I saw her at some friends. She looked terrible. She was crying and saying; 'I can't do it on my own' and was threatening to kill herself.

Worker: Why do you think she left?

Husband: She gets ... real upset, angry. Last fall, we had friends over and we got into a big fight. She said I never stick up for her. She ran out of the house and went driving off in the car drunk.

Worker: What does that have to do with her leaving?

Husband: Well, I come home drunk some nights ... (pause) I do drink a bit too much sometimes. I came home drunk, it was late, she was pissed off ... she's real strong. She punched me in the eye, so hard that I had to go to the hospital. She was hysterical.

Worker: O.K. so what made you call me today?

Husband: Three weeks ago she threw the baby (age three), he was stand-
          ing up, she's really strong, she heaved him against the chester-
          field ... He smashed his teeth. We took him to emergency. They
          sent us to see Dr C. at his office.

Because the caller was a private individual, a husband, his claims
were bracketed such that veracity had to await discovery. The possibility of veracity could emerge only through a dialogic construction
rooted in my questions and his responses. I evaluated his responses
to questions by looking for reasonableness of argument, contiguity,
contradiction, temporal sequencing, logic, emotionality, and possible
corroboration. As a social worker, I needed to determine if an actual
incident of child abuse or neglect had occurred and if the child was
in immediate danger. Any information the husband provided that
was not addressed to the work of discovering if there was 'a child in
need of protection' became irrelevant noise and distraction. My focus
as the social worker was to select and document information that
would determine if this call was a proper report of child abuse. I had
to find out if there had been witnesses. Were there perceivable
injuries? Was there medical attention? Was there a past history or
even a file on the family?

When this man called to report an instance of child abuse or
neglect, I bracketed not only his claims, I tested alternative accounts.
I needed to demonstrate that I had handled his call professionally. To
demonstrate this, I inserted the husband's claims into professional
schemata to account for motives, desires, problems, and conflicts. For
example, the schema of marital dispute suggested that the husband's
call might be retributive. The child custody schema suggested that
the husband's call was an attempt to discredit his wife's parenting
while advancing his own claim to be a capable parent. The alcohol
abuse schema caused me to speculate that perhaps the husband was
actually the one with an alcohol problem. I wondered if his accusa-
tions about his wife's drinking were just alcoholic rationalization,
denial, and projection. The family violence schema forced me to wonder if the husband was trying to pre-empt a complaint from his wife
by lodging his own complaint first. Indeed, I worried, 'Why did his
wife leave him?'

My invocation of background professional schemata meant that the
sense I made of the husband's claims was not necessarily the sense
that he intended to convey. The man's claim that his wife could not

get along without him sounded my alarms. As a social worker, I was familiar with the patterns of wife battering. I recognized that abusive men force their wives into a dependent position. His comments sent up danger flags. I recognized the need to consider wife battering schemata to recover professional sense from his story. I could not accept his claims at face value. How could it be that his wife could not get along without him? Was she mentally disturbed? Was she mentally handicapped? Yet, if there was a mental health or psychiatric problem, I expected some form of mental health history or prior intervention.

Indeed, on the basis of my work with feminist social workers, I seriously doubted the husband's claims. From inside feminist discourse, I recognized that the husband was using fairly standard male tactics for asserting his power over his wife. Thus, he asserted that (1) his wife cannot survive without him, implying that as a woman she is by nature emotionally unstable and dependent; (2) therefore, as a woman and a mother, to be a stable parent, she needs a man in the home;[2] (3) her decision to leave him was a mistake, and she needs him back in her life; (4) until this happens somebody, preferably a professional, had better check on her and the children; and, finally, (5) as a social worker, I was bound to convince her to return to her husband for her own and the children's sake. By recognizing the husband's talk as an instance of male power, I was forced to wonder if he was battering his wife and whether this was why she had left.

My recognition of possible wife abuse inverted the husband's claims. Although he phoned to alert me to his wife's abuse of the child, in the course of our conversation I had become more concerned about the possibility of his abuse of his wife. I worried that he might actually be a child abuser. As the social worker, I needed to raise these questions with his wife.

Similarly, the repeated references to drinking – at least twice in this single segment: (1) she drove away from the house 'drunk' and (2) she objects to his drinking – alerted me to the schema of alcohol abuse. Through this schema I heard the husband minimizing his own drinking, while attributing excessive drinking to his wife. I wondered if she alone was the alcoholic or if both husband and wife had an alcohol problem. By raising the potential problem of alcohol abuse, I was forced to ask: Is the parenting of either the husband or the wife adequate? Are both the husband and the wife alcoholics? Perhaps neither is a competent parent? Perhaps neither should have custody?

Perhaps the child is in need of protection regardless of which parent has him?

As I did my work – informed by the relevances of a professional and organizational discourse – there was a danger for the caller. Would I arrive at understandings, and would I take courses of action contrary to the interests of both the caller and his ex-spouse? The caller, by reporting his wife, risked setting into motion courses of action which he had neither anticipated nor desired.

The husband's call raised a series of questions and concerns. Just how responsible was this husband? How concerned was he for the safety of his child? I wondered why, if he was genuinely concerned about the safety of his child, he had waited three weeks before reporting the incident to my office. Why did he wait until after his wife left the home before he reported the inadequacy of her parenting? Why did the doctor or nursing staff at the hospital who supposedly examined this child with smashed teeth not report the physical injury to my office? Why didn't the dentist report? What was this call really about?

Although, the veracity of the caller was suspect, he did make a substantive allegation of child abuse – 'She heaved him against the chesterfield ... He smashed his teeth.' An investigation was required.[3] Regardless of the caller's motives or veracity, his claim that there was an incident of child abuse leapt out from a series of other claims. I had to treat the call as a report. For the caller, the incident of child abuse – if it did occur – seemed less important than the 'fact' that 'she left me.' Because I was a child protection worker, my focus, however, was on an alleged incident of child abuse.

By rigorously pursuing the call as a possible report and by focusing exclusively on providing child protection, I was able to search the caller's talk for incidents that warranted an investigation. All that was relevant for my work was the claim that there had been an incident of child abuse, that is, the child was thrown. This single incident warranted an investigation.

This call, like private calls in general, placed me in an awkward or difficult professional situation. As a social worker, I needed to preserve a standpoint of organizational objectivity and impartiality. Yet, this caller had created a potential situation where I could become his ally. His call threatened to enlist me in his conflicts and marital antagonisms. Was he trying to use me as his own private detective to check up on and supervise his wife? I feared that I would find myself doing the husband's 'dirty work.' I faced a dilemma. Despite the organizational imperative to work objectively and impartially, I could easily become party to the husband's manipulations and designs. The call from the husband threatened the professional integrity of my work.

As the social worker handling the husband's call, I had to ensure that I maintained my place inside organizational courses of action. I had to ensure that I accounted for my work as an instance of good objective practice. I had to construe some sense from the talk on the phone by following professional and organizational courses of action. My focus on organizational courses of action to provide protective services to children allowed me to cut through the bulk of the information provided by the caller. In this example, I was obliged to do a home visit with the wife for no other reason than that I had received a report of an incident, that is, 'she heaved him.'

By following the courses of action established by legislation and policy, I incorporated this instance as one warranting investigation. From my institutional place inside policy, I had to assure the husband that the matter would be investigated, yet beyond that my involvement with the husband was conditioned and limited by the provisions of confidentiality. As a professional, I had to maintain the confidentiality of my work with the man's estranged wife. I was not free to report back to him about the findings of my investigation. Indeed, not only did policy not require further contact with the reporting party, further contact had to be guarded to avoid disclosing confidential information.

CLASS TRANSFORMATIONS

I argue that calls to our office – colloquially, 'calling the welfare' – index class relations. Calls from relatives, friends, neighbours, baby-sitters, and co-workers, come from people who share a class situation. Poor people, Native people, and people out of work belong to a class that has only its labour power to sell. Some are fortunate enough to be able to sell their labour power for years at a time in unionized workplaces, while increasingly a great many others, if they can find work at all, must do so for minimum wage or on a part-time or seasonal basis. Minimum wage proves to be an insufficient wage. Minimum wage is a wage of poverty. Additionally, those who are forced into unemployment or minimum wage work are often the most marginalized groups in Canada. I have lived in two northern single-industry resource towns. In these towns Native people comprised at least 30 per cent of the population, yet, they formed only a small percentage of the work force employed in the major unionized industry, whether pulp and paper or mining. Throughout the north, Native people have suffered the racist policies of large corporations that screen and reject them for employment. Once forced onto the margins, Native people are compelled to accept seasonal employment at an inadequate wage in areas where no provision exists for their families or children.

When employment is unavailable or denied and unemployment insurance has expired welfare is all that remains. It is welfare that will issue income assistance to the woman who leaves her husband. It is welfare that will speak to the kids, to straighten them out. It is welfare that will talk to the 'old man' who drinks too much. It is welfare that neighbours call when kids are left at home alone. Welfare can refer the husband to an alcohol treatment program. It can refer the battered wife to the transition house. It can refer the problem teen to a group home.

Welfare is an essential resource for marginal and poor working class people. Not only do social workers identify working people as the targets of their interventions, but poor and marginal working people refer themselves and their families to welfare for service. They often have little choice but to contact welfare and child protection workers. Once contacted, social workers and other helpers take up what people say, their utterances, claims, and calls for help, into the frames of professional and organizational discourse. Once entered into this discourse, people's problems are transformed. They themselves become individual cases marked by disorders, disequilibrium, inadequacies, or needs.

In my practice in a small northern community, most of the private calls I received on intake were some kind of request for service. In the course of making the request, the caller would often mention some matter that could be professionally construed as untoward or problematic, that is, as child abuse or neglect. For example, I frequently received calls from Native people – uncles, aunts, grandparents, brothers, and sisters – who complained because they had been 'left with' a relative's child. Usually, the child had been left with the relative while the parent had gone off to find work or to work in an inaccessible or inappropriate place for children, for example, a logging camp, a hunting camp, a remote mine site, a fishing boat, a trap-line in the bush, or a remote cannery.[4]

As a rural social worker, I knew that Native and other northern parents often had to work in situations where employers made no provision for child care or family life. In addition, I recognized that economic upheaval throughout single-industry communities, caused by closure of primary resource production facilities, such as pulp mills, sawmills, canneries, and mines, only worsened unemployment and transience. Throughout northern communities, chronic economic crisis produced considerable disruption in people's lives and families.

As a social worker, I have worked inside state laws, programs, and policies that proceed as if it is just 'business as usual.' Although parents may move from town to town and camp to camp in search of work, their children are required by law to attend school. To attend school, children need a stable home in a community with a school. As a result, children are left behind with relatives and friends in settlements with schools while parents go off to work. Consider the following call:

Relative: I'd like to get some support for looking after my two grandchildren. Art (their father) gave me no money for them this month. He gave me $250 last month, but I haven't got nothing this month. I'm living on a pension. I can't get by.

Worker: Do you know where Art is?

Relative: I don't know. I haven't heard from him since he gave me the money last month.

Worker: Do you know where their mother is?

Relative: She don't want nothing to do with the kids. I don't know where she is.

Worker: Who has custody?

Relative: Art has them. They live with him.

Worker: Yes but, does he have legal custody, does he have papers giving him custody.

Relative: I don't know.

Worker: How long have the kids been with you?

Relative: About three months.

Such calls are brought to the attention of the social worker only because the grandmother, aunt, uncle, brother, sister, or friend, cannot cope financially with the added burden of caring for extra children. The children are not neglected, abused, or even unwanted. Rather, the relative cannot afford to keep them. The people who call live on welfare, unemployment insurance, or work at low-paying, non-union jobs or are seasonal labourers. These people rely on a wage, welfare, or U.I. for their survival. Their ability to be generous is limited. Yet, because the law places financial responsibility for children with their natural parents, such calls when received could properly become reports of child neglect.

As social workers, we are often able to avoid treating these calls as reports of neglect by encouraging the relative to keep the children and by offering financial support through a child in the home of a relative (CIHR) agreement. However a CIHR agreement requires that (1) the parent be contacted; (2) the parent sign a copy of the agreement; (3) the parent be financially incapable of supporting the child as determined by an income test – disqualification occurs at income levels just above welfare rates; and (4) the relative agrees to care for the child. Difficulties arise when the parent cannot be contacted, refuses to sign the agreement, or does not qualify because of 'excessive' earnings, or when the relative refuses to continue caring for the child. Under these conditions, a social worker has little alternative but to enter into a voluntary short-term care agreement with the parents or to apprehend the child.[5] Either way, the child becomes a temporary ward of the agency.

On those occasions when the call for help results in an apprehension, the caller's interests are displaced by an organizational mandate. Workers are forced to treat the financial problem of supporting extra children as child neglect. Yet, such treatment represents a 'peculiar eclipsing' (Smith, 1987: 17) of social reality by addressing the social problem of poverty as an individual problem of parental failure. Social workers' understandings of the situation within the schema of child abuse and neglect preclude explication of the problematic character of daily life. The professional situation begins outside the demands, relevances, and problematics of clients' lives. People's immediate experience of not having a job, not having enough money to buy groceries, having to buy second-hand clothes, having problems with the kids, not having day-care services, and living in poor housing, when taken up into professional discourse become a series of discrete problems, that is, unemployment, poverty, and neglect.

MARKING OFF PRIVATE FROM PUBLIC

The personal interests and motives of private calls automatically require different procedures for investigation than are required for calls from public organizations and professional sources. When a report is received from a private caller, no further contact or discussion of the case is required. A private caller is not entitled to receive nor do they receive a follow-up report on the investigation. In the example where the father accused his ex-wife of abusing their child, if it is found that the mother is incapable of caring for the child, and if the child is apprehended, the social worker is not required to return the child to the father. Indeed, for the father to obtain custody of the child, he would have to initiate separate legal action under different legislation, for example, through a family relations act. Under child protection acts, social workers usually must return apprehended children to the 'parent apparently entitled to custody.' This often means returning the child to the parent who last had legal custody of the child. By interpreting legislation in this manner, social workers avoid becoming embroiled as partisans in marital disputes over child custody. Furthermore, even if for exceptional reasons the husband was given custody of the children, the social worker would not be obliged to give him details of the case other than as they might affect the safety and health of the child. However, when social workers work with professionals from other institutions, they routinely share information from their investigation with the reporting agency. Professionals within institutional settings routinely request, upon reporting, that they be informed of the results of the investigation and of any future action taken by the child protection agency. Such sharing of information is not only legitimate but conforms to interministerial protocols established in policy manuals, for example, 'In the co-operative sharing of information between Departments and other professionals necessary to the process of investigating, monitoring and providing service to ensure the safety and well-being of a child, the social worker is acting within the legal mandate of this section' (author's name confidential).

This type of cooperative information sharing which occurs between professionals is not possible between professionals and private individuals. Sharing the results of an investigation with ex-spouses, relatives, friends, and neighbours is not only technically illegal, it is unethical. To disclose information to a private individual would violate the professional value of confidentiality. In specific circumstances, social workers do share information with other family members, but workers must be careful to justify why this is appropriate. Social workers are much freer to hide behind a shield of confidentiality when dealing with private callers than they are when dealing with professional callers.

The veracity of reports from professionals is taken for granted. Like social workers, other professional callers are understood to share a commitment to the universalized codes of conduct, values, and knowledge characteristic of an organizational discourse. Even during those exceptional occasions when professional callers are discovered to be too involved or in a conflict of interest situation, impropriety is attributed to the individual caller not to the profession or to the organization. The caller is understood to be acting unprofessionally.

When child protection workers receive calls from professionals such as teachers, psychologists, nurses, and doctors, they document the time of the call, the name of the caller, the capacity of the caller, the nature of the complaint, witnesses, family history, and so forth. To document the case, the social worker will create running records, reports, and memos, which will be placed on file. Reciprocally, professionals located in other organizations can be expected to produce their own records. Whatever records a social worker produces for a child protection agency will most likely be paralleled by records in those other agencies also involved in the case. Just as the social worker documents receiving the call, she expects that the professional caller will document making the call. Both social workers and professional callers recognize that recording the occurrence of the call is a necessary precaution if a child is critically injured or dies and their work becomes the subject of scrutiny. Additionally, calls from professionals are often accompanied by a follow-up. Again, this reinforces the need for the social worker to document her progress on the case.

In contrast to organizational callers, private individuals do not normally document their contacts with a child protection agency. Social workers do not expect private callers to record their call, to note the name of the worker, or to leave any documentary account of the information exchanged in the call. If there is a dispute between a social worker and a private caller, whatever records the social worker has at hand, even if incorrect, will have more authority than the mere memory or recollections of a private caller. The social worker always has recourse to the response, 'Sorry but my records show ...' Unlike organizations, daily life does not demand documentary records of day-to-day practice. A neighbour, aunt, uncle, or grandparent calling the child protection organization is not required to record that she has done so. Accordingly, social workers recognize that when they receive calls from public organizations they must exercise far greater caution than is required with private calls. When managing public calls, the social worker must ensure the routine production of documentary evidence that is part of an adequate investigation of a report. When managing private calls, social workers can employ far greater discretion in record keeping. They do not have to worry about a parallel documentary record that could either contradict or corroborate their own claims.

PROFESSIONAL REPORTING

As a front-line social worker who was routinely assigned to intake, roughly half of all the calls I received reporting child abuse or neglect came from professionals – notably teachers, school principals, doctors, public health nurses, public housing workers, and social workers in other agencies.[6] Calls from professionals, by definition, are expected to be disinterested, unbiased, impartial, objective, and guided by formal discursively organized codes.

Professional claims to represent a 'case of abuse or neglect' have an authority and objectivity that indexes a location inside organizational work processes. In this location the practice that follows negates the professional's subjectivity as a matter of importance in the reporting work. Professional reporting activity, although concretely embodied as the work of a knowing subjectivity, produces its self-negation. A professional's location in discourse makes this self-negation possible. For a professional's claims to be heard as warranted, simultaneously requires a skilful self-negation and constitution of an abstract organizational standpoint.

A properly objective report is embedded in professional and organizational language. The professional call, even as it is being told, as it unfolds, and as it is dialogically elaborated, is marked by a process of reciprocal matching between the caller and intake worker, who jointly cue and guide each other's responses. In telling a story of child abuse, professional speakers employ the warranted or accepted forms of professional discourse for sorting out certain particulars as relevant to the work at hand. They employ the categories of the discourse of child abuse or neglect such that the report as a case of child abuse or neglect will be there already to be seen in the talk itself. Examining a call from a school counsellor reveals the discursive organization of a claim of child abuse:

Counsellor: I'm phoning about a possible case of abuse. I have a stu-
                  dent in my office, a fourteen-year-old girl. Peggy. She
                  claims that she has been hit on the head by her aunt who
                  is caring for her. I've looked at her head and there is a
                  scab and some red marks. She said she was hit about two
                  weeks ago. Her aunt also keeps her home from school to
                  babysit the other kids. Peggy thinks that she's treated
                  different from the other kids; the same rules don't apply
                  to her.
Social Worker: Has she been seen by a doctor?
Counsellor: No. She should be seen, you know, she could have a con-
                  cussion, or something. Peggy wants to leave, but can't go
                  live with her mother ... She says this (episode) isn't the
                  first time; her aunt has hit her in the face with her fist,
                  about two months ago. Peggy, says she was back talking.
                  She was hit in the cheek, and she (the aunt) pulled her
                  hair.

In this example, the social worker takes for granted that the professional caller is phoning from her office, in both senses of the word, that is, from the physical site as an office and from her position, holding the office of school counsellor. First, the physical location, although taken for granted, provides critical background information to the social worker who needs to sort out the situation at hand. The identification of the school by the counsellor enables the social worker to grasp a series of background relevances. For example, the counsellor could work at Queen Elizabeth, the senior secondary, or Sir Charles Tupper, the junior secondary, or at Prince Charles, the elementary school, which immediately identifies the general age of the child and thereby allows the worker to begin to assess the degree of risk. Furthermore, the physical site of the school is often a familiar setting, visited by the social worker in previous liaison meetings, case conferences, and workshops. Additionally, particular schools may have a reputation as problem schools, may have disproportionate numbers of poor and Native children, may be in the less affluent parts of town, may have less competent staff, or may have an inexperienced or overreactive counsellor or principal. Finally, the school is another organizational site that is guided and governed by rules, regulations, policies, and legislation, much like the child protection organization. The professional caller at the school engages in a work process that parallels that of the social worker in a child protection organization. The office as a position also informs the background relevances for constructing a call as a report. Social workers hold both tacit and explicit understandings about the work of school counsellors. It is assumed that the school counsellor is also an office holder, in the sense addressed by Weber, for she fulfils the duties of an office as her work (1978: 959). She calls the child protection social worker because a problem has been brought to her attention through her work within a school. She is calling about not just any child, not her own child, nor the child of a friend, but about a child as student. The organizational specificity of the student–counsellor relation is rooted in an educational apparatus and a division of labour involving teachers, support staff, special education instructors, counsellors, principals, school superintendents, and elected school trustees.

The school counsellor demonstrates her professional competence by providing a clear focus from the start, that is, she begins by addressing her call as reporting a case of abuse. This is followed by a systematic outline of the problem. Her claims are explicitly oriented to the schema of possible abuse. The provisional character of her formulations demonstrates that she remains open-minded and not committed to a particular finding. She wants to see that an impartial assessment of the situation is carried out. Yet, despite the apparent provisional character of her claims, she ventures specific evidence as 'facts' that point in the direction of a probable finding. Certain bruises, cuts, stories, and relations are easily construed as untoward and as deserving investigation. The school counsellor establishes a sequence to her call which demonstrates her adherence to logical, rational, and orderly presentation. She begins by identifying the reason for the call. She identifies the child by name. She outlines the child's story, describes the corroborating evidence, the 'scab and some red marks,' and she relays some history to show that there may be a pattern of abuse. Finally, the counsellor opens up organizational sources for corroboration through a documentary record that shows reasons for concern, that is, school days missed, poor grades, and disciplinary action. Both the school counsellor and the social worker can identify the warrant and good sense in the order, specificity, and nature of the particulars. Both are competent to speak about such matters. They may even formulate some tentative explanatory hypotheses. The aunt provides inadequate parenting. The child's own parents have rejected her. The aunt has made the child a scapegoat. The family dynamics are dysfunctional.

The school counsellor's call directly addressed the issue of neglect and provided only those particulars that could be construed discursively as relevant to the work at hand. For the intake social worker, the form and content of the account displays the caller's professionalism. The order and ready sensibility of the call affirms the probable authenticity of the caller's claims. That Peggy really told the counsellor that she was hit by her aunt is accepted as fact, although Peggy's claim that this actually occurred is subject to the usual scepticism directed to all private reports. Did Peggy have a fight with her aunt after acting out? Was Peggy seeking revenge? Did Peggy accuse her aunt to punish her?

Finally, it is important to note that although the school counsellor's interview with the child is a work process, the procedures she employed to elicit, select, and assemble the information she provides are not addressed. These skilful moves towards assembling a story comprise an unseen background of expected competencies that lend legitimacy and warrant to her professional report.

Just as the report of the school counsellor is embedded in the work processes of the school, so too are the reports that are received from other organizational sources embedded in institutionalized work processes. Many reports received from police are about children who have violated the law either by being picked up for shoplifting, arrested for illegal activities, or found to be in unsafe surroundings (usually teens engaged in acts of public mischief and vandalism, or runaways). Hospitals and emergency ward staff report when a child is admitted with injuries that are not consistent with the explanation provided by the parents, or when an injured child is brought to the hospital by a parent who is intoxicated, belligerent, or unwilling to follow prescribed medical advice, such as leaving the child in the hospital for twenty-four-hour observation.

Public health nurses, working closely with the schools, report cases of children arriving to school consistently dirty, stinking, infested with vermin, or suffering from untreated medical problems. These are children who have not received their routine inoculations or who, when examined, show signs of neglect, such as poor dental care, poor hygiene, parasitic infections, unattended sores, or malnutrition. Even provincial housing authorities are frequent reporters of abuse or neglect, as caretakers notice that certain apartments emit noxious odours, tenants have drunken parties, and children are left to wander about in halls or are left alone in at home.

In short, most of the calls from professional sources arise through their routine and day-to-day organizational work. The poorly cared for child places an extra burden on the teacher. The drunken family disrupts other housing tenants. The juvenile delinquent or lost child takes up a cell and uses police time for extra supervision. The uninoculated or vermin-infested child poses a health risk of infection or infestation and extra work for the public health nurse. By submitting a report to the child protection agency, professionals transfer specific work problems to other authorities. Other institutional and professional workers anticipate that the child protection worker will eliminate or at least reduce the problem.

To conclude, social workers use different methods to manage calls received from professional sources against those received from private individuals. Social workers when receiving a call from another professional can usually assume that the caller's claims are organized by the contexts of organizational work and by the professional responsibility to refer cases of child abuse and neglect to child protection authorities. Like social workers themselves, other professionals can be relied on to produce knowledge that pieces 'facts' from people's daily lives into discursively structured categories, schemata, and theories. Additionally, social workers can locate professional callers in the spaces of familiar organizational contexts, whether a doctor's office, a school, or a hospital. Calls from private individuals, on the contrary, are located in the ambiguous and often dangerous contexts of daily life. The challenge for the social worker is to devise practices for bringing these dangers under the control of the organization. The work which binds people's lives to organizational realities, as we have seen, begins when the social worker first receives the call, and, as we see in the next chapter, continues in the investigative work and courses of action that follow.

8

Child Protection Work

As the intake social worker on a Thursday afternoon I received a phone call from the caretaker of an apartment building who complained, 'Donna Trout is drunk again. She smashed her fist through the god damned kitchen window. Last I saw her she went staggering off, swearing, saying she was going to go the hospital. She's left one hell of a mess. She's left her kid alone in the apartment, and sure as hell I'm not going to take care of it. You guys had better do something about that woman. I've come down here several times, after neighbours complained, to tell her to be quiet. She'll party all night if you don't stop her. I've had my belly full of her BS, and I want her out of my building.' When I asked, 'How do you know what happened?', he responded, 'I was upstairs cleaning the hall when I heard glass breaking, a commotion going on – a hell of a lot of hollering and screaming. I went down to the ground floor and found Donna staggering about the hallway. She was drunk out of her mind and bleeding like hell all over my floor. She'd slashed her arm, putting it through the window.'

The Sea View apartment building was a familiar stop for me. I had other clients in the same building. It was slum, sub-standard, and low-cost housing. Its exterior had gone years without paint. The windows over the entrance doors were shattered. Graffiti was scrawled on the hall walls. The building stank of urine and filth. The floor tiles in the apartments were cracked and broken. The wooden front steps were rotting. The grounds were unkempt and littered.

The owners lived down south in the city. They bought the building as an investment. My other clients who lived in the building had problems getting repairs for leaky plumbing, broken refrigerators, broken ovens, and faulty electrical wiring. Most of the tenants were welfare recipients, handicapped, unskilled workers, single-parent families, and Native Indians unable to get better housing.

As soon as I arrived at the apartment, about fifteen minutes after the call, I tried to find a focus for a case. I tried to sort through myriad sensual details to recover a professional standpoint. I noticed that the caretaker was outside at the side of the building boarding up a blood-streaked window. As I entered the building and walked down the hall I saw two older people were clutching each other outside an open apartment door. They looked very upset. They were Donna's parents. When I introduced myself, they told me, 'We just got here.' They said, 'We came because Donna called us from the hospital.' This last bit of information seemed important. It suggested that Donna had taken reasonable steps, following an obvious injury, to ensure supervision for her child in her absence. However, the grandfather continued, 'We won't take care of Edith (the child). This sort of thing has happened too damn many times before.' The possible strength of Donna's efforts to ensure 'continuity of care' weakened as a factor in her favour.

Although what usually mattered was quite simply whether or not a responsible adult was available to care for the child, I saw that in this case there were other factors that needed to be considered. It looked like there might have been a pattern of drinking, drunkenness, and grandparents being called out to pick up the pieces.

Donna's father groaned, 'She has been drinking a lot since Christmas. We warned her that she had better stop.' He added, 'She wouldn't listen. I wish you still had the old interdict[1] list. I used to be on it, and I couldn't get any booze. Donna should be on it too!' The grandmother demanded, 'The welfare should take the kid, teach her a lesson, she's got to stop drinking.' Again, to cover myself, and to ensure that the grandparents were making a decision that they would not regret, I repeated my request, 'Are you prepared to take the child?' Again they both refused.[2] Donna's father burst out, 'We've bailed her out of trouble too many times. She never learns that girl.'

From this exchange I learned several vital pieces of information for building a case of neglect and for legitimizing my intervention. First, I saw the signs of drunken incapacity by the blood smeared on the window and the obvious absence of a parent. Second, I heard the grandparents' story about Donna's continual drinking. Third, I heard the grandfather admit to a drinking problem. This suggested a pattern of alcohol abuse in the family. Fourth, I heard the grandparents refuse to take the child into their care.

The grandparents' reasons for being at this doorstep were embedded in social relations of parents, family, and kinship. These relations did not bring me to the doorstep. It was their daughter's arm that went through the window. It was their daughter's blood that lay in pools in the hall and was smeared on the apartment walls. They faced a moment of their daughter's life whose meaning was recovered through a lifetime past and a lifetime yet to come. Whatever they felt, and I could only guess, horror, disgust, a sense of sadness and personal failure, and whatever they did, whether speaking harsh words at the door, turning down their heads, crying softly, or holding each other for comfort, theirs were hot actions fused into their daughter's life. They shared a personal history that extended back through intimate and day-to-day spaces. That moment at the doorstep was fused by the flashes of remembrance. Their tears were sparked by the mysteries of shared time. What were these parents feeling? How were their tears shaped by the hard labour of Donna's birth, their pride as she toddled across a wooden floor, her tantrum for candy, her withdrawal when Daddy was drunk, her sullen resistance to school, and her confused tears when she discovered that she was pregnant?

These people, who came together at this apartment 'grow old together' (Schutz, 1973). This was not my world. Their history was not mine. I was at this doorstep to do child protection work.

CLASSIFYING THE EVERYDAY

As I surveyed the scene at the doorstep a case began to congeal. I could see signs of alcoholism, family disorganization, and what Seligman (1975) has called 'learned helplessness.' I discovered that the father, like Donna, had a history of alcohol abuse. Was there a family history of excessive drinking, disruption, possible violence, and dysfunctional adaptation? Had Donna's family background denied her healthy opportunities to learn to cope? Did the mother's reference to 'the welfare' indicate that this family had had a history of economic dependence and marginality?[3]

Even as I spoke with the grandparents I saw their dark skin, black hair, brown eyes, their stature and faces. I 'knew' that they were

Native Indians. I knew how to see them as members of a racial and cultural type. I saw through their bodies to recover a knowledge about race, culture, and class. In my 'professional gaze' (Pfohl and Gordon, 1987) I inscribed these people's physical appearance into a discourse.[4] I read their bodies to understand their physical and mental health, lifestyle, attitudes towards change, and social membership. I considered whether or not they were fat or thin, neatly groomed or dishevelled, clean or dirty, fashionably dressed or out of style.

In addition I knew how to 'class' these people. I saw that both the man and the woman at the door were 'overweight.' The man had oiled hair combed into a duck tail. He was dressed in drab olive work pants and a torn white T shirt. The woman's dress was old and worn. The flower pattern that had once been brightly coloured had faded into a dim jumble. As my eyes scanned these people it was not necessary for me to say anything. My assessments needed only be noted mentally. Later these observations would be reworked into a report, for example, 'Mrs X presents as a middle aged Native women who dresses neatly.'

I recognized that these people were out of fashion. They were dressed in the clothes of poor people. Their physiques told me that they were not preoccupied with diet and shape as are middle class folk. I did not voice my judgments of their appearance; nevertheless, I read race and class from skin colour, clothing, and style. Colleagues, court lawyers, and the judge would also read these appearances. From such reading we would generate tacit accounts of people's relative education, intelligence, power, prestige, and social status.

Even as these people spoke, they opened up a space for evaluation. Speech, like dress is tacitly assessed and framed to assess people's education, intelligence, authority, power, and status. When the grandparents spoke, my ears heard the distinctive local accents and grammar of Native Indians in the area. Sh's disappeared into s's and the alliteration of the words had a guttural style over-emphasizing 'g's; thus, 'I gow by Selly's, then wi'll go sopping.'[5] Although negative evaluations of accents were rarely stated, they remained, nevertheless, an important data. If a client had a 'good' vocabulary, spoke well, and had a sophisticated urban accent, then this could be noted, for example, 'Client presents as articulate, urbane, and intelligent.'

In Canadian society race and class have meanings that extend far beyond mere colour, accent, income, and heritage. In Canada race and class are socially grounded in complex 'practices which organize relations among people' (Ng, 1988: 21). Racial and class membership become the source for powerful valuative attributions such that 'being' Native Indian, East Indian, Black, on welfare, or unskilled means being subject to a series of negative typifications.

Social workers would never dare to state that they apprehend children because they come from Native families or poor families. Report after report, however, affirms that Native children and children from poor families dominate among children in care (Warry, 1991; McKenzie and Hudson, 1985; Johnson, 1983; National Council of Welfare, 1979). Race and economic class provide essential tacit data for professional assessments of problems, pathologies, weaknesses, and deviance.

Imagine how different my work would have been if I had arrived to find a white 'gentle-man,' in his late fifties with stylishly cut greying hair. Imagine if he were wearing a houndstooth sports jacket, cravat, and dress pants. At his side might stand his wife. She might wear a fine cream-coloured silk dress offset by a pearl necklace. I would look at these people and try to imagine why they were at the doorstep. I would recognize that they did not belong. Was their daughter a 'drop-out' who had rejected her parents? Was she a rebellious cast-off from an affluent family? Had she fallen in with a bad crowd?

As professionals, social workers know that they must arrive to work and to court 'properly' dressed. They expect to be corrected by a judge if they appear in court without a jacket and tie or if female, not in a dress. Many clients, however, arrive in court dressed in blue jeans and T-shirts. Certainly, a judge, although not making any direct comment, evaluates a client's appearance to understand better the case before him or her. Similarly, while social workers would rarely make a direct remark to clients about their appearance, evaluations of appearance are continually being made in reports, in conversations, and in coffee-room chit-chat.

As social workers, we are skilled in the use of proper grammar, general vocabulary, theory, and organizational language. As professionals, we correct our students, our children, and even on occasion our colleagues for poor grammar and improper usage. We have been evaluated and judged in our essays, papers, and theses on such matters. We know that good presentation has definite consequences for how we are treated and for our life prospects.

SEEING ALCOHOLISM

As I looked at the shattered blood-smeared glass I imagined Donna's arm smashing through the window. I felt sick and overwhelmed by the senselessness of self-mutilation. I imagined my pain if it had been my own arm. I recoiled from the image. It was too painful, too senseless. Somewhere, though, there had to be sense. I recovered sense and meaning by seeing the episode as a moment of drunkenness and alcoholism. From the time of the caretaker's call to the grandparents' words at the door, the repeated reference to alcohol rendered the scene at hand sensible, expected, predictable, and meaningful. The alcoholism schemata provided a version of 'what actually happened.'

By seeing the destruction about me as signs of alcoholism or as signs of a disease my focus shifted to an abstract space, not to these individual's actual lived spaces. As Foucault observed, 'If one wishes to know the illness from which he is suffering, one must subtract the individual, with his particular qualities' (1973: 14). Alcoholism, like most diseases, is an abstraction. Alcoholism possesses its own relevances, its signs, its course, its symptoms, and its treatments. Particular individuals present signs of the disease. They are alcoholics.

In Canada alcoholism is often combined with race to produce understandings about the special character of 'Native alcoholism.' Skilled social workers will make referrals to specialized Native alcohol treatment centres. They will focus intervention efforts on helping Native clients adjust to the transition from Native to white culture (Thomas, 1981). They will work to strengthen traditional family and clan supports. They will implement prevention programs on reserves (May, 1986), and so forth.

Clearly, while the alcoholism frame allowed me to recover a professional sense from a chaotic, and seemingly not sensible situation, it simultaneously obliterated the integuments of Donna's lived reality. It discarded her concrete ground in the world. It allowed for the replacement of concrete ground with the abstracted and generalized schemata of the particular disorder and disease.[6]

PRODUCING EVIDENCE

I entered the apartment and moved from room to room to record, mentally, particulars worth documenting. I noted the pools of blood by the shattered window, the bloody trail of chaotic hand prints smeared on the walls (signs of a stumbling, halting, and confused movement), empty beer bottles strewn across the floor, the dark hair of a man apparently 'passed out' on the couch, the stench of booze, urine, and unwashed bodies, and the filthy and disordered state of the apartment.

Moving to the back bedroom I found an infant, perhaps ten or twelve months old, lying asleep on top of filthy sheets turned brown by dirt. I saw that she lay on a bed not in a crib. I knew that a child that age should not have been left unattended on a bed. I anticipated a series of potential dangers against which the mother failed to protect her child. The child could have accidentally rolled off the bed and could have been injured in a fall. If the child survived the fall uninjured, she could have crawled to other more dangerous areas of the house, for example, cupboards with cleaning supplies or towards stairs.[7] I looked at the child's body to note that she was wearing only a feces-soiled and urine-soaked diaper. Feces had dried to cake her torso and face. This showed that the child had been left unattended for several hours without attention to her needs.

When I picked the child up I saw that the back of her skull was flattened. I assumed that the flattened skull was not natural. I guessed that it signified the parent's failure to attend to the child by rotating her while sleeping or to pick her up when awake. The flattened skull could be an invaluable piece of evidence before the court. It was a graphic sign of abnormality resulting from serious neglect. It showed that the child had been left alone lying on her back hour after hour and day after day.[8]

I looked under the diaper and saw that the child had a red rash and had a small patch of two or three open sores. Her face had several infected scratches about her nose and eyes, probably from her fingernails, which were jagged and unkempt. I made a mental note to myself, 'remember to have the group-home parent take photographs of the flattened head, the sores, and the scratches.'[9]

As I stood in a dimly lit room, and breathed in putrid air, I held a groggy child who was beginning to emit frightened cries, yet, my mind was focused on an institutionally defined problem. I had to establish that this was a child in need of protection. I had to compile sufficient evidence to win the case before the judge in court. Although I wanted to apprehend the child, I needed to proceed cautiously and to assemble facts and particulars that would stand as compelling evidence of child neglect and that would affirm the warrant of my actions. I anticipated a battle in court. To win the battle, I needed enough facts to tell a convincing story of neglect. I could tell a story of alcohol abuse by referencing the empty beer bottles strewn about the living room, the half-empty bottle of rye whisky by the couch, the empty wine bottle on the kitchen table, and the sickly sweet smell of alcohol from body pores that permeated the apartment. 'Neglect' was signified by the putrid smells of feces, urine, and filth, and by the state of the child. From experience doing child protection work I believed there were enough indicators to sustain an apprehension before the court.

I asked the grandmother to find a clean diaper while I took the child to the washroom, where I placed her under warm running water in the bathtub. I washed off the feces and was able to do a quick check of the child for bruises, scars, and other injuries. I assessed the severity of her sores, and tried to determine if there were other more serious injuries, which would have required taking her to the hospital for observation or treatment.[10]

I made a final surveillance of the apartment. I noted the piles of dirty and smelly clothing littered about the bedroom floors. I moved to the kitchen, opened the refrigerator, gasped at the stench, and noted that it was empty except for a few wilted carrots and two open bottles which contained mouldy food remnants. The cupboards were almost bare except for an abundance of small black droppings. The apartment was infested with mice. The kitchen sink was filled with dark water and grimy dishes. The counter and stove were littered with unwashed pots, plates, bottles, and cutlery.

As I sat on a chair in the kitchen, I passed the child to the grand-mother, and pulled out my black notebook (daily log) from the satchel that I had deposited on the kitchen table earlier. Log in hand, I began to ask a series of routine questions. I wanted to establish the particulars of the case. I asked the grandmother: 'What is your daughter's full name? What is her birth date? What is the name and birth date of the child? Who is the father? Where does he live? (I had already gathered that the father was not the drunk the grandfather had roused and ordered to leave.) What do you know about what happened here today? How do you know Donna was drunk? What is your name, address, and phone number? How long has Donna been drinking? How many times before have you had to take the child? Are you willing to testify in court?'

I had to make a decision about this case. As we talked two crucial 'facts' emerged: First, the child's grandparents were not prepared to assume custody. Second, they claimed there had been a series of incidents that could be considered to be child neglect.

I talked with the grandparents to gather information to uphold and support my decision to apprehend the child. Was the child Edith Trout in need of protection? Within seven days I would have to explain my actions in the report to the court. The report would need to describe the 'circumstances warranting an apprehension.' My interview with the grandparents was guided by this background knowledge and by my expectations about the operations of the court. I knew that I needed to establish satisfactory evidence and to demonstrate that there were sufficient grounds to warrant the apprehension of the child.

PRODUCING PARENTAL FAILURE

As I moved about the apartment I was building a case. I heard the grandmother's anger with her daughter: 'I warned her about her drinking. She started when she was fifteen, when she began hanging around with Eddy. Eddy's no good. He spends all his money on dope, ... Uh, ... you know, we warned her, stop drinking or the welfare will take your kids.' The grandfather repeated the message he gave at the door: 'You guys should have one of those interdict orders, it did me good. You know, I went to jail, got sobered up, and quit drinking.' As their words buzzed through the air I selected only those 'facts' that were relevant for making a case of neglect. Their pain, their sorrow, their anger, and their fear for their daughter and granddaughter were all largely incidental for my work at hand.

Could Donna have accidentally put her arm through the window? Could Donna have been locked out of the apartment? Had she called or banged on the door to try to waken her drunken friend inside? Did she smash the window to regain entry to protect her child? First, the location of the shattered kitchen window revealed that Donna could not have accidentally fallen into it. Second, even if Donna had been locked out she could have contacted the caretaker to let her back into the apartment. Third, even if she could not find the caretaker she could have picked up a board or a rock, rather than used her fist, to smash the window. Clearly, Donna had not acted rationally. She had not taken proper care of herself. If she could not care for herself, how could she care for her child?

I quickly appreciated that the apparently simple facts at hand could easily be assembled to produce a case of immediate parental failure. However, I also recognized some troublesome details that threatened this account and that needed to be contained by my story. First, Donna's self-mutilation required immediate absence from her child. She had taken the precaution of phoning her parents to ensure continuity of care. Had she appreciated that leaving her child in the care of the man 'passed out' on the couch was not adequate? However, she did not wait until her parents arrived before leaving for the hospital. Could anyone expect that Donna could have waited? Would Donna have bled to death if she had waited? The large pools of blood on the floor indicated that Donna probably could not have waited for her parents. What would a physical examination of Donna's wounds reveal? Had Donna taken reasonable steps to ensure continuity of care in her absence?[11] Could Donna be faulted for leaving her child without adequate adult care? Partially. Could an apprehension be sustained on this point alone? Unlikely. It seemed most important that Donna's wounds were self-inflicted. The severity of the injury signified Donna's disregard for her own care. Furthermore, her parents, although at the apartment, had refused to assume responsibility for the child. Their claim that 'this type of thing has happened before' was important. It suggested a pattern of drunkenness and parental neglect. Finally, these elements could be combined with the sensory evidence of prolonged alcohol abuse and resulting neglect, for example, the filth, disorder, stench, and, most importantly, the physical condition of the child.

Implicit in my construction of Donna's parental failure was the normative model of a rational actor. If I showed that Donna's actions were irrational, this would be sufficient grounds for claiming that she had failed to exercise her duties as a parent. If I could prove that Donna's actions were irrational, then others would have to intervene in Donna's life to protect her and her child.

SEEING THE TEAR

This work which described Donna's action as irrational was not innocent. Its good sense articulated a domain governed by the dual imperatives of rational action and mastery of self and others. Smith understands that the normative model of the rational actor is problematic; it is a model of action that is grounded in the social relations of a ruling apparatus: 'The rational actor choosing and calculating is the abstracted model of organizational or bureaucratic man, whose motives, methods, and ego-structure are organized by the formal rationality structuring his work role. At work his feelings have no place. Rationality is a normative practice organizing and prescribing determinate modes of action within the bureaucratic or professional form. Responses that do not conform to these modes of action, by virtue of how they are excluded from these domains, are constituted residually as a distinct mode of response and being' (1987: 65). Smith argues that the lives of women, and I add Donna's life and the lives of clients in general, do not conform to this voluntaristic model of rational action.

As a social worker, I created a professional account of Donna's actions as not rational. In my social work accounts Donna was drunk, irrational, and out of control. I developed a tentative history that suggested links between this moment and other moments. I was beginning to see a pattern of parental failure. The patterns that I saw emerged as visible through the connection of case details to professional understandings about normal family life, child development, and personal care. Patterns emerged as I wove together the caretaker's and the grandparents' statements, the evidence of disorder about the apartment, and, most importantly, the child's flattened skull, diaper rash, uncut fingernails, and scratches.

At the moment of raising her fist, hurling her hand through the window, and ripping it back through shattered glass, Donna expressed her place in a lived world. Just as there are realities of fantasy and of dreams (Schutz, 1973) so too is there a reality of alcohol intoxication. Beyond the alcoholic reality is the social organization of 'being' drunk. These forms of being evidence their own irrational codes, for example, license, spontaneity, disinhibition, and animality. Although the alcoholic reality lies outside the logic of organizational space and documents, it was important for me to grasp the nature of Donna's reality on that Thursday. Surely, Donna's act gave voice to her place in a world. This may have been a world whose boundary was a locked door, a window, a shabby apartment, a cry from her child inside, her yelling and banging, the lack of response from the man inside her apartment, a mounting sense of anger, desperation, frustration, and rage, and ultimately a fist hurtling through glass.

When Donna slammed her fist into the window, she gave voice to something real for her. She meant to do it. Her's was a voice not necessarily expressed in words – perhaps other than through a scream or a profanity – but in a particular form of action that flowed from her history and her lived world. When the tip of her knuckles first touched the glass, her voice lacerated the tranquility of glass. Her voice shattered a silent second. When her hand withdrew, jagged and ripped, her voice was pain and rage. Her voice reverberated through a lifetime.

In my report to the court what disappeared – as not worth reporting – were the conditions of Donna's life expressed from her standpoint. The report to the court did not address her situation nor her understanding of what it meant to be a Native Indian, a young woman (nineteen years old), a single mother, a grade eight drop-out, and disabled. Certainly, as a social worker I could guess that Donna's life had not been pleasant. Her father had already told me enough for me to know that he had had a serious drinking problem. Later, Donna told me that she, her brothers, sisters, and mother had all been victims of his rage, beatings, and abuse. But this information was peripheral to the work at hand of determining whether or not there was a child in need of protection.

PROFESSIONAL ENTRIES AND EXITS

As a social worker, my entry and my work upon entering was structured by my location inside an organizational work process. I entered as a professional, not as a friend. As a social worker, I entered Donna's home to do child protection work. I did not tisk-tisk, shake my head, or cry over my friend's injuries. I did not mop and sweep up the floor, rouse the drunk, and wait for Donna to return home. I did not put on a pot of coffee, sober Donna up, talk about what was wrong in her life, or agree to take the child for a few days until she sorted things out. I acted as an agent of the state with the legislated authority to enter her home, to investigate, and to apprehend her child.

I had neither the time nor the authority to wait at the apartment. Indeed, while I was at the apartment I was consuming precious organizational time. I had a pile of work waiting for me back at the office, people waited for me in the reception area, applications had to be completed, and forms had to be filled in.[12]

Having made the decision to apprehend the child, I left the grandparents my business card. I instructed them to have Donna call me first thing in the morning. At this point the organization had assumed custody of the child through my action as agent.

PLACEMENT

I left the apartment to go to the receiving home. The receiving home was an approved 'group living home' as defined by the act. A legal contract specified the organization of the receiving home, the number of spaces (beds) available for children, the types of services provided in the home, the group-home parents' responsibilities, and a budget for salaries and services.

The receiving home had become available for placement of children only after it was approved by our agency. The building was inspected by the fire department and by city health officials. The home's parents were interviewed, investigated, and approved as caregivers by social workers. A contract was signed between them and the district supervisor and the regional manager. Only after these procedures were in place could the home's parents receive children.

Clearly, the processes that produced the receiving home differed from those processes that produced the child's home, or for that matter, our own homes. In our own homes, we speak of the social relations as family. We are husband and wife, mother and father, sister and brother, son and daughter, and so on. Such relations, although occasionally contractual, particularly in the form of marriage and marriage contracts, are not institutional. The relations in a receiving home, however, are expressed as group-home parent, child-care worker, foster child, permanent ward, resident, and so forth. These names designate institutionally produced social relations.

As a social worker, I knew that the receiving home had a free 'bed'[13] for an infant and that the group-home parents would have to accept the child. I had worked with these group-home parents many times before, and I expected that I could rely on them to carry out my instructions and to provide good child care.

When I entered the receiving home I left behind the worlds of daily life. I left behind people's pain, chaos, and disorder. I was entering a familiar setting. The receiving home was a part of an institutional world occupied by co-workers employed in child protection work. I had moved from the disorder of daily life into an administered and mandated order. In the receiving home, I could begin to relax. I knew the group home parents and the child-care workers, so they invited me to sit down at the kitchen table for a cup of coffee. As I sat at the table, I calmed down and organized my thoughts. As I talked about what I had seen and what I had done, I began to assemble a coherent version of my intervention work. Again, just as it was after every apprehension, in telling the story I searched for and received support and encouragement. On that Thursday, the group-home parents helped me see that my actions were necessary and that the child would benefit from placement in their home. We talked, and they shared their understandings of what this particular child would need. I appreciated their knowledge and they acknowledged the propriety of my actions.

My knowledge that the receiving-home parents would assess and monitor this child gave legitimacy to my action. I knew that the child would be safe in their home. The work of the receiving-home parents and their reports to me would provide important information to present to the court. I expected that the receiving-home parents would assess the child's intellectual and emotional development and look for behavioural or emotional problems. I also expected that if the child's mother requested and was granted scheduled visits with her child, the receiving-home parents would report whether or not she showed up, and they would provide an assessment of the visits. Simply, I expected that the daily work of the receiving-home parents would provide additional information for building a case.

In the modern kitchen chair and sitting before a clean table, I had entered into friendly and supportive institutional relations. Inside the receiving home, I found like-minded people who understood my work and the language I employed. Together our talk affirmed the correctness of our enterprise. This comfort was in contrast to the world from which I had come. There I had entered as an intruder, a stranger, as someone unfamiliar with people's histories and daily lives. Despite such ignorance, I was empowered to intervene dramatically in their lives.

I hunched over the cup of fresh coffee and breathed in the aroma. It erased the lingering stench of urine cloying in my nostrils. The sparkling cleanness of the kitchen washed away my memories of patches of blood on a floor. In the calm of this kitchen, I continued my search for order in the disorder that had become a memory. I searched for a pattern. Once away from the chaos of the front line, I was able to slowly recover a frame of mind and a centre of being essential for the work. Inside the safe space of this kitchen, I could reconstruct a professional persona, detached, objective, observing, emotionally controlled, evaluating, and acting in accordance with regulated policies and protocols. I was out of danger.

Despite the obvious sensibility of my professional self, there remained an inner unmediated fragment. Behind the social worker who calmly sipped his coffee, there remained an insecure man. I sensed that what I had done and what I could do as a social worker failed to adequately address Donna and her parents' pain and problems. As a child protection worker, I was unable to remain at the apartment to await Donna's return from the hospital. I did not stay with her until she sobered up. I was unable to take the child for a few hours and return her later. I was unable to work with Donna to help her resolve the practical conditions of her life.[14] Although my actions of investigation and apprehension were properly executed as defined by legislation and policy, I felt that I had failed. I felt that I had not done enough and that what I had done was wrong.

My doubts remained silent. My words briefed the receiving-home parents. I pointed out my concerns. I gave them a list of instructions: 'Observe the child to assess her mental development. Pick up the child's permanent medical record form at the office tomorrow. Take the child to the doctor for a full medical examination. Ask the doctor to make a report concerning the flattened occiput. Ask her to look for other signs of neglect. Make sure she submits the bill and report to my office.'

I interrupted my coffee to take a trip to the washroom, where the child-care worker was giving the child a more thorough bath. Again, I checked the child's buttocks, back, chest, and legs for signs of old bruising and deformity. I looked for signs of neglect that I might have missed during my first hasty examination. However, no additional signs were visible. I had been away from the office for almost two hours. I had to return to the work waiting for me.

9

Producing a File

When I left the office, I moved towards worlds where people smash their fists through windows, where razor blades course across wrists, and where people hurt others and are hurt themselves. These are worlds where rage is expressed, tempers explode, threats are made against people's lives, people scream, lash out, and move in ways that are not acceptable in the office. When I left the physical space of the office, my movement was in one sense a break with the office. In another sense, I was an agent of the office. But, as we saw in the last chapter, I had to return to the office. I had to document my practice. I had either to create a file or enter my notes onto an existing file. This production of a documentary record of my direct intervention affirmed that my activities were conducted for the child protection agency. This production of a file affirmed my organizational power.

When I stood at the door of a client's home I was embodied and vulnerable. As I sat at my desk and wrote, the writing effected a transformation. As the author of reports and documents on file, I assumed an Archimedean standpoint to gaze back onto my practice and the lives of my clients. My writing activities produced an 'objectifying gaze' (Pfohl and Gordon, 1987) through which sensations, movements, confusion, and chaos were rewritten into discursively coherent patterns.

When I arrived at the doorstep of the apartment building, I had to manage my body, a churning stomach, trembling hands, and a quavering voice. Back in the office, I had to manage my thoughts. When my hand sped the pen over the paper, I created flat words on a flat page. At the doorstep, I stood all at angles in a dangerous space. At the doorstep, I had to regulate the cadence and tone of my voice. On paper, my voice became the measured word, the formal phrase, and the organizational imperative. At the doorstep, my voice asked, 'Can I come in? Can I talk to you?' On the page, 'I requested entry.' When I wrote of the apprehension, my documents silenced my struggles to manage fear and anxiety. In the documents, I could speak without being present. Even the physical form of my scrawl would be rewritten and erased when my report was typed up by the secretary. Ultimately, my words stood in black and white. My words merged into a text to form the measured expression of a discursively ordered account.

As I sat at my desk, writing my report, I actively worked to erase my material presence. The controlled rituals of writing an organizational report soothed the hot physical sensations of making an apprehension. By writing up the experience, I transformed the confused blur of sensual memory into a logical, orderly, and linear account. I transformed my activities on a Thursday afternoon into the protocols and policies of a work process.

My writing activity and the account I produced were bound to the regularities of the office, the familiarity of my desk, the safety of the blank sheet, loops of ink on a page, and a computer screen. My account would become yet another document in a client's file. In the report, I transformed my sweaty hands on a steering wheel into the regulated movements of a social work 'investigation.' In the report, I arrived not as Gerald de Montigny, but as the child protection worker. Through the story in the report, my action, my eyes, my hands, and my thinking did child protection work. I was an agent. I embodied the legislation.

FILE FUNCTIONS

This chapter returns to the office to follow the production of a case file. But before examining the pieces of a file, it is necessary to identify some key organizational functions it performs. First, the file brings together multiple documents into a space where they can be merged and combined to produce a veridical account of both the case and the social worker's efforts. Second, the file collects important 'facts' for managing a case, hence, it provides details about clients (names, birth dates, addresses, phone numbers), provides an assessment, highlights key problems, outlines dynamics, and proposes intervention strategies for managing the case. Third, as noted above, the social worker in the process of producing forms, records, and reports for the file thinks through the case. To inscribe the case into agency forms, the social worker must sift through details of the case using the relevances of discourse. Fourth, for administrators, the file records work performed by subordinates and the services provided by the agency. When taken up by administrators, the file becomes a tool to evaluate the assessment and intervention skills of front-line social workers. Finally, files also serve administrators as a documentary resource for planning and program development.

Despite the clear organizational utility of files, many workers view them with suspicion.[1] Over the years I have met scores of social workers who take pride in asserting, 'I never read the file until after I have met with the client.' Social workers continue to mistrust files. They suspect that files may not accurately represent the case. They fear that the 'facts' on file may be wrong, that a previous worker was biased, and that the file is merely another worker's opinion. Despite the reservations of social workers about files, once they are assigned to a new case, they themselves must produce a string of documents that will become part of a file. As they produce the documents on file, they strive to ensure that their reports are empathic, fair, open-minded, and non-judgmental. They struggle to avoid the supposed errors made by their predecessors. Social workers' sense of professional integrity demands that their records on file record what they really did, what really happened, and what really caused the problem.

Inside the covers of a simple brown file folder, the everyday worlds of Donna Trout and her child were bound to the orders of an institutional reality. To the uninitiated, Donna's file might appear to be a conglomeration of various scraps of paper carelessly bound together. Inside the folder, one would find papers of different sizes, colours, and degrees of wear. Some papers would be typed, and some would be handwritten. For the initiated, however, there would be a clear order among these pieces of paper; they would represent an order determined by rules for file management. These rules require that specific types of paper be grouped together, for example, legal documents are attached to the left inside cover. The most recent legal documents are placed at the top, with the oldest documents at the bottom of the stack. On the inside right are agency forms and running records. Once again, the newest entries are at the top.

The scraps of paper in a file folder claim to reveal something about a client's life. They claim to represent my work as a social worker, the services I have provided to a client, my assessment of the situation, and my plans for intervention. The scraps of paper I and other social workers have produced for a file coexist in a propinquity that itself is suggestive of a connective order. The physical space of the file, much like the oral space of a tongue, allows seemingly unconnected words to mingle in a 'common ground' (Foucault, 1970: xvi). However, unlike mere spoken words, the words in a file are bound by the discipline of an organizational format. In clients' files their lives become a series of incidents on record. Inside the file, a social worker may pick up, hold, and read a report, the court orders, and forms. The reality of the documents is a material 'fact.' They may be touched, handled, pulled out for review, read to a client, and passed on from one generation of workers to another.

The file assembles discrete entries into a coincident structure where they may be mingled, mixed, and combined into diverse new accounts. The file brings together records that may be combined into hybrid assessments and novel understandings. The words on the pages allow for a fusion of new interpretations, understandings, and strategies for intervention.

OPENING A FILE

When I apprehended Edith Trout I was expected to open a file on the case within a week. Although the actual construction of the file was a clerical duty, I needed to provide the clerk with rough contents in a draft form. Whatever information I provided to the clerk was usually sketchy and incomplete. In this case, I had been fortunate to have met the grandparents at the doorstep of the apartment, however, in many other cases, I have had to apprehend children with no adult present. Often I have had to provide emergency services where a parent or guardian was not available, or, when parents were present, they were drunk or high on drugs and were unable to answer questions. In these circumstances, I had to postpone my paperwork until more complete information became available. As work on the case progressed, I was expected to collect more complete information. Indeed, over weeks, months, and years, and occasionally decades, a client's file may grow to several volumes as generations of social workers are employed on the case.

Following my intervention into Donna Trout's home and the apprehension of her child Edith Trout, I had to open two files, a family service and a child in care file. Each of these files was assigned an individual file number. The files were cross-referenced to each other and to any other existing files. If Donna had received service from our office in the past, I expected to find a file. If there were a child in care or a family service file, it would have to be reactivated. If there were a file for a different type of service, such as, foster placement, adoption, or income assistance, it would have to be cross-referenced with the new file.

When I rose from my desk with the paperwork completed, I handed my longhand notes and forms to the clerk. I expected that she would open the files and type up my notes onto the appropriate organizational forms. As my work on the case progressed and new documents were created, notably running records, child in care activity forms, and routine medical examination forms, these too would be entered into the file. Once the clerk completed her work on the files, they were returned to me for review and signature. Once the forms were signed, copies would be sent to regional and central offices to alert them that a case had been opened.

The collection of documents that I compiled in the files purported to be a veridical record of my work, the problem, and the client's life. Through the ongoing work process and entry of contacts into the record, files would grow to provide a history of the Trouts' case and the Trouts' relation to our agency.

CHECKING THE CHILD ABUSE REGISTRY

A proper check on the case demanded searching the office file index for any previous record of contact between Donna Trout, her child, and our agency. My search turned up only an open income assistance file. The failure to locate a prior family service or child in care file suggested that this was probably Donna's first contact with our agency on a child welfare matter. As a matter of routine I also phoned the provincial child protection registry. Phoning the registry allowed me to determine if there was a prior record of child abuse or child neglect that might have been recorded in a different district. When I phoned the child abuse registry I expected that my request for information would be documented there. That documentation would affirm the thoroughness of my investigative work in the event of a future review. Reciprocally, I documented in Donna's file that I had contacted the registry. I reported that there were no records in their files.

Checking the records allowed me to determine whether this episode was connected to past episodes and past reports or was the first time the family had come to our attention. Such information would be critically important in a court case. The determination that this was not a first contact would signify a pattern and suggest that there was a reduced possibility for effective intervention. A lack of prior records would be in Donna's favour, as it would signify that she should be given another chance to learn to be a good parent.

THE APPLICATION FOR MEDICAL SERVICES

When I took Edith Trout into care, the policy demanded that she be given a routine medical examination. As noted in the previous chapter, before I left the child at the receiving home, I instructed the receiving-home parent to take the child to the doctor the next day for a medical examination. To ensure that Edith Trout was examined, one of the first documents I produced was an application for medical coverage.[2] It was necessary to apply for medical coverage for children in care because so many of them came from poor families that did not have medical coverage. Policy demanded that the social worker when taking a child into care routinely apply for medical insurance coverage for that child.

By applying for medical coverage for Edith Trout, I took the first documentary step to make her case organizationally visible. My application assigned Edith Trout to a specific case type (a child in care) with specific rights and benefits, (paid medical insurance and medical coverage). Through the documentary production of an application for medical coverage, Edith Trout became an individual case eligible for medical services. She could be examined by a physician, admitted to hospital, and provided with medical care. On those occasions when I apprehended a child in need of immediate medical attention or examination, I would take the child directly to the hospital even in the absence of necessary documentation. However, when I returned to the office either that day or the next, I would complete an application for medical coverage, but use a retroactive activation date to cover those services granted before the number was assigned.

Before Edith Trout could receive medical coverage, her situation had to be translated into the categories of legislation and policy. First, the application for medical coverage on file affirmed that Edith Trout was eligible for medical coverage as defined in policy. Second, the application for medical coverage established a proper individual identity for her as a legal person before the law, that is, her name was Edith Trout, her birth date was 1 April 19XX, and she was the daughter of Donna Trout whose birth date was 1 July 19XX.

The information provided on the application for medical coverage allowed medical services branch staff to delete Edith Trout from her mother's medical coverage account (if one existed), establish a separate account for the child, and assign her a group and identity number for billing purposes.

Also included on the application for medical coverage was information that identified the origin of the application: my office address, organizational code, and my name as the social worker. This information ensured that the application was duly authorized. The application for medical services was completed in duplicate. Both copies were sent to the head office of medical services. However, to ensure that our office had proof of making the application, it was routinely photocopied. The photocopy was kept on file until the approved copy with the assigned group and medical plan number was returned to our district office.

THE CHILD'S PERMANENT MEDICAL RECORD

After completing the application for medical services, I completed the relevant portions of the child's permanent medical record. This form replicated much of the information provided on the application for medical services, but it also contained several extra pages for doctors' notes. Again this was a signed and dated form. Group-home parents are usually asked to pick up the form from the social worker's office receptionist shortly after a child comes into their care. The group-home parents are then able to take the child to see a doctor. The doctor is expected to complete the relevant sections, turn it over to a secretary, who in turn ensures that a record is made of the medical service provided and that a copy of the form is returned to the social worker's office indicating any medical problems or assessments of injury.

The child's permanent medical record often provides an invaluable documentary record of a physician's diagnosis of neglect or abuse. A case of child abuse and neglect usually depends on a physician's medical investigation. Although a social worker may document gross signs of neglect and abuse, a medical examination is necessary to confirm that the etiology of physical injuries is inconsistent with parental explanations. A medical finding is required to support claims that a child's injuries are not consistent with accidental trauma but are likely the result of abuse (J.E. Smith, 1984; Kempe, Cutler, and Dean, 1980; Radbill, 1980). The social worker can only note the suspicion of injury, while the physician has the power to define and determine the nature, extent, and probable cause of the injury. As Schmitt notes, 'the recognition of inflicted injuries will continue to be the responsibility of primary care physicians and nurses' (1980: 128).

Medical professionals, not social workers, make determinations about the etiology of bruising, scarring, lacerations, and fractures.[3] Determining the etiology of physical injury is work that itself has developed into medical specialties, notably those of pediatric radiology and forensic pathology. This medical monopoly over physical diagnosis places social workers in a dependent and subordinate position. To produce a warrantable diagnosis of physical trauma, social workers have to enlist medical professionals (Larson, 1977: 38) into child protection work. Physicians alone have the warrant and expertise to provide a medical examination of a child and a diagnosis that can be sustained in court.

The child's permanent medical record was not designed to provide an assessment of the etiology of specific trauma. Rather, as the name implies, the form was designed to provide a record of routine medical attention a child may receive while in care. The requirement to have a child examined when coming into care was designed not to detect abuse, but to ensure that a child who might not have received routine medical care was examined and treated if necessary. The routine examination also allowed the agency to detect any infections and communicable diseases that might be passed on to other children in a home.

The child's permanent medical record serves to collect evidence of routine medical examinations, evaluations of a child's health, and attention to medical conditions. As an organizational document, the child's permanent medical record is proof that the agency has attended to a child's physical needs while in care.

If a child comes into care with injuries that the social worker suspects are the result of abuse, then the social worker is supposed to request a written medical report from a physician. Unfortunately for front-line social workers, a physician's diagnosis of a trauma from suspected abuse is not covered by the medical services plan. As a result, front-line social workers are required to receive approval from their district supervisors before requesting a medical report. The burden of extra cost and the need to secure the approval of the district supervisor make the formal medical assessment of abuse an exceptional rather than a routine document. Additionally, all the doctors in our community at the time recognized that a medical report for court alleging child abuse would likely be submitted as evidence to the court. They realized that any evidence they produced might also result in their being subpoenaed to testify. Of course, if they were subpoenaed as expert witnesses, they would have to cancel their medical appointments for the day, wait in court until called, and face cross-examination about their medical judgments. The anticipation of legal annoyances, lost wages, and possible embarrassment led doctors in our community to simply refuse to do formal medical reports for court. The combined effect of these factors was that front-line social workers in our office rarely, if ever, requested a formal medical assessment of abuse.

To fill our needs for a medical assessment of a child's injuries, we used the child's permanent medical record.[4] We hoped that the doctor would note any exceptional injuries on the form and that the information he or she provided could be presented to the court. Furthermroe, the routine character of the child's permanent medical record was important, as doctors were more willing to complete it than an extraordinary medical report.

Through the child's permanent medical record, we were able to gather indirect information about abuse or neglect. Although our use of the child's permanent medical record was outside official parameters, we used the form to secure information that otherwise would not have been available. Reciprocally, senior administrators recognized that by making a medical report an extraordinary item, front-line social workers would save the agency the expense of paying for medical examinations. They also recognized that front-line social workers would use the child's medical record to gather information about abuse and neglect.

The use of the child's permanent medical record to gather information on abuse and neglect reveals a reciprocity of understanding between administrators and front-line workers. Through an interlocking weave of both explicit and tacit practices, front-line social workers and senior administrators ensure, albeit for different reasons and from different standpoints, that the problem of assessing a child's health and injuries is taken up within the routine documentary structure of the child's permanent medical record. At the same time, the routine character of this record ensures that physicians will be willing to complete it. The general focus of the form on the child's health, rather than an explicit focus on the cause of injuries, allows physicians to complete the report with a greatly reduced risk of being subpoenaed to appear in court.

THE RUNNING RECORD

This section examines the practical production of the running record. The running record tracked my efforts as a social worker on a case, as well as the life events of my clients and their children. Running records were chronologically ordered, with the most recent entries at the front and earlier entries progressively buried towards the back. Taken as a whole, they were a detailed textual representation of my professional involvement with a case. As the social worker responsible for a case I signed and dated each entry in the running records. The operative concept organizing the running records is that they are a professional product that expresses my assessment, planning, and treatment activities. The running records represent the goodness of my professional practice on a particular case.

Good running records provide an indispensable defence if our interventions on a case are ever questioned: if a client goes public by complaining to the media; if a child dies and an inquest is held; if a case goes bad; or if we have to justify our work on a case. Through the skilful construction of running records, we display our professional insight, efficiency, skill, and integrity, while generating a documentary record that affirms that work has been performed.

The specific contents of our running records, although not formally structured by policy directives, are structured by professional and organizational discourses. In my running records, I would note every significant contact with a client, whether this occurred through a home visit, a chat on the street, an office interview, or a telephone call. If contact with a client did not occur at some expected rate, particularly in cases with a mandatory supervision order, I would list my efforts to establish contact in the running records. The running records would document why contact had not occurred, for reasons such as avoidance behaviours by the client, client out of town, conflicting appointments, client not at home.

Running records vary considerably from file to file and from worker to worker in length, detail, and theme. As a general documentary form they address our work with and for our clients. Furthermore, we use the running records to present our work as proper, as conforming to policy, and as professional. The relatively unstructured nature of our running records makes them distinct from all other organizational documents on file. They are organized primarily by professional discourses rather than by preset structures of an organizational form. They come the closest to being our professional voice. As a professional voice, their detailed focus on individual client's life events, the social worker's interventions, and social work assessments of the case make them unsuitable, however, for administrative consumption. Unlike preset forms that present the 'facts' of the case, our running records present the multiple problems, dynamics, confusions, breakdowns, and chaos of clients' daily lives. Running records are retained only in the office files. Our running records were not copied, nor were they sent out of the office for review by administrators in central offices.

Running records address our mundane activities as front-line social workers. They record what we do, when we do it, how we understand and make sense of people's problems, how we discover and produce the 'facts' about an incident, and how we organize these facts into a case. Through our running records, we begin a preliminary professional sift or envelopment of situated problems into professional discourse. Our running records are a textual terrain that allows for preliminary and relatively ad hoc expressions of potentially good social work sense. In our running records, we begin to sort out particulars, make theoretical connections between incidents, assess problems, develop tentative plans, and work out strategies for intervention.

Our running records have an emergent quality. Contacts, episodes, observations, guesses, hunches, and suspicions are were all jotted down in the running record. For example, consider the following extract:

16/05/XX Call from Mrs Moore, re. 15 year old daughter Joyce. Joyce acting out at home. Mom requesting Short Term Care Agreement.

18/05/XX Interview with Mrs Moore, she is adamant that Joyce go into care. Mom does not want Joyce back home as she can't manage her. Joyce has been living with her grandfather but was kicked out on Saturday after coming home drunk. Grandfather is not willing to have Joyce return. This worker reluctantly agreed to the Short Term Care Agreement, placed Joyce at Pine Tree group home.

05/06/XX Jake, group home parent at Pine Tree, called to report that Joyce told him that she is pregnant. Joyce was very upset, as she is three weeks overdue. Called Mrs Moore to communicate this information. Set up an appointment for 10/06/XX to meet mom and Joyce.

10/06/XX Joyce and Mrs Moore into office. They were both quite unresponsive and uncooperative. They continue to refuse to address the problems in their relationship. Both hide behind defense of sarcasm, claim that they can't remember, and irritating grins. Dorothy insists that Joyce have an abortion. Joyce seems to agree. She is to see Dr Maltet on 1 July 19XX. They were warned that unless they make a more significant effort to work on their relationship that I would terminate the Short Term Care Agreement.

14/06/XX Mrs Moore into office to discuss situation. She informed me that when she was 16 she too had had an abortion. She is very fearful for her daughter. Encouraged her to share this information with Joyce.

25/6/XX Jake, group home parent at Pine Tree, caught Joyce in bed with Henry Redfern in the morning of 24/6/XX. Jake warned her about this before as he found her naked in Henry's bed a week earlier. He has expelled her from the house and does not want her returned.[5] Contacted Mrs Moore, informed her that I was going to terminate the Short Term Care Agreement.

28/6/XX Provided medical allowance for a CIC to fund Joyce's trip to the city for the abortion.

This example of a running record places a string of incidents, insights, interventions, and analyses together on a set of pages. As proximate textual entries in a file, the notations in the running record allowed me and other social workers to scan the pages of information to get a sense of the case. By using our professional knowledge, we could read the running record as providing essential information about a case. We understood that the running record might give us a clue to long-term dynamics and patterns that might not be visible through a single contact. Thus, a social worker might read the running record presented above as indicating a series of dysfunctional and problematic matters that involve the communication between mother and daughter, intergenerational premature sexual acting out, sexual rivalry between mother and daughter, and maternal failure to establish firm parental boundaries.

By sitting down and writing our running records we are able to think through our cases systematically. Writing the running records demands thinking as social workers. Our running records have to prove that we are probing the case, trying to assess its dynamics, and beginning to design an intervention plan. To effect a competent demonstration of our thinking and our practice on the case, we connect case details to professional knowledge about systems, family, developmental, psychodynamic, and ecological theories. To demonstrate our professional virtue, we use our running records to communicate our evaluations of the right, good, and proper forms of everyday life.

THE CHILD CARE ACTIVITY FORM

When the agency was granted custody of Edith Trout by the court, I had to complete a child care activity form for admission. This is a detailed form that integrates the decision of the court with organizational procedures. The child care activity form provides clerks in the central office with the information they need to begin paying foster and group-home parents for children in their care.[6]

The child care activity form also allows administrative staff to monitor the social worker's activities, while guaranteeing centralized administrative control over disbursement of funds to child-care resources. Most of the information requested in the form is designed to identify financial responsibility for the child and to determine methods for payment. The form seeks to determine if the child is the legal responsibility of the agency, another province, or another country. It asks if the child's parents are on welfare. If the parents are on welfare, their workers are notified, and the family's welfare rate is reduced to account for the removal of dependent children from the home. The form also asks if the child is a Status Indian under the terms of the Indian Act. When Native children come into care, the province bills the federal government for the child's support. The child care activity form also requests the name of the person who received the Child Tax Benefit. This allows the department to apply for the benefit, ostensibly on the child's behalf. Additionally, the form requests detailed information about authorization for payment to 'substitute caregivers.' The social worker has to indicate whether to pay regular foster home rates, special rates, group-home rates, or per diem rates. Finally, the form asks if there has been a court order for the parents to provide payment to the agency.

The second critical function of the child care activity form is to provide the central office with statistical information necessary to account for organizational activities over the fiscal year. In this case, the form was completed in quadruplicate, and it provided central offices with information to enter Edith Trout, born 1 April 19XX, as one case among several thousand children admitted to care in 19XX under the terms of the act. The child care activity form and its counterpart the child care change or discharge form provides statistical information on children in care which can be assembled for annual reports and budget planning. These forms are completed whenever a child is brought into care, moved into placement, its legal status is changed, or it is discharged. The forms provide the central office with statistical information about activities in the field. It also allows staff in the central office to 'track' the movements of individual children through the child welfare system. The forms provide information about the reasons a child is admitted to care, the legal status of the child in care, the child's racial origin and religion, the child's number of siblings, the siblings who may have been admitted to care with the child, the social worker's plans for the child, whether or not the child attends school, the names of the parents and their marital status, and the estimated length of stay in the present placement.

REPORTS OF INVESTIGATION AND FINDINGS

The report and investigation of a child in need of protection is an essential document on all child abuse and neglect files. It must be completed within thirty days of the report. This form is used to keep the provincial child abuse registry up to date. The form requests the name and address(es) of the child, the mother, the father, and the abuser. The nature of the incident as alleged is checked off as either physical abuse, sexual abuse, or neglect. The form asks that the social worker provide the approximate date or period in which the alleged incident is believed to have occurred. The worker is requested to provide additional comments about the incident, for example, 'The child was stabbed in the leg with a pair of scissors during a fight and scuffle between the parents. Three stitches were required at the hospital for the wound.' The identity of the complainant is requested, and a series of eighteen possible categories are provided, including a relative, friend or neighbour, the homemaker or baby sitter, a mental health or hospital worker, a doctor or nurse, school, preschool or day care personnel, police, an involved child, or anonymous. Although workers recognize that the categories do not always fit, or that a complainant might fit into several categories, they work to transpose situations at hand into the warranted spaces of the form.

The next section of the report and investigation of a child in need of protection asks for the investigator's findings. Again, the social worker faces a predefined set of mutually exclusive options. Under the category 'allegation is unfounded' the options are: 'facts misinterpreted,' 'report mischievous/malicious,' and 'injury was not due to abuse or neglect' or 'death was not due to abuse or neglect.' The social worker indicates whether her investigation found physical abuse, sexual abuse, neglect, or other, for example, psychological abuse or questionable parenting practices, requiring 'no professional medical care,' 'medical care,' 'hospitalization from —— to —— ,' or the 'child died.' Finally, the document requests information on the situation, whether or not family service is continuing, is the abuser still in the family, and has the child moved? The social worker finishes the work on the form by signing it and then getting it signed by the district supervisor. When the district supervisor signs the form, she signifies her approval of the contents, as well as of the propriety and correctness of the investigation.

The report and investigation of a child in need of protection is accompanied by a form requesting details of the investigation. This form lists the sources of information contacted by the social worker as she pursued her investigation. These include district office files, central registry, hospitals, doctors, and police. The contacts are to be listed and named and may be referenced at a future date as indicators that the worker has pursued the investigation in a proper, thorough, and professional manner.

WRAPPING UP THE FILE

Social workers understand that the file contains information of variable reliability, truthfulness, objectivity, and accuracy. They appreciate that some documents present hard 'facts,' for example dates, names, and court orders or findings, while the correspondence to reality of other documents is vitiated by bias, worker ignorance, administrative scrutiny, and organizational contexts. The challenge for workers is to sort through the vast array of documents collected in a file to produce a version of 'what actually happened.' Most of the documents addressed in this chapter, except for the running records, purport to establish documentary evidence of the 'facts,' thus, (1) the names and relations of people involved in the case; (2) the dates a worker engages in specific activities, such as, an apprehension, presenting a report to the court, attending a hearing, and making a home visit; (3) legal documents or orders, such as, short-term care agreements, foster-home agreements, and court orders; (4) the workers' understandings, assessments, and plans concerning the case.[7] The various completed forms, such as the running records, the applications for medical service, and the child in care activity form, are all framed as representing child protection work. The file that the worker produces will continue to exist through the years as the voice of not just a particular social worker's work, but, more importantly, as the work of the organization.

The documents on file connect a case with services, mandates, policies, and protocols of a variety of organizations, such as, court, police, public health, alcohol treatment agencies, child care services, and day care. The documentary connection and coordination of action into an institutionalized web is essential for a ruling state apparatus. When I apprehended the child Edith Trout, I was not acting alone, but in concert with a court register, a provincial court judge, a district supervisor, and departmental administrators. The coordination of professional activities through documentary records builds isomorphic organizational categories, procedures, and knowledge for managing situations at hand.

The documents I produced for Donna and Edith Trout's files were instrumental for coordinating the elaborate division of labour centred on their case. These documents connected my activities to those of nurses, doctors, health officers, housing authorities, and alcohol treatment centres involved with this particular case. The documents on file coordinated the actions necessary to manage this case. The documents provided for payment for services, proper authority for the case, and case transfer, for example, from one district office to another. Documents coordinated organizational action on the case.

For social workers, documentary work becomes just another tiresome routine in a generally overwhelming work process. Our paperwork has to be done on time or else we face embarrassment and possible reprimand from administrators. Our paperwork is essential to provide services. It ensures that payments are made to the foster parents, children receive medical attention, a teen gets new clothes for school, a little girl gets a bicycle, a case proceeds to court on time, and an adult is forced to stop abusing a child. Documents demonstrate that we have a plan and purpose for intervening in a family's life. Documents legitimize our practice.

For administrators, our paperwork allows them to not only see but to manage and control our practice in the district offices. Through our paperwork they are able to measure the number of apprehensions in each district office, in each region, and across the province. Our child care activity forms allow them to answer critical administrative questions, such as: Are more children being apprehended this year than last year? Is there a trend towards institutional care? Are the numbers of permanent orders decreasing? Are certain ethnic groups disproportionately represented in any category of service? Are more Native Indian children coming in care than white children? Do Native children remain in care for longer periods than white children?

Statistics compiled from forms filled out in district offices are used to answer myriad administrative questions. Administrators use our paperwork to assemble statistics which speak to managerial places inside the organization. The statistics they produce would allow the minister and deputy minister to argue for the department's budget, to justify policy, to implement new programs and so forth. Statistics are used to justify current expenditures, to demonstrate average costs for children in care, to rationalize cutbacks, to negotiate renewed funding agreements with the federal government, to develop new programs, to modify services, and to project future budgets. In short, social worker's paperwork provides a major source of knowledge for administrative staff. Our paperwork allows administrative and management work to proceed.

As social workers, we use our documents and files to artfully manage the confusion we face in the everyday worlds of clients' lives. We need to manage our own fear and the terror of everyday experiences. We need to rationally account for the irrational. Our written words, modulate the screams, the stench, and horror into a series of ordered, predetermined, replicable, photocopied, stapled-and-bound accounts. In our documents, there are no explicit ruptures or disconnections between 'what actually happened' and what is addressed by policy as a proper case or instance of service. In the documents the everyday world becomes a domain that is properly manageable and properly managed. Our documents are a textual waiting room that lines up people's lives into a string of cases.

10

The Report to the Court

After I apprehended Edith Trout, I not only had to complete the standard documents required to open the family service and child in care files, I had to prepare a report to the court. The report to the court, by entering my activities on the doorstep and inside the apartment that Thursday afternoon into a formal document, did two things: (1) It provided my activities with the sanction of a legal apparatus and determined that the apprehension of Edith Trout was properly executed, warranted, legitimate, and legal; and, (2) it provided for a formal organizational appropriation of my practice as sanctioned work performed for the child protection agency. This chapter explores the documentary activity of completing a report to the court to highlight how I and other social workers practically inscribe the everyday worlds of our work and clients' lives into institutionally manageable forms.

To complete the report to the court, I, as other social workers in our office, was guided by the *Forms Manual*, which provides instructions and facsimile reproductions of all forms, including the report to the court. No deviations nor modification of standardized forms are allowed. For the report to the court to be seen as complete, accurate, neat, legible, and professional, it has to conform to a predetermined format.

The report to the court is a four-page document that includes a one-page affidavit or sworn statement of fact. It interlocks my activities as a social worker engaged in child protection with a legal apparatus. The report to the court envelopes my actions into properly prescribed legalized form, where they are subjected to scrutiny, evaluation, and eventual legal sanction by the court.

The mundane truthfulness of the document called a report to the court depends on an institutional and historical matrix that includes child protection legislation, prescribed agency forms for case work, policies and protocols, and past judgments and legal precedents. The report to the court and the court work that follow articulate highly ritualistic language, grammar, rules, and codes.

Even for social workers, the rituals of the law and court are strange. However, I, like most other social workers, quickly learned how to manage work in court.[1] Although many of us may be unfamiliar with the specific nature of the law and court, we do know how organizations operate. We do know how to generate proper documentary accounts of daily life. We do know how to inscribe the everyday into the organizational. As we will see in greater detail below, for most clients, however, the law and court remain a strange and foreign realm. Court work confuses them as its order and codes are outside their experience. Although many clients may have been confused by court, they clearly recognize the power over their lives of the people who run the courts, and the courts themselves.[2]

THE COVER PAGE

The report begins by identifying the legal jurisdiction of a provincial court over a particular matter as defined in the legislation. A typical first page of a report to the court reads:

IN THE PROVINCIAL COURT OF (PROVINCE)
IN THE MATTER OF THE ACT.
X.X.X. 19XX–Chapter XX
and
IN THE MATTER OF THE CHILD
Edith Trout.
Report to the Court

1.
Section X(x)   I, Gerald Alexander Joseph de Montigny am duly authorized, pursuant to Section X(x) of the Act, by the Child Protection Agency of the (Province), to present this written Report to the Court.

2.

Interpretation

Section X.   The Child listed below is under the age of 19 years and is hereinafter referred to as 'the child.'

The Child	Birth date
Edith Trout	1 April 19XX

3.

Section XX(1).   The child was apprehended on the 1st day of January, 19XX in Viking, (Province) by Gerald Alexander Joseph de Montigny.

4.

Interpretation

Section X.   The child was apprehended as being in need of protection by reason of being:

(a) abused or neglected so that her safety or well being is endangered.

This is 'Exhibit A' referred to in the Affidavit of 2 January 19XX, sworn before me at Viking, (Province), this 2nd day of January 19XX.[3]

The cover page provides a warrantable account of practical social work activities as a legally mandated course of action. The account developed in the report to the court is organized by the relevances of legislative provision and authority, by policies governing the use of legislative provisions, and by the requirement to document and to receive sanctions for applications of legal power. The specific site, time, and people involved in the exercise of legislatively mandated authority are documented. The legislative provisions that warranted action are cited as the basis for specific actions, viz., 'the child was apprehended as being in need of protection by reason of being abused or neglected.' Finally, the document references the practices of oath taking and the swearing of truth.

The second page of the report elaborates particulars that are intended to sustain a case of abuse or neglect. Social workers construct an account of their activities that is typed into the four inches of blank space provided under the heading Circumstances of Apprehension. The section begins, 'The circumstances that resulted in the apprehension of the child were as follows.' The accounts provided, although varying in details from case to case and from worker to worker, have to be professionally recognizable as concise and warrantable. The account addresses the time and place of apprehension, the people encountered when apprehending, their involvement and conduct (if relevant), and the condition of the child(ren). The account generates a base for seeing that there are legislatively defined grounds for apprehension. For example, a child is apprehended by reason of being: '(a) abused or neglected so that his or her safety or well-being is endangered; (b) abandoned; (c) deprived of necessary care through the death, absence, or disability of his or her parent; (d) deprived of necessary medical attention; or (e) absent from his home in circumstances that endanger his or her safety or well-being' (author's name confidential). In the case of Edith Trout the Circumstances could read:

Attended at apartment 102–304 Zenith Drive, at 4:30 p.m. after receiving a report from the caretaker, Frank Valley, that a child Edith Trout was unattended in the apartment. Met the grandparents of the child at the doorway. They refused to assume custody. The child was found unattended on a filthy bed. She was covered in dried feces, had diaper rash, and appeared to have been unattended for several hours. The back of her skull appeared flattened, indicating inattention. The apartment was filthy, empty liquor bottles were evident. Donna Trout the mother was not present, as apparently she was drunk and was at the hospital receiving care for self-inflicted wounds. The child was apprehended and placed in the receiving home.

The above would stand as a fairly detailed version of the circumstances. Shorter versions were also possible, such as, 'Attended at 102–304 Zenith Drive to find the parent absent and no responsible adult present willing to assume custody. Apprehended the child, placed her in the receiving home.'

Regardless, of how I or another social worker might present the circumstances, we would focus on one issue alone, namely, whether or not we had reasonable grounds for believing and acting as though this was a child in need of protection. All other information that does not directly address the issue of child neglect and inadequate parental or other adult supervision falls outside the legal definition of a 'child in need of protection.'

After I provided the circumstances in the report to the court, I supplied the names, addresses, and marital status of the parent(s). This information is often not available in veridical documentary form, for example, a certificate or license of marriage. Indeed, on rare occasions, particularly in cases of abandoned children, the name of the child and her date of birth are not available. However, the process of naming identifies, for this moment in the process, the people who are considered the subjects of the case, and who might, following the report to the court, be served with notice of hearing. Finally, the second page requires that the social worker address the present whereabouts of the child. In the Trout case, I indicated that the child 'remains in the custody of the child protection agency ... pending further investigation and assessment.' In other cases I might have indicated that the child 'has been returned to the parent(s) apparently entitled to custody pending further direction of the court.'

Finally, the report of the court requires that a short-term plan for the child be created by the social worker. Is the child to be retained or returned? Can the parent(s) care for the child? Should temporary wardship be requested? If so, what amount of time would be necessary to correct the situation in the family? Three months, six months, a year? Should crown wardship – a permanent order – be requested? Should the social worker merely request a supervision order?

The third page of the report to the court addresses the interim order requested. Proper completion of this page requires that the social worker checks off the particular order requested from the possibilities provided for by the act. For Edith Trout the interim order requested was:

XX(2)(c)
The child protection agency requests that the Court order that the child protection agency retain custody of the child until an order is made under Section YY of the Act.[4]

Although this example employs a legal provision for maintaining custody, in the majority of cases the child is returned to the parents without proceeding to a court hearing. Frequently, children are picked up who have become lost or who have wandered away from home.[5] For example, one afternoon I was called to the police station to pick up a three-year-old child. Apparently, he had wandered into the local taxi stand to ask for candy. He could only tell people his name and did not know his address or how to get back home. I picked the child up and took him to the receiving home. When I got back to my office, the boy's mother was there to meet me. She was frantic with worry. She told me, 'I lay down with him for his afternoon nap. I must have dozed off. I guess he got up, undid the safety latch on the apartment door, and wandered off.' The woman explained that she did a search of the apartment, the building, the grounds, and then the neighbourhood. Finally, in tears she phoned the police. By the time she had phoned, I had already picked the child up and taken him to the receiving home.[6] This set of events, although happily resolved, was nevertheless an apprehension, which requires a report to the court.[7] In this circumstance I requested the following order:

Section XX(2)(a) The child protection agency requests that the Court make an order approving the child protection agency's action in returning the child to Madeline Trouve at 93 Perdue Boulevard, Viking, who appears to be the parent apparently entitled to custody[8] pursuant to Section XX(2)(a) of the Act.

PRODUCING THE FORM

After I had written out a longhand version of the report to the court regarding Edith Trout, I submitted it for typing. I placed it in an 'Urgent' box, with a short note attached requesting that the clerk also type an affidavit (all the information she needed was contained in the report). The clerk usually gave the request top priority, generally typing it within an hour or two, and returned it to me through my intake box. This mundane office organization of In and Out boxes, plus boxes marked Urgent organized the flow of work through the office.

Specific rules exist for workers using such an office system. It is assumed that social workers will not place work in the 'Urgent' basket unless it genuinely is urgent. All court documents and overdue work are considered urgent. The routinized systems for regulating workflows allow social workers to take for granted an orderly productive background of clerical practices to produce documents in the warranted forms. The day-to-day and routine character of office organization allows clerical staff, social workers, and others to take documentary work for granted. The remarkable quality of documentary production is lost in the sedimentation of experience and familiarity with office routines.

THE AFFIDAVIT OF SERVICE

After the report was typed, I proceeded to another social worker's office to swear an affidavit. After the affidavit was sworn it was attached (stapled)[9] to the report to the court. The affidavit read,

IN THE PROVINCIAL COURT OF (Province)
IN THE MATTER OF THE ACT
X.X.X. 19XX–Chapter XX
Edith Trout

1. I, Gerald Alexander Joseph de Montigny of Viking make oath and say as follows:
2. That I am the person whose Signature appears on the report dated the 2nd day of January 19XX, and attached as Exhibit 'A' to this my Affidavit.
3. That the information contained in the said report is true to the best of my knowledge, information, and belief.
   Sworn before me in Viking, (Province) this 2nd day of January, 19XX.

My affidavit, like all other affidavits, was produced through a formal procedure for taking affidavits. To produce an affidavit, social workers enter themselves into a highly ceremonial and routine set of activities. The ceremony and the routine of these activities provides for an invariant construction of specific oath-taking occasions, such as doing an affidavit of service. After I signed my signature, which stood as a matter of documentary record in the designated blank on the affidavit, the social worker who acted as the commissioner would ask:

Commissioner: Are you Gerald de Montigny?
Gerald: Yes.
Commissioner: Is this your proper name and signature?
Gerald: Yes.
Commissioner: Do you swear that the information you have provided is true to the best of your knowledge, information, and belief?
Gerald: Yes.

As social workers, we are instructed by supervisors to adopt an invariable procedure for swearing affidavits. We are warned that we might be compelled to testify before the court regarding the subject of an affidavit (details of a report) which we have either sworn or witnessed. If this occurs we need to sustain our claim to properly swear an affidavit, by referencing our use of an invariant procedure. If challenged to demonstrate how we could know that the affidavit was properly sworn, we could reply, 'I always swear an affidavit in this way. It is my habit. I never swear an affidavit differently.' This process of swearing and witnessing implies a possibility of conflict, variation in lived memories, and the indeterminacy of situated forms of being itself. The institutionally controlled acts of swearing and witnessing are designed to transcend the equivocalities of the everyday which even permeate our office work.

When we take a sworn oath, this ceremonial act constitutes a relation between a particular document and ourselves as social workers. Oath taking absorbs particular actions as candidate members of universal courses of action and legal sanction. Swearing an oath creates a bridge between the social worker and the law, such that the sequence of events we pursue, the investigation, entering an apartment, apprehending a child, and so forth, are properly identified for the court as being our actions performed for the child protection agency. Swearing establishes that this person before the court is the one who saw what we did and pursued this course of action.

THE COURT ORDER

Once the actual form was completed, I took photocopies of the report to the court, placed those in the file, and, with the original in hand, walked to the courthouse, and gave it to the clerk in the Court Registry. The court clerk assigned my report to the court a file number, date stamped it as 'Received,' placed it in a court file, and assigned it a date to be heard before the court (the next Wednesday, as was usual).[10] At the same time, I deposited a copy of the report to the court in a file folder for our lawyer, who also had a box at the Court Registry.[11]

By duly registering the report to the court, I complied with legislation and policy that demand legal review of a social worker's activities by the court. Once my work at the registry was completed, and a date had been set for the report to be presented, I tried to deliver a copy of the report to the parent(s) 'apparently entitled to custody.'

When the following Wednesday arrived, I appeared in court at the scheduled time to present my report to the court. In the case of Edith Trout, I requested an interim order for custody until the hearing. The interim order was produced from the work of the social worker, the lawyers, the court clerks, the court stenographers, and the judge. The interim order affirmed that my activities on this occasion were properly conducted on behalf of the child protection agency.

COURT CEREMONY

Court work is accomplished in a rigorously symbolic manner. The physical organization of a court places the judge at the front of the room. She or he sits behind a raised dais, beneath the national crest, and is surrounded by a solid oak 'bar.' From this dais, she or he presides over all who enter the court. The judge's power in the court is symbolically articulated to the power of the monarch and the state. The authority of the judge is expressed through her or his dress. Her or his honour is cloaked in a long black robe and a scarlet collar.

The symbolic construction, ceremony, and continual reliance on legal precedent and protocol in court allow participants to generate the transcendent and universal character of their work. The visual, ceremonial, and symbolic practices for managing the court, allow members to construct the practical links of the occasion, the time, and the place with the power, authority, and order of an extra-local and transcendent legal apparatus. Any presently enacted court transcends the immediate situations of its producers.

The specific occasions of court work intend in their genesis a discourse and a division of labour that records, documents, and sanctions people's performances as properly constituted court work. Through the practical articulation of activity to transcendent relevances, participants produce an effective claim to power. The combined articulation of participants' performance of a legalized code provides for the appropriation of a specific occasion by the court itself. Through iterative practice forms, the members perform the court as the actor, and proper subject, that produces a court order. They write themselves into the abstracted forms and rule of law such that it is the court, not they personally, who have the authority. The people who do the court's work are themselves subject to institutionalized processes for managing situations, producing decisions, and continuing legal rule.

Our particular court operated according to the rule of law, as do courts across the province and across the country.[12] As knowledgable participants in the court, we relied on universalized forms of (legal, ceremonial, classed, and gendered) action to accomplish the court's legitimacy. Matters that were brought before the court, such as my report to the court, were subject to the law, and accordingly were reviewed, assessed, and judged within the matrix of legality. Particular matters at hand were addressed as occurrences subject to the law.

The legislative requirement for review of social workers' child protection work expresses the juridical discourses about people's rights. Throughout the past two centuries, people have struggled to protect themselves against arbitrary, discriminatory, and unjustified actions by the state or other institutions. They have sought protection from arrest, entry, persecution, and harassment. The report to the court reviewed the propriety of my actions as a social worker and as a representative of the state. The report to the court is designed, at one level, to safeguard and uphold the rights of citizens against arbitrary violations against their privacy, property, and person.[13] As the judge (the court) reviewed my report to the court, he sought to determine whether or not my entry into Donna and Edith Trout's private lives was justified under the act.

If my entry into these people's lives was sustained in court as justified, then my actions became organizationally appropriable. They became work performed and sanctioned on behalf of the child protection agency. My activity of apprehending Edith Trout was properly subjected to a narrow range of considerations, as defined by the act.

THE INTERIM ORDER

The deliberations of the judge who considered the matter brought before his court resulted in a court order. The act required that the court shall do one of the following: '(a) make an order approving the child protection agency's action in returning the child under section XX (5) where he has done so; (b) order the child protection agency to return the child to the parent apparently entitled to custody; (c) order that custody of the child be retaken or retained by the child protection agency until a further order is made under section XX; (d) make an order under section XX(1)' (author's name confidential).[14] The legislation provides sanction of the child protection agency's actions.[15]

Only after a court order is issued can the social worker proceed to the next stages of child protection work, to make either an application for a hearing or seek approval to return the child.

When a judge hears evidence in court he or she poses a series of questions both explicit and implicit based upon knowledge of the law. Were the social worker's actions justified by the law? Did the social worker have reasonable grounds to make an apprehension? Did the social worker take all reasonable steps to avoid an apprehension? Has the child been returned to the parents since the apprehension? Was this a reasonable and proper decision? If the child was not returned, should the child remain in care? Should the matter proceed to a hearing? Once these questions are answered to the judge's satisfaction, a ruling is made on the case which is documented as an interim court order.

From the moment I answered the call regarding Edith Trout, did the investigation, and apprehended the child, my practice articulated this moment in court. This moment in court, in turn, served to retroactively subsume my situated and particular work activities into general and universalized policies and law. As a social worker does child protection work, he or she collects evidence that may provide sufficient material for presenting a case in court. In turn, the court considers the evidence brought before it to appropriate the social worker's activities and to produce an interim court order that affirms and validates the social worker's practice. This twofold dance between situated practice and court review produces a hermeneutic circle that establishes the hegemony of the institutional sphere over the spheres of daily life. Institutional hegemony is constructed in textual activities, which themselves intend legal review, the presentation of documents in court, the textually mediated assessments and reviews of those documents in court, and the interim court order that frames particular activities as instances of generalized institutional practice. Smith has observed: 'The articulation of different segments of these social relations are [sic] not obvious, yet they create the actual linkages between a lived actuality and the event as it becomes known in the documentary forms in which it circulates for further work. Whatever else may be going on in this interchange between the professional discourse and the institutional structures of state control, it is a process which continually integrates, circulates, feeds back and coordinates the continually changing relations of the bureaucratic apparatus to the actuality of everyday life.' (1990: 147).

What emerged as the situation of this child, Edith Trout, her life, her history, her relationship with her mother, her mother's history, their situation as Native, working class, unemployed, and struggling to survive in a hostile capitalist society, dropped out of sight as irrelevant for the immediate court work at hand.

11

The Hearing

A notice of hearing might read as follows:

IN THE PROVINCIAL COURT OF (PROVINCE)
IN THE MATTER OF THE ACT
X.X.X. 19XX–Chapter XX
and
IN THE MATTER OF THE CHILD
Edith Trout
Notice of Hearing

To Donna Trout

Take notice that on the 4th day of February 19XX, at 1:30 o'clock in the afternoon, a hearing will take place at the Provincial Court, at 100 Market Place, Viking, (Province), to determine whether:

The Child	Birth date
Edith Trout	1 April 19XX

is in need of protection by reason of being
(a) abused or neglected so that her safety or well-being is endangered.
And further take notice that at this hearing the Child Protection Agency will recommend that an order be made under Section XX(1).
(c) Custody be awarded to the Child Protection Agency for a period of three months.
And further take notice that if an order is made that the Child Protection Agency assume custody of your child, the Child Protection Agency becomes

the guardian of the said child and the Court may make an order that you pay a sum of money towards the child's maintenance.

Please be advised that:
(a) You are requested to be present at the hearing.
(b) You have the right to be represented by legal counsel.
(c) An order may be made in your absence.
(d) You have the right to appeal any order within 30 days from the date the order is made.
Dated at Viking, (Province), this 14th day of January, 19XX.
(signed Gerald de Montigny)

Just like the report to the court, which we reviewed in the previous chapter, each section of the notice of hearing indexically references a section of legislation to address the courses of action that will follow. Simply, a hearing will occur on a specific date, to determine if this child 'is in need of protection' within the terms of the legislation.

Unlike the report to the court, the notice of hearing requires that the social worker establish the proper legal identity of 'the proper parent' of the child. To meet this legal requirement for identity, only a certified copy of the registration of live birth – for all children born in the province – or an equivalent document, such as a notarized adoption order, will do. To get a certified copy of the registration of live birth, the social worker applies to the central office. The clerk in the central office will apply, in turn, to the provincial department of vital statistics or to a similar office wherever else the client may have been born. Once a registered copy of the registration of live birth is obtained, it is forwarded by registered mail to the social worker in the district office. The registration of live birth is an essential documentary record that establishes for the court, the name, date of birth, place of birth, and the maternity and paternity of the child.

Unfortunately, for social workers some single mothers refuse to divulge the name of the father of their child. Women's motives for their refusal vary. A woman might fear that the father of the child will try to obtain custody of the child if he discovers that the child has been apprehended. She might fear the man's threats and physical assaults. She might even want to protect the child's father because he is married to another woman. In spite of whatever fears and objections a child's mother may have, the social worker is required to secure the registration of live birth. The social worker has to determine the identities of both the mother and the father to ensure proper service of the notice of hearing. In special cases, when the social worker encounters a particularly recalcitrant woman, an application can be made to the court to waive service of the notice of hearing on a father. This step becomes necessary when there is no record of the father's name on the registration of live birth and a mother refuses to divulge the father's name.[1] A judge may also choose to waive service if a woman presents compelling arguments justifying why the child's father should not be served, such as, he has never provided support, he has never had any contact with the child, or, he has a record of physically abusive treatment towards the mother and child. In these situations either the woman or the social worker may apply before the hearing date to have service waived. However, service on the father may not be waived without a court order.[2]

The demand to present a registration of live birth to the court relies on taken-for-granted processes for 'naming' and 'dating.' Such taken-for-granted processes are profoundly dependent on institutional procedures and bureaucratic work. Through bureaucratically organized work social workers, clerks, and various officials take everyday events, such as births and the giving of names, and enter these into a formal record as incorrigible matters of 'fact'.[3] Similarly, the facticity of the information contained in the notice of hearing itself depends on a bureaucratic work process for producing 'facts' as matters of record. Dates of birth, maternity, paternity, and other such matters, may be treated as given, or 'incorrigible propositions'[4] (Pollner, 1974), only as a result of carefully monitored, secure, and structured bureaucratic work practices. The mere 'birthness' (Smith, 1974) represented by a registration of live birth relies upon interpretive procedures for producing a veridical documentary reality (1974: 265) that transcends the vicissitudes of daily life.

SERVING NOTICE

A notice of hearing has to be served on the parent(s), the child welfare director, and, when the child is Native, the Indian band. The process of preparing the notice of hearing closely parallels that used to prepare the report to the court, which was reviewed in the previous chapter.

When, as a social worker, I checked the birth registration, the father's name, the mother's name, and served them both with a notice of hearing, possibly against the wishes of both, I did so because my practice was mandated by legislative provision. As an organizational agent, I was required to serve a notice of hearing. If I failed to serve a notice of hearing, this would have been regarded by the judge as a serious matter. It would likely have resulted in some form of censure, reprimand, or punitive action against me or my agency.

The legal requirement to serve a notice of hearing is designed to protect the rights of the parent with regard to the child. The demand to serve a notice of hearing ensures that the parents are informed of the time and place where the hearing will occur. It ensures that they may be heard in Court if they wish to tell their story or to defend their position. Social workers in a liberal state must protect rights. They must make 'every reasonable effort' to locate parents and to ensure that parents are served with a notice of hearing.

The notice of hearing has to be served according to strictly set rules. In some cases, fulfilling the demands of service is a simple task, especially if the child is non-Native, the parents live together, have a telephone, and are home during the day. However, it seems that for the most part serving notice is exceedingly time consuming. Frequently, the child is Native, the band is located outside the geographic jurisdiction of the office, the parents are separated, the father lives in another province, a parent cannot be located, the parents do not have a phone, no-one is at home, or parents have left town.

Even when difficulties do not arise with service, proper preparation of notices of hearing is time consuming. Every 'fact' on the notice of hearing has to be shown to be correct. Any slips or errors on the notice, if recognized by the judge, may result in her or his refusal to proceed and the adjournment of the case for up to a month. The judge is entitled to reject any notice of hearing that contains errors of 'fact' or that do not comply with the legislation.

Our judge in the Trout case was exceedingly scrupulous about the details in the notice of hearing. For example, he insisted that the notice to the Indian band specify the full legal name and the position of the person who had been served. Difficulties arose because the judge would only approve notices that indicated that the person served was the 'band manager' or the 'band social development officer,' for, as he argued, these position titles were the only ones identified in the child protection legislation. The judge reasoned that only those people who occupied positions with these titles were eligible, under the law, to receive notice of hearing for the Indian band.

On actual reserves, however, those position titles are not necessarily used. Frequently notices served on bands by social workers in other district offices come back, either lacking a position title or using a position title such as 'band chief' or 'band social worker.' When this occurred our Judge simply refused to proceed until 'proper' notice was served on the band. On one occasion, I appeared before his court with a notice that was not properly completed. The judge revealed a wry smile that betrayed a peculiar satisfaction, and then asked, with feigned confusion, 'Who is this person named on the notice of service? What is his position, I cannot tell?' Unfortunately, for me, the child in custody, and the parents, the judge postponed the hearing for thirty days until proper notice of hearing could be served.

Even beyond ensuring that the details of service are 'correct,' serving notice on the Indian band 'under which the child is registered' often proves exceedingly difficult. Unfortunately for social workers, many children are registered with Indian bands that they had no contact with. A band might be served which is totally uninterested in the fate of the child. Such situations arise because under the federal Indian Act, children born out of wedlock are registered under the mother's band. However, if a child's mother marries or remarries, her band membership remains the same (unless she makes a special application to Ottawa), as does that of her child who was born out of wedlock. Band lists are particularly problematic in some areas, as federal legislation demands that membership be recorded patrilineally, while traditional settlement patterns and tribal membership operate matrilineally.[5]

The problem of service on Indian bands is compounded by the possibility of a conflict between parental rights and band rights. A Native parent is legally entitled to request that the band not be served. The parent's request has to be presented before the hearing date to the court where the judge could decide to waive service on the band. The potential conflict between the parents' rights and the band's rights arises from a fundamental disjuncture between western conceptions of children as private property and Native notions of children, not as parents' property, but as communal and spiritual beings.

AFFIDAVITS OF EFFORTS TO LOCATE

If a social worker cannot locate a parent to serve with a notice of hearing, this creates serious problems. Social workers expect that judges will examine their practices to ensure that they have pursued every reasonable channel to locate and serve the parents. Before social workers are able to prove that they have explored every channel, they need to do a great deal of tedious and detailed work. They have to write up their attempts into a signed affidavit of efforts to locate. Child protection policy advises that 'efforts to locate a person should include contacting known relatives, placing advertisements 'to whom it may concern' in newspapers with circulation in the area where the individual was last known, contact with employers, or through engaging the services of the attorney general's skip tracing unit.' As social workers in our office pursued the measures outlined, we made entries in our daily logs. These entries would record all our efforts to locate and serve a parent, and later, when we had exhausted all reasonable avenues, these log entries would be written into running records. Our running records would become a reference point for drafting a list of efforts to locate. This list, complete with times, dates, and corroborating witnesses, would be submitted to the agency lawyer. The lawyer would use these notes to produce an affidavit of efforts to locate, which the social worker could then present in court. The social worker could take the stand in court to give oral or viva voce evidence to affirm the 'facts' in the affidavit.

The affidavit of efforts to locate has to conform to the protocols established for all court documents. It has to indicate the legislation, the name of the parties involved in the case, the names and position of the persons who swore the oath, and the geographical jurisdiction of the child protection agency. The affidavit has to be presented to the court at least seven clear days before a hearing.

If the judge is satisfied that a social worker's efforts to locate are thorough and reasonably executed, he or she may approve a request for substituted service. This requires reproducing the notice of hearing as an advertisement in the personals section of the local newspaper on the dates specified by the judge. Normally, however, the notice of hearing has to be served personally in a face-to-face meeting between the social worker and the person named on the notice. After each notice of hearing is served, the social worker must swear out the affidavit of personal service on the reverse side of the form. In the Trout case, it stated:

I, Gerald Alexander Joseph de Montigny of Viking in the Province of _____, Social Worker, Make Oath and Say:

That I did on the 15th day of January 19XX, serve Donna Trout at 102–304 Zenith Drive, Viking, XX.

This affidavit, like all affidavits, was sworn before a commissioner – another social worker – who was entitled to take affidavits in the province.

Serving the notice of hearing on an Indian band inside our district office's jurisdiction often required that the social worker charter a plane and fly to the reserve or village. It was only occasionally that we were fortunate enough to have either the band manager or band social development officer visit our town within seven clear days of the hearing. When the Indian band was outside our office's jurisdiction, the notice had to be mailed or dictated over the phone to a social worker in the district office responsible for the band. That social worker had to serve the notice face to face, swear out the affidavit of service, and return the signed original to our office.

For front-line social workers, such complex procedures absorb tremendous amounts of our time. To avoid embarrassment or delays in court, social workers must be absolutely scrupulous to guard against errors of fact or procedure. If an error is detected on the notice of hearing, the entire process has to be repeated, provided there is enough time before the hearing. If there is not enough time, the social worker will still present the documents before the court with the hope that the judge might miss the error or that she or he might decide to proceed even with the error. However, realistically social workers expect that if a notice of hearing contains an error, the judge will adjourn the hearing.

BRIEFING LEGAL COUNSEL

To prepare for the hearing, social workers also have to consult with agency lawyers. Inside the court, our lawyers acted as the spokespersons for our agency. They presented the case to the court. In our province, social workers who did child protection work were not authorized agents of the court. Although it is social workers, not legal counsel, who are intimately familiar with case details, social workers do not present the case to the court. Social workers may only speak in court to give evidence.

The exclusion of social workers from direct participation demands that we generate a detailed documentary record to guide the lawyers in their presentations. To brief legal counsel, social workers complete one of three possible forms: (1) supplementary information for counsel, (2) brief for legal counsel for consented temporary and permanent orders, or, (3) brief for legal counsel for contested orders.

The brief for contested orders differs from the brief for consented orders as it provides detailed information to argue a case and to counter challenges from parents and their legal counsel. The brief for legal counsel for contested orders outlines much of the information contained on file. It addresses the efforts of the social worker to resolve the problem situation, the professional assessment of risk to the child, and it documents why custody is necessary. The brief for legal counsel for contested orders attempts to make a strong case for why the child needs protection. It addresses the relevant information for arguing and winning a case of child abuse or neglect. The brief for legal counsel for contested order listed:

1 All the orders since the most recent apprehension,
2 The service of notices and any problems which resulted from service,
3 The position of the parent regarding the proposed order,
4 The evidence to be called, including witnesses,
5 Other social workers' involvements,
6 The goals or expectations social workers had of the parents, such as, alcohol treatment, psychiatric hospitalization, involvement in rehabilitative programs,
7 Medical involvement,
8 Police involvement,
9 Service of subpoenas,[6]
10 Long-term plans for the child,
11 Information on incidents for cross-examination of parents,
12 The name of the child's counsel,
13 History of previous apprehensions, and
14 Legal documents to be presented, such as, registration of birth and marriage certificates.

The wealth of information the social worker provides the lawyer is gathered from extensive research and work with file documents and through telephone and face-to-face interviews.

To prepare a difficult case involves working with a variety of agencies, professionals, witnesses, and experts who are prepared to give testimony. Making a case demands that the social worker cover all bases by engaging in intensive consultations. Preparing the case means meeting with lawyers, other social workers, foster parents, child-care workers, family-support workers, and infant-development workers, as well as psychologists and physicians, the natural parents, and other family members. Witnesses have to be briefed and prepared for court. Their testimony has to highlight and reveal information that best supports the case of child abuse or neglect. Sometimes parents have to be subpoenaed. Subpoenas have to be drafted and delivered to the court registry to ensure that they are served by a sheriff. From out of such complex activities social workers struggle to produce sufficient evidence to sustain not only their case in court, but also their status as competent professionals. Court is a trial not only of the parents' capacity to care for their children, but the social workers' capacity to do their jobs.

THE COURT HEARING

When the time for the hearing arrives, if the social workers are properly prepared, they usually can count on getting the orders they request from the court. Occasionally[7] a parent contests a custody order, secures an energetic lawyer who is willing to plead their case, and wins. Such occasional defeats for social workers are necessary to sustain the legitimacy of the court. Social workers' advantage in court is rooted in their ability to tie their presentations and claims to detailed records assembled in a file. Through collaborative work with professionals across organizational settings, social workers, unlike parents, can arrive in court armed with the facts and the documentary record.

A social worker can present a client's case history through the file and its wealth of detailed facts. A social worker can report that the client has had three psychiatric hospitalizations, that a report of child abuse was investigated in 19XX, that a psychologist reported that the mother was immature and incapable of nurturing her child, and that a court order was issued in 19XX, giving the agency temporary wardship for six months. The importance of the documentary record for organizing a social worker's presentations in court is reflected in Turner and Shield's advice: 'The preparation of his evidence should be concise yet comprehensive in a clear written document, either the report to Court or brief to legal counsel. Written documentation is essential, presenting the letter of authority or affidavits or even being prepared to inform the Court of his credentials and experience to avoid challenges to his credibility. The social workers should also enter the Courtroom familiar with the data. The case file should be complete and up-to-date and should be available since the Court may require it' (Turner and Shields, 1985: 121). The client, however, usually has recourse only to a verbal story supported by the vagaries of memory. Additionally, many clients are assigned legal counsel through legal aid only upon entering the door of the court house. On several occasions I have seen the clients meet their lawyer for the first time only minutes before their cases were about to be heard in court.

In addition to extensive preparation for the hearing, social workers have the advantage of knowing how to operate inside the language of the law, legislation, precedents, and policies. Simply put, social workers know how to use the discourses of power. Child protection clients, however, who are usually the most marginalized and vulnerable segments of the population, are excluded from the discourses of power. Clients often remain caught inside life and class situations of their immediate experience. They use a language of daily life, not an organizational language.

When I would arrive in court I knew how to be seen as a respected professional participant. I knew how to operate to ensure that my words, opinions, and presentations were given full consideration. When I entered or left the local court, I displayed my respect for the court by bowing. When called to the stand, I assumed a confident posture. When called on to speak, I did so 'clearly, slowly, and loud enough' (Turner and Shields, 1985: 121) for the judge to hear. When I moved in court, I conducted myself to reflect a 'measure of respect and decorum that is expected in such serious proceedings' (ibid.: 121).

Male social workers are expected to wear a shirt and tie with either a suit or sports jacket. Female social workers are expected to wear clothing of appropriate style and modesty. When social workers speak in court, we are expected to use proper grammar and proper language and to employ a tone of voice that conveys our respect for the authority of the court. When we are called to the stand, we know that our words are to be directed to the judge, not to the audience in court.

Predictably, our clients are unfamiliar with the rules of the court. Either consciously or accidentally, they arrive in court dressed in ways that violate appropriate dress codes. They wear T-shirts advertising 'Moosehead Beer' or bearing slogans like 'Boogie till you puke.'

They wear torn blue jeans, or arrive dishevelled or even drunk. When called on to testify, they act in ways that the judge will interpret as rude and not showing proper regard or respect for the authority of the court. Through simple errors they display their 'ignorance' – and this is where the analysis usually stops – of the codes, protocols, and behaviours that produce the court.

When people violate the tacit codes of the court, they reveal their place outside the circles of power. They subject themselves to the negative judgments of those in power. Once clients are identifiable as not being respectable, suitably deferential, informed, proper, well mannered, and so forth, they are placed at a disadvantage. When their actions, behaviour, or demeanour is negatively perceived, this necessarily influences how the judge makes sense of the case. If a father who is accused of being abusive arrives in court with a defiant swagger, Harley Davidson tattoos on his arm, wearing leathers and torn jeans, the judge will certainly judge this appearance. The man's appearance will be read to construct a match between the accusation of abuse and his character as a father. Simply put, a man who looks like a brute will probably be judged to be a brute. A judge will try to determine if the parents' presentation in court is indicative of their behaviour in general and whether this indicates that the child needs protection.

Such evaluations of people's presentations and performances in court do not need to be explicit. Except from those rare occasions when a parent threatened the decorum and order of the court, by acting in an aggressive, loud, drunk, or demanding manner, our judge never made negative comments in court about the people who appeared before him. Although the judge was clearly loath to make explicit negative comments about clients, he was prepared to make complimentary remarks about clients who he felt presented well. For example, when Mrs Jones arrived in court wearing a fashionable dress, spoke with a broad vocabulary, used a sophisticated grammar and accent, and argued logically and persuasively in her defence, the judge commented, 'Well Mrs Jones, you don't look like the sort of mother who would neglect your children.' The judge also expressed a sense of confusion and asked, 'I don't understand how such an articulate, obviously educated, and attractive young woman could find herself in this situation.'

Once the hearing begins the child protection agency's lawyer, who has been given all sworn notices of hearing beforehand, submits these to the court as proof of service. Each notice is backed by a sworn affidavit, which makes the fact of service a matter of sworn oath, subjected to legal sanction. Furthermore, if social workers are required to give evidence in court, they have to take another oath on the stand. As social workers take the stand, they take the Bible in their hands, identify themselves by name and agency position, and swear a promise to tell the truth. By taking an oath, social workers subject themselves to the laws governing perjury. If they lie under oath, they risk their professional reputation, jobs, and even penalty, including fines and incarceration.

The hearing addresses the issue of whether there is parental failure, whether the child continues to be in need of protection, whether the child protection agency should be granted custody for a temporary period, or whether the child should become a permanent ward of the court.

As evidence was presented before the court, the judge in the Trout case engaged in a process of legal deliberation from which eventually would emerge a court order. The order began by identifying the court and its jurisdiction, the legislation, the child's name, and the specific date on which the hearing occurred. The order identified the judge by name and outlined the specific orders:

ORDER

Upon this matter coming on for hearing this day in the presence of Robert P. Power, counsel for the child protection agency; Patricia M. Plebe, Counsel for the mother; the mother Donna Trout; and the father Edward Lightening;
And upon hearing allegations and those allegations not be challenged by the mother or by the father and upon no evidence being called on behalf of the mother or the father, and by consent;
The Court finds that the child is in need of protection within the meaning of the Act.
It is hereby ordered that the child protection agency retain custody of the child for a period of six months, pursuant to section 15(1)(c) of the Act, expiring on the 4th day of August 19XX.
Approved (signatures of Robert P. Power, Patricia M. Plebe, and Judge.)

ENFORCING THE COURT ORDER

After a court order is granted for temporary custody, the social worker has to ensure that her efforts are not faulted or found lacking if the family problem is not resolved within the specified period. For the social worker, the court order creates a new set of difficulties. Simply put, children are then no longer in the custody or guardianship of their natural parents, but in the custody and guardianship of the child protection agency. This separation makes reparative family work extremely difficult. The social worker has to develop schedules, places, and mechanisms to bring parents and children together from separate locations. Parents who experience the power of the court to remove their children are usually extremely suspicious of working with a social worker.

The loss of the children brought about by a court order also creates negative consequences for parents. For example, by losing her child Donna Trout, who lived on welfare as a Unit 2, became a Unit 1. The loss of a dependent child also meant that she was no longer classifiable as unemployable, and, as a result, her welfare rate dropped dramatically. Furthermore, her allowable shelter costs as a Unit 1, were half what they were as a Unit 2. Donna was no longer able to afford her rental accommodation. She had to give up her apartment. Other clients in Donna's position defaulted in their rental payments and lived in their apartments until evicted. But even this option has risks as these people then gain a reputation of being bad tenants. Even those parents who live in public housing lose their apartments. Housing authorities are unwilling to allow parents without children to occupy two- or three-bedroom units beyond a few months.

The court order rather predictably produces unpleasant complications in poor people's lives. Forced relocation poses a series of new difficulties as single mothers have to solve a string of new problems. A single mother who is evicted from her apartment often has to move her belongings without a vehicle, pay moving costs, or find storage for belongings that the landlord has thrown into the street. Where can she store her furniture? What is she going to do with the children's things? How can she find a place to rent without a reference? How can she survive on even less money than she had as a parent?

Maintaining contact with the children also poses problems. How is she to get to the foster home located across town? Can she secure visiting rights? Where can she meet her children while they are in care? Will the foster mom be 'keeping her eyes on her' when she visits? How can she prove that she is a good mother? How can she get her children back?

In our community mothers who lost their children to the courts and who were reclassified as employable by the welfare worker often had no choice but to move to those downtown hotels that rented cheap rooms by the month. Unfortunately for clients with alcohol problems, relocating to a downtown hotel usually proved disastrous.

Mothers in downtown hotels had the added burden of arranging to visit children who were located in group homes away from the downtown core. Travel for mothers from their downtown hotel rooms to the group or foster homes where their children lived was difficult, as welfare income prohibited paying for taxi fares, and the distances made walking hard and time consuming. If a mother wanted to have her children for a weekend, and the social worker approved, special provisions were needed to approve the mum's home as a temporary placement. Women caught in the child protection system often suffered homelessness, discomfort, loneliness, isolation, and rejection from their children, family, and friends. Many clients' personal lives were seriously disrupted following the court order, as their lives worsened rather than improved.

The court order does not herald the beginning of help and rehabilitation, but a worsening of already bad conditions. The period after a court order is marked by a rise of crisis and increased need for support and service. However, for the social worker, once the custody order or a supervision order is granted, the immediate pressure to work on the case is relaxed. Indeed, behind any single case, there is a procession of other cases that also need to be processed through court. The intense character of child protection work and the demands of court work compel social workers to direct their efforts to the most immediate and urgent cases at hand. Once a case proceeds past the hearing and an order has been granted, it is no longer urgent or pressing.

Social workers do appreciate that for clients the immediate period following a court order is one of terrible emotional turmoil, loneliness, a sense of failure and loss, and life crisis. After a court order parents have to cope with losing a child, and possibly their home, and with facing family and friends with the 'fact' that they are inadequate parents. We appreciate that this is an agonizing period for parents, yet our work demands require that we turn our attention elsewhere, to other cases. In effect, we withdraw from the case.

Even when mandatory supervision orders are granted, social workers find it difficult to arrange and keep appointments for home visits. Many welfare clients can no longer afford telephones. To maintain contact, we can only drop in with the hope of contacting people when at home. Even when a meeting is scheduled, social workers have to rely on the client remembering the meeting, wanting to meet, and staying at home until the social worker arrives. As expected, many meetings do not occur as scheduled. Meetings when they do occur are usually accidental, hurried, and unsystematic.

If there are other crises in the client's life, the social worker has to respond. As a social worker, I received calls from the hospital when a parent had attempted suicide, from the police when they picked up one of my clients for drunk and disorderly behaviour, and from a probation officer when a client was arrested for shoplifting. Even when we feel unable to help people, as social workers, we have to look as though we are able to help. To appear helpful, social workers make referrals for clients to any number of other resources. For example, I assigned an infant development worker to supervise and to instruct a mother about caring for a 'special needs child'; I sent a child's father to an out-of-town alcohol treatment centre; I referred a mum to a mental health facility for counselling; I arranged for an appointment between a client and a public housing office. Even, inside our agency, we could refer clients to ancillary services. These included a rehabilitation officer[8] who, if funding was available,[9] could send a client to school for job training, involve her in the 'incentive program' (subsidized work placements) or develop an 'individual opportunities plan' (usually funded upgrading or job training). We also provided family support workers to work intensively with parents to improve their capacity to care for children, and child-care workers to do intensive supportive work with children in high-risk situations.

LOOKING HELPFUL

Yet as services and programs are phased out because of government cutbacks, it becomes increasingly difficult for social workers to sustain, both for themselves and others (that is administrators, judges, lawyers, or colleagues) the appearance of providing adequate service for clients. Family support worker positions are being wiped out, child-care worker positions are being cut, day-care funding is being reduced, and specialized programs for teens and for the physically and mentally disabled are being eliminated.

Cutbacks mean that social workers have fewer resources for clients. The elimination of resources erodes our ability to make successful referrals for clients to other services. By making referrals to other services we had been able to appear to be actively involved in a case and to provide concrete resources for clients. However, as resources disappear or became more restrictive, our prospects for securing successful referrals decreases. Front-line workers wanting to refer a client for service face lengthy waiting lists, increasingly stringent criteria for acceptance, and reduced numbers of spaces. As resources become tighter, it is increasingly difficult for front-line social workers to protect themselves (by demonstrating that they have provided appropriate services) and their clients (by actually providing those resources).

To cope with budget cuts, administrators demand heightened levels of accountability and increased levels of authority to approve spending. Those of us at the front line as social workers, have been caught by our professional obligation to help, declining resources, increased demands for accountability, and increased demands for paperwork to justify our actions. Even if social workers provide few concrete services and although our time for face-to-face contacts with clients becomes threatened, we may survive if we at least document our efforts. What matters is not that we provide the services we believe should be offered, and certainly not that we engage in professional interventions, but that we provide statutory services and that we document our efforts to do so. For example, a court order that requires a mandatory home supervision can now be fulfilled through a five-minute visit to an apartment, an entry logging the visit in the running record, and the presentation of the record in the court. Although, many of us believe that we should be able to use home visits to provide therapy and counselling, the constraints on our time vitiate achieving these objectives. What matters is not the particular character of the visit but rather the 'fact' that it occurs and that it can be documented to have occurred.

Similarly, a social worker can arrange sessions between a mother and a foster mother to encourage the mother to learn effective parenting techniques. If the mother does not attend, the worker only has to document, 'Although arrangements were made the mother failed to follow through.' Such documentary practice allows social workers to sustain the apparent adequacy of their work. As long as we adhere to institutional courses of action and document our practice, it matters very little what happens to our clients. We can use the documents, the policies, and the law to argue that we do our best and that we fulfill our duty. We manufacture a documentary reality, embodied in notices of hearing, sworn affidavits, and reports on file, which cumulatively demonstrate that at the very least we do what is organizationally required.

Yet, as social workers we remain plagued by questions, doubts, and guilt. I often used to ask: What have I done to change these people's lives? Have I managed to help them? Will these children be safe? Even if I keep the children, will they be better off then at home? When will the next crisis arise? Unfortunately, despite the appearances of doing the job, the voice of guilt tells us that we do very little to benefit our clients. For clients, the result of our work is the imposition of institutionalized authority and order over their lives by social workers who seem able to blame but unable to help.

12

Conclusion:
Dirty Social Work

Relations among men are not the sum of personal acts or personal decisions, but pass through things, the anonymous roles, the common situations, and the institutions where men have projected so much of themselves that their fate is now played out outside them. (Merleau-Ponty,
1973: 32)

Supper was over. Edward, Norman, and I sat on the cedar deck
digesting our meal with the help of a few beers. We had come together
at a faculty party. It was a typical prairie summer evening. The air
was hot and dry. Hints of dust and pollen swirled invisibly and
danced in my nose to cause a slight tickle. I listened as Edward, who
argued, 'Social workers should not work for any agency which requires involuntary services. We should not be involved in coercive
work.' Norman pragmatically asked, 'Where then would any social
workers work?' Edward, ignored his question, and expanded his
argument, 'As professionals we must ensure that our clients come to
us freely, and that we contract with them for services.' He went on,
'If we mean what we say about self-determination, then we cannot
coerce our clients into accepting services.'

Norman and Edward both repeated their arguments, expanding,
and elaborating points. Their debate droned on as static electricity
crackling in the hot summer air, while I drifted off into my own
thoughts. Edward and Norman's intense concentration on their
debate allowed me to feign attention and to retreat into an inner
world. My deafness was a blessing. Drifting off was easy. I felt content. Perhaps it was the beer? Perhaps it was the sharp-tailed swal-
lows which swooped through the sky? Perhaps it was the orange-

washed sky itself? Perhaps it was the echoes of steel mop handles striking the washbucket wringer?

What was I doing there? How had the years erased my focus on erasing dirt marks on nine-by-nine tiles? How had my gaze shifted from dirt marks to intellectual discussions about social workers' power? What paths had I taken to allow me to comprehend this discussion? What obstacles had lain in my path? What forced me to examine where I was going? Why had I not taken these paths for granted?

As I listened, and reflected on my own life, I realized that being a social worker for me meant crossing a class divide. It meant learning how to perform in spaces, in language, and in social occasions, in, what were for me, new ways. Being a social worker meant being different from what I was. Being a social worker meant constructing my place inside a distinctive reality. This is a reality where Edward and Norman's talk made sense. This is a reality where abstractions, generalizations, and universal concerns are cogent, meaningful, and worth bothering about. Social work and my own practice of it were part of an epistemological domain of control and power.

I listened, and I wondered about the 'quiddity' of the profession. I played with that silly word – quiddity. I wondered what is it that makes social work what it is? What is it that makes social workers what they are? How can people represent their actual day-to-day practice as social work? What magic do they perform to transform sitting at a kitchen table and talking with Mrs X into 'an interview.' How do I make myself into a social worker? Am I a social worker just because, 'I am paid to do a job?' Is it art or magic that allows me to be a social worker?

The caragana hedge was alive with the electric whine of crickets' song. Their rhythm whirled my thoughts into pulsing charges. I repressed a smile. I repressed my thoughts. I drifted back to hear Norman clarify, 'The reality is that most social workers work in prisons, in child protection agencies, in psychiatric hospitals. We would be out of work if they refused to work for agencies with coercive power.' Edward countered, 'To be true to our values we cannot work for agencies which provide involuntary services. We can't deprive people of the power to determine their own lives.'

Norman spoke of the 'real.' He was the pragmatist. Edward spoke of the ideal. Norman argued that we must try to teach workers to do the best possible practice in agencies. He insisted that social work educators could give graduates the tools and skills to reform organizations. Edward countered that good social work practice requires relations with clients based on 'mutuality, reciprocity, trust, respect, and equality.' He added, 'developing this way of working is difficult if not impossible within many agencies.'

At one level, I sided personally and politically with Norman. He was a progressive faculty member in the social policy stream. He acknowledged that front-line social workers have tremendous power over clients' lives. Yet, he argued, 'Social workers should try to humanize their work and make their work more responsive to people's needs.' I agreed. But how can workers humanize their practice? Is the education we give our students congruent with this imperative? What constraints do agency policies impose on progressive workers? In answer to my silent questions, the debate shifted. Edward recalled the names of two or three excellent former students whom both he and Norman knew. He pointed out that they had moved into senior management positions at income security offices. He then asked Norman whether he thought that these offices and their policies represented examples of 'good social work practice.' Norman, was aware of recent controversy surrounding income security. He had to agree that they did not. Edward proceeded, 'If even our best and most promising students are co-opted by work within authoritarian agencies, how can we expect more from our average students?' Norman nodded his head in agreement with Edward's assessment that the people named had 'betrayed professional values' – a point gained for Edward – but added, 'Our challenge is to educate students to help them avoid being sucked into the system.'

I resented Edward telling me that I should not have earned my living by doing front-line child protection work. I resented Edward's claim that thousands of social workers are violating professional ideals by working for a living. Neither my colleagues nor I could afford Edward's purism. Edward's claim that 'involuntary services' require that social workers engage in coercive practice is certainly true. However, Edward did not see that professional social work practice itself, that is, as the self-alienated, managed, and controlled activities of actual social workers, arises inside a complex matrix of institutionalized power.

Professional social workers' practice effects our own self-negation. Its very forms of expression produce those aspects of the organization that Edward saw as problematic. Whether social workers work in involuntary or voluntary agencies, they claim expertise, authority, objectivity, and specialized knowledge to influence others and to change others' lives. In a society of profound inequalities of status, prestige, influence, and access to resources the BSW, MSW, and DSW degrees are signs of power. The language, grammar, and talk of professionals are signs of power. The salary is a sign of power, as are the commodities it purchases. The clothes, demeanour, and comportment of social workers are signs of power. Although social workers may not command the power of some professionals, compared with the power of most Native clients, single-parent women, welfare clients, and members of racial minorities, they have considerable power.

What then is the solution? Can social workers salvage a liberating practice from inside organizational and professional forms of action? Can progressive social workers ever help clients? Norman urged that progressive social workers act like soldiers inside a Trojan horse within organizational walls. Norman believed that progressive social workers should conduct forays in the night to change organizations. He suggested that progressives infiltrate the organizational city to press for reform from inside. At the core of Norman's strategy is a deception and the danger of being found out. How hard can progressives push for change before they are either marginalized from colleagues or fired? How can progressives survive when each day compels them to engage in practices that conflict with their beliefs? What happens to beliefs that are held internally, yet are violated concretely, and in practice each day? In the face of such difficulties, Edward argued that social workers once entering organizations will be converted and co-opted. I played with the metaphor. What did we as progressives seek to achieve by constructing a Trojan horse? Conquest? Plunder? Power? Hegemony? Could we use our power differently? Would we just produce a new organizational city? Where should we begin to look for clues for building a progressive practice? How should we work to build this practice? I have argued that we must begin not in the clear blue heavens built on abstraction but in the muddied grounds of day-to-day life.

THE DANGERS OF PLAYING WITH DIRT

My work has looked at social work practices that are not sanitized, distantly theorized, and safe. I have tried to address social work that is both dirty and dangerous. I have examined social work that is contaminated by daily life, with regard to both clients and social workers. Social work cannot be scrubbed clean. Social work is like the nine-by-nine tiles I washed as a child. Real people with dirty shoes track across the order, the wax, and the polish of the organizational floor. Real floors and real social workers get dirty week after week. Their lives and the lives of clients cannot be scrubbed clean.

Despite the dirt and the danger of practice at the front line, the solution is not to succumb to terror. Social workers must resist the temptation to flee into the safe and managed spaces of professional discourse. Indeed, as social workers, we need a practice that celebrates the equivocal, the confusing, the chaos, and the mystery of the everyday. We must abandon the deceptive power of work that manages, contains, and orders. Social workers need a practice that is not simply work and a practice that does not work simply. Social workers need to practice in ways that are alive to their own location, partiality, and fallibility. Social workers need to play at work and to work at play. Although child protection is 'serious' work, social workers must bracket the opposition between work and play (Baudrillard, 1975: 40).[1] They must acknowledge their work as a form of play. By recognizing the play in social work, social workers question the 'serious' work of the organization. Recognizing the play in social work means challenging propriety, order, formality, and authority. It means bending, molding, and playing with the rules for organizational action. Social workers must stop taking themselves seriously, they must stop being deferential to power. They must respect people not positions.

Indeed, there is much about social work that is already play. Some of us appreciate that good work at the front line is filled with 'discharge, waste, sacrifice, prodigality, play and symbolism' (ibid.: 42). This is what makes our work worth doing. We are not only wearied, but challenged by the queue of clients moving through our offices. We feel alive when we produce change. We feel alive when we subvert policy, and 'get away with' providing exceptional services to clients. We feel bold and righteous when we 'take a client's side.' We rejoice when we help a client to see the world differently. We celebrate when clients act differently. We experience honest pleasure when we 'get to know' other people. We enjoy entering people's daily lives and learning how they put their lives together. We like to learn from our clients. We like to teach people how to understand their lives in new ways. We become electrified when a client questions harmful relations and ideas. We are lured by the wondrous possibility of imagining ourselves inside clients' lives. While we sometimes cry with our clients, we often laugh, chuckle, and share tales.

To play at social work is dangerous. Social workers, despite our desires for a liberating practice, are caught not just by clients but by organizations. We cannot simply repudiate the pleasures of our power (Pfohl and Gordon, 1987). We cannot simply decide to not work for a living. We cannot survive without a salary. We cannot easily risk becoming unemployed, out of work, and like our clients.

To work inside organizations, we reduce clients to things. Clients are studied. Their lives are penetrated. Most importantly, clients must change their lives according to our rules, according to the values of rationality. As social workers, we survey clients' lived worlds through an 'objectifying gaze.' We must measure, classify, cut up, and master people's lives. We must produce case facts. We survey clients' lives with a 'carceral' gaze (Pfohl and Gordon, 1987). We look towards containment, management, and control. We write over the realities of clients in universalized and objective professional forms. As social workers, we act as though there are normal subjects. We act as if we know what is normal. We work to make our clients normal. We differentiate us from them (Pfohl and Gordon, 1987).

As social workers, we do not merely help our clients. Instead, clients' lives become the terrain for exercising our professional powers. When clients are 'served,' their lives are inserted into organizational and professional discourses. Clients' lives are absorbed by a power that transforms their experiences, their lives, and their stories into alien, universal, and formal terms. However, the absorption of people's lives by an institutional reality is not seamless. The process is never complete. For example, rural social workers are often unable to be 'proper' professionals when working with clients. They find themselves working with neighbours, friends, and even family. Rural social workers lack the distances and spaces that allow for separation and differentiation from clients. In small towns, clients live on the same block or in the same neighbourhood. They shop at the same stores. They play in the same parks. They drink in the same bars. They attend the same dances as social workers. Their kids know your kids. Their spouses know yours. When clients are also neighbours, friends, and relatives, the organizational imperative to create a regulated and controlled professional standpoint becomes painfully visible. The size and relative anonymity of the city, however, allows social workers to more readily assume a professional and organizational orientation to the work. In the city, social workers can sustain stylized and regulated professional relations with clients. They can separate themselves from clients through consumption, accent, vocabulary, grammar, theorization, dress, manner, and esthetics.

BEYOND TIDY ENDS / LIFE WHERE THE ENDS NEVER MEET

This book is not about 'clean' social work. Daily life is not a tidy house where china ornaments are arranged in tight rows for display. In daily life, china is shattered, the shelves are knocked down, dirt is tracked across the carpet, and screams shatter the mirror.

My work at the front line was not clean, neat, and tidy. I lacked the comforting illusion of being able to plan an intervention strategy. I was unable to address specific problems with calculated interventions to produce measurable solutions. Instead, I found myself working with families who had been known to our office as 'multiproblem families' for generations. I met parents and children who moved in and out of crisis, often two or three times a year. I worked with children who had moved from foster home to foster home. I faced problems that just would not go away.

In my practice, I recognized that there was no beginning or visible end to the difficulties and sufferings of those who were clients. How was Michael, a twelve-year-old boy, responsible for 'acting out' and running away? He had been moved through thirteen foster homes, receiving homes, and treatment facilities in six years. What could sixteen-year-old Peggy do, after she accused her stepfather of sexually abusing her? Her mother rejected her and called her 'a lying little slut.' She was not wanted back home. How could she survive on the street other than by prostitution? Did her difficulties end when I found her a 'bed' in the group home? Was the problem the stepfather's victimization? Was it her mother's dependence on the stepfather? Was it exploitation by 'johns' on the street? Was it the lack of resources for teens? Even when a client took positive action, their problems did not end. For example, Mary left her husband and returned to school. He tracked her down, broke into her apartment, and beat her. She went to court and got a restraining order. The husband was released on probation, and Mary lived in constant fear of another attack.

As a front-line worker, I struggled to see inside the confusion, impulses, and conflicts to understand my clients' lives. I did not stop there. I also struggled to see how my own understandings were structured by my place inside professional and organizational discourses. My place at the front line constricted my vision, however. I needed to find some understanding, some solutions, and some interventions where I could help in small, practical, and visible ways. I saw that there were serious needs. I had to try and get Michael and Peggy off the street. I needed to find them homes. I needed to strategize with Mary to explore how she could protect herself and her children from further abuse. Yet, beyond obvious critical interventions, these people's lives remained dangerous places.

Life at the front line required meeting people where they lived, talking to them in a language they could understand, and developing a practice that met their needs, largely as they, not I, defined them. I did not abandon my beliefs or my convictions. I tried to use my practice to create links and connections between individual or family situations and socially organized relations. I struggled to help clients develop a politicized view of their situation within class, race, and gender relations. For example, one day on intake a young man came into our office to request welfare – social workers in the office handled welfare cases. He was extremely despondent and ashamed. He blamed himself for failing his family and not finding a job. Like 850 other men and women, he had been laid off from the mill during a prolonged shutdown. Like many other workers at the mill, he had to turn to the state for assistance. As we talked, I connected his predicament and pain to broader social forces:

1 He was not alone. Many other families in town were suffering similar hardships since the mill had closed. Social workers in our office had processed hundreds of claims.
2 Although he was entitled to unemployment insurance, Canada Employment had been criminally slow processing claims. People were being forced to wait at least eight weeks before receiving benefits which they should have received after two weeks. It was the failure of Canada Employment policies that led him to our office.
3 The welfare office had created policies to discourage people from applying for and collecting welfare while pending their rightful unemployment in-

surance benefits. He and hundreds of other families were caught in the middle of a dispute between two different organizations.

4 As a working person he had a right to 'welfare.' If there were no jobs how else could he and his family survive?

5 The shame he felt was produced by a social welfare system that was highly stigmatizing. His shame was produced by a daily barrage from media, government officials, and employers. Unemployment was blamed on working people.

6 Finally, as a working man, he needed to question the good sense of what it means 'to be a man.' Was asking for help 'unmanly'? Was being unable to 'provide for the family' a sign of failure? Have those who talk about responsibility, pride, and manliness faced a plant shutdown and loss of income?

My front-line work was a process of critical pedagogy. I tried to help clients make connections between personal and family problems and broader social forces. I struggled to politicize my clients and to help them voice the social organization of their lives within a classist, racist, and sexist society. I was not a neutral. I rejected a narrow definition of 'individual, family, and group work' as therapeutic, neutral, and objective. Instead, I struggled for a practice that allowed clients to understand critically the social organization of my power as a social worker, the mandated power of the organization, and methods for surviving contact with 'helping agencies.'

SENSUOUS SOCIAL WORK

Liberating social work begins by acknowledging the fear that arises when we leave the office. It turns towards that fear to ask, 'Why is the office safe? What makes our clients' worlds so dangerous?' We must question the organizational demand to enter clients' lives and to restore safety and order. Safe social work remains inside the regulated boundaries of the code. Liberating social work is dangerous. It takes risks. It smashes the simulacrum of synthetic images encrypted by the predictive regularities of an office, discourse, and power. Social work must risk taking a stand with the clients. We must take sides. We must not be afraid of the word enemy, nor can we avoid the practices of conflict. We need a social work that is subversive. We need to eat away at the inside of the beast. We must distort policies to favour clients. We must struggle to see strengths, rather than pathologies. We must differentiate between blame and responsibility and between punishment and empowerment.

Social workers need to recognize the structured regulations posed by a clock and an organizational calendar, and they must struggle to build a practice regulated by the beats of a heart, the cycle of seasons, and the paths of a social life. As social workers, we must not abandon judgment, but we do need to identify the relations of power and inequality between the judgers and the judged. We need to examine critically our own judgments. As front-line workers, we need to take the side of clients to formulate new judgments. We need to judge our practice and our organizations alongside, or in solidarity with those who are clients and those who are poor, Native, black, and marginalized.

Liberating social work is not without values. However, our values must be bound to the mundane places where we live and work. We must create values that are catalysts for practical action. We need values that demand decent housing, ending exploitation of working people, fighting racism, sharing wealth, and building communities. As front-line social workers, we need values that put us in danger. We must repudiate the safe values built on an alienated terrain of an institutionalized rhetoric. Nietzsche said: 'You exert power with your values and doctrines of good and evil, you assessors of values; and this is your hidden love and the glittering, trembling, and overflowing of your souls ... he who has to be a creator in good and evil, truly, has first to be a destroyer and break values ... Let us speak of this, you wisest men, even if it is a bad thing. To be silent is worse; all suppressed truths become poisonous' (1961: 139).

Notes

1 INTRODUCTION

1 The invocation of hegemony at this point in the text is embedded in my historical standpoint as a young political activist in his twenties during the 1970s. In this sense 'hegemony' denoted the sites of resistance and intractability that I and my fellow activists encountered in our struggles to change the world. Hegemony spoke to my sense of disconnection between the world as I could see it and the dominant or popular forms in which that world was represented to me and for me by an institutional apparatus. Hegemony expressed the socially organized boundaries of desire, the limits to imagination, and the constraints to action. Hegemony was produced in locations other than my own, by actors I did not know, and inside life spaces I only dimly understood.

2 The notion of 'intellectuals' is borrowed from Gramsci who insists that 'all men are intellectuals,' but goes on to insist that in a society such as ours 'not all men ... have the function of intellectuals.' Clearly, professionals such as social workers have a key intellectual function in relationship to their clients. In the social worker / client relationship, it is the social worker who ultimately has the authority, power, and expertise to construct warranted organizational accounts. The naming and ordering work that is part of investigations and assessments have an 'intellectual' function.

3 To pass my second year practicum, after my adviser decided that I demonstrated a lack of commitment to the profession, poor professional judgment, and a problem with authority, I was compelled to engage in a consciously constructed practice to display my suitability as a social worker. To establish commitment to the profession, I routinely voiced

professions of faith in cardinal social work values and recited social work formulas and principles as outlined in key texts. To display good professional judgment, I confessed my errors, got a haircut, shaved my sideburns, bought white dress shirts, wore a tie, and appeared respectable. To show that I no longer had a problem with authority, I ingratiated myself with my supervisor, and eliminated my objectionable socialist vocabulary when in her presence. These efforts worked. I passed.

4 The mainstream social work literature works up our experiences into the manageable form called burn-out (Zastrow, 1985; Bourgault and Meloche, 1982; Maslach, 1982; Freudenberger and Richelson, 1980). Notable exceptions are H.J. Karger in his paper 'Burnout as alienation,' and Gillian Walker's 'Burnout: From metaphor to ideology' (Walker, 1986).

5 Often social workers can identify each other's reports and running records by virtue of a worker's preoccupations with certain problems and themes. It is not uncommon to find that a social worker will write similar reports about quite different clients.

6 As Althusser (1977), Poulantzas (1978), Therbourn (1980), and other structuralist Marxists have argued.

2 IDEOLOGICAL PRACTICE

1 The book even contains an afterword by Susan Silva-Wayne, a Children's Aid supervisor, who reorders and reframes the author's story to produce a compassionate account of why some parents abuse their children.

2 Nigel Parton's work *The Politics of Child Abuse* is a notable exception. Parton employs the sociology of social problems to analyse the social construction of child abuse. He analyses the case of Maria Colwell, a seven-year-old battered to death, to outline the components that frame the construction of social problems in the press: 'First there is a framework of concepts and values which classifies events into story types, such as crime, welfare, human interest, and shapes the meaning of the event, implicitly defining it in a number of ways ... The second component is more distinctly professional and is supplied primarily by the professional imperatives of journalism. These professional imperatives constitute what is seen as newsworthy events and is structured by an orientation which defines events as abnormal.' (1985: 87–8) Parton speaks of the media constructing a circle in which social problems are defined and recognized as existing in the world.

3 Attention to 'practice' as profoundly social and as grounded in the forms of life within a class society appreciates ideology as more than a method that practitioners can freely take up or discard at will. Rather, ideological practices are grounded in social relations of power and authority – specifically the power and authority of some people to order and control other people.

4 An informed social worker might attempt to assess the severity of neglect and the degree of risk to a child by either ad hoc or formalized schemata outlining standards, such as those developed by Polansky et al. in their 'childhood level of living scale' (Polansky, et al., 1981).

5 I often felt troubled when I listened to the stories provided to me by those clients who had experienced psychiatric hospitalization or other forms of intensive involvement with 'helping professionals.' It became very clear that the generalized and universalized sense provided by professional categories had become their own common sense. For example, an ex-psychiatric patient had learned to speak of his 'ego defence mechanisms fostering his paranoia'; a sixteen-year-old single mother involved with child welfare talked about, 'my problem bonding with my child'; a teenager in trouble with the law talked about 'my need to control my aggressive impulses,' and so forth. What troubled me about such narrative accounts was the loss of the client's own feelings, understandings, and senses of reality and their replacement by a stock set of professional formulas. For these clients, the professional language provided a mask or a gloss under which the equivocality, the struggle, and the tenuousness of everyday life were contained, managed, and denied. The formulaic understandings and prognoses that clients found in professional categories while sometimes comforting, unfortunately occasioned a false sense of understanding, closure, and control in life worlds that were marked by profound ambiguity and uncertainty.

3 CONSTRUCTING A PROFESSIONAL STANDPOINT

1 The school where I completed my MSW degree was very clinical and, accordingly, politically conservative; furthermore, the systems approach had not yet been fully integrated as the base of social work. Therefore, many of the factors I sought to introduce into a case analysis were not yet acceptable for social workers. With the promotion of the ecological approach, social factors are at least recognized, though the focus on the 'psychology' of stress, with its insistence that 'stress is not only a

transactional phenomenon ... but is also a perceptual phenomenon'
(Germain, 1982: 3), places the responsibility for a 'maladaptive per-
son/environment relation' largely with the individual.

2 He had had a minor conviction seven years earlier. Prior to his arrest
for the latest crime he had worked for a large automobile manufacturer
for five years. His crime consisted of smashing a store window and
grabbing a statue of a horse for his wife. He was extremely drunk at
the time.

3 This thesis employs the ethnomethodological concern with how members produce sense and meaning, but addresses 'the day's work' dialec-
tically. Although 'the day's work' is in one aspect a particular whose
sense and meaning are bound to the concrete spatial and/or temporal
activities of members, in another aspect its very accomplishment as
such, that is, the intentionality that accomplishes and the interpretation that accounts, articulates the producer's or knower's socially
organized ground in transcendent and universalized forms of action.
Social work occasions, even at the moments of their specific and practical accomplishment, are thoroughly social. Particular occasions are
rendered accountable and reportable through universal and extra-local
discourse. The essential questions are: (1) How do social workers produce a professional identification? (2) How does this professional identification advance the work? (3) How does the social organization of the
ground structure the phenomenological horizon of the social workers?

4 Use of the article 'the' constructs the noun that follows as an object.
For the readers to recover sense, they adopt discursively organized
practices for transforming social relations and social action into an
object, viz. the profession.

5 Throughout the 1980s fundamental conflicts arose between social
workers and employing organizations that relied for funding upon the
state, as government pursuit of monetarist economic policies resulted
in a continuous erosion of services and working conditions. In Great
Britain under Thatcher, the United States under Reagan, in Canada
under Mulroney, and in the Canadian provinces under the likes of
Devine, Bennett, Van der Zalm, and Getty, social services and social
workers were under direct attack. They were doubly threatened, for as
salaried employees they faced lay-offs and unemployment, and as professionals they faced a steady attack on their programs, work projects,
and most deeply held beliefs.

6 The often used social work notions of goals and objectives are organizational effluvia indexing an institutional consciousness that constructs

the appearance of control and perspicuity. By referencing documented goals and objectives, the institutional actor can demonstrate, following the accomplishment of some piece of work, that the product of the work conforms to the goals and objectives. Such an accomplishment requires that the event can be artfully matched to the goals and objectives as though they were identical.

7 Supervisors and social workers expected that their professional training would enable them to handle difficult financial assistance clients more ably than the semiskilled welfare workers. In our office, social workers, not financial assistance workers, were assigned the most difficult, explosive, chronic, and disagreeable welfare cases.

8 For an interesting discussion of workplace 'antics' as escape, see Donald Roy's 'Banana Time' (Roy, 1959–60). Also see Paul Willis's Learning to Labour (1977) and his discussion of the 'lads' techniques for surviving the authority of the school.

9 A member of the clerical staff who yells at a client she finds aggravating may be forgiven, for example, because she does not have the skill to manage such situations. No such indulgence would be granted to a professional.

10 I borrow Goffman's notion of a performance (1959), but expand the terms under which people perform so that proper professional performance involves not merely specific settings and actions before specific observers (1959: 22), but designates a mode of life for professionals, and therefore a class position.

11 Bolger et al. contend 'we see all those who are wage labourers or those who have only their labour power to sell as being a part of the working class.' They extend this 'Marxist' formulation to argue that welfare workers are therefore also part of the working class (1981: 22).

4 PROFESSIONAL DISCURSIVE POWERS

1 Terrance Johnson, in Professions and Power, discusses the preoccupation to develop a concept of the profession through 'more or less abstract' models and concludes that such enterprises 'abound in the literature' (1972: 22). Johnson observes critically that professions' own definitions of themselves, although often couched in altruistic terms, most often serve to 'make life easier for practitioners at the expense, one way or another, of their clients' (1972: 26).

2 The problem of coming from a working class background was that I

would consistently not 'get it right.' The problem was not just employing the words and expressions, but grasping the tacit social situations of power, authority, and control that were implied in the daily use of the words. The problem was learning how to locate myself and operate properly within an institutional standpoint.

3 Field instructors often demand that students do audio recordings or video recordings of interviews and group work with clients. Although recordings appear to represent 'what really happened,' warranted interpretations of those recordings remain discursively organized. The interpretation of action presented in the video is systematically cued to the relevances of discourse (Silvers, 1977).

4 Laura Anderson talked to students in an inner-city affirmative-action BSW program about their experiences. Anderson and Munoz's fieldnotes reported the following comments from a student: 'Going into social work we were forced to look at social problems and I started using myself as someone to relate it to. I had to relate my existence to what I was learning.' (1986). Selected pieces of interviews were produced in an educational booklet, *Flowers Through the Sand.*

5 Over the past two decades, systems theory and its variants, such as the ecological and life models, have become dominant for mainstream social work. Social workers have discovered in systems theory a powerful device for conceptualizing, legitimating, and accounting for practice (Germain, 1991; Anderson and Carter, 1984; Germain and Gitterman, 1986; Germain, 1982, 1981; Hearn, 1969).

6 Volosinov asks 'how actual existence (the basis) determines sign and how sign reflects and refracts existence in its process of generation' (1973: 19).

7 Where I worked, a management information system (MIS) was proposed. Practitioners were to be seconded from district offices for a two year period to do the research necessary to get the MIS operative. Clearly, administrators recognized that doing the research required full-time dedication to the project. Funding was cut, however, and the MIS project was shelved.

8 In the months prior to its election defeat, the Conservative government of Brian Mulroney initiated a process of major governmental reorganization that results in the elimination of both the Secretary of State and the Department of Health and Welfare. Various functions of these departments are reassigned to newly constituted departments including Canada Heritage, Human Resource Development, and Health Canada. Necessary Senate approval of these changes was delayed by the defeat

of the Conservatives and the election of the Liberals to government. Approval is expected early in 1995.

9 Barlow and his colleagues in the works *Single Case Experimental Designs* (Barlow and Hersen, 1984) and *The Scientist Practitioner* (Barlow, Hayes, and Nelson, 1984) attempt to repair the perceived rupture between researchers and practitioners. They state: 'The overriding consequence of the lack of an appropriate research methodology for practice has been a disillusionment with research on the part of professionals in training in all health and educational fields. The oft-noted observation that research is viewed as a hurdle to be circumvented if possible, on the way to the professional degree, and the observation that relatively few trained practitioners with the inclination or skills to do research are doing any research at all, confirms the general disillusionment' (Barlow, Hayes, and Nelson, 1984: 23).

10 In Zimmerman's account of 'Record Keeping and the Intake Process in a Public Welfare Agency,' he described how novices learn to take up 'the investigative stance' (1976: 333).

5 AD HOC SCIENCE: CONSTRUCTING CHILD ABUSE

1 This approach parallels that employed by Lynch who states: 'Although it is not the task of this volume to systematically confront or refute romantic ('storybook') or formal-rational versions of science in the science studies literature, the observations of scientific work which are reported here are perspicuous for the incongruities they reveal between science as practical action and science as presented in extant science studies.' (1985: 4). Similarly, I examine causal accounts as a technique for generating organizationally congruent sense.

2 Erika Deglau (1985) has written an excellent paper entitled, 'A Critique of Social Welfare Theories: The Culture of Poverty and Learned Helplessness,' which outlines the politically conservative effects produced by using these theories.

3 These questions can be formulated in a professional style as follows: What types of behaviour endanger a child's safety or well being? What evidence is needed to establish a finding of child neglect? In this form, the actor who sees, evaluates, and considers is eliminated. The result is that these discrete acts can be constituted as rules, formulas, and guidelines for decision making.

4 Operational definitions, while providing an important sense-making device, nevertheless require what Garfinkel addressed as the 'ad

hocing' practices employed by line workers to 'recognize what the instructions are definitely talking about' (1967: 22).

5 Karger develops the term 'scientistic work' (1983: 202) to designate work that appears to be science.

6 The victim blaming nature of *Damaged Parents* was recognized, albeit in a positive light, by Thomas Young in his review of the book (1982). Young praised *Damaged Parents* as a 'truly remarkable book' that arrives at a notion of 'infantilism,' which Young recognizes to be 'an unpopular view of the problem.' He elaborates, saying that 'Polansky does not back off in the face of what his data has revealed' (Young, 1982: 161). What Young ignores is that the method used to create the data, and the categories themselves, may have produced this 'unpopular view.'

7 These are considerations for the 'relatedness dimension – absence of apathy-withdrawal' in the Maternal Characteristics Scale (Polansky et al., 1981: 252).

6 PRODUCING GOOD SENSE

1 The continual use of the masculine gender is not accidental. Mandated courses of action produce a transcendent objectivity and 'factual' domain that historically have been integral to the social relations of male power and the relations of ruling (Smith, 1987: 7).

2 See Gillian Walker (1990) for her discussion of struggles and debates inside the women's movement to create a language to express the problems faced by women who were being beaten, abused, coerced, and brutalized by men. Walker also notes that the choice of the term 'battered woman' allowed women to connect their plight to that of 'battered babies,' and to a legal discourse governing 'assault and battery' (1990: 97).

3 The paragraph quoted, from the third edition, differs from the paragraph in the second edition. In the second edition, Shulman wrote, 'Clients perceive workers as 'authority people' with power to influence them.' (1984: 33). Shulman's change between editions is not inconsequential. It is likely that he recognized that his use of the phrase 'authority people' tacitly ascribed a pejorative characterization to clients. By employing the grammatically incorrect phrase 'authority people,' rather than 'symbols of authority,' as he did in the third edition, he attributed quaint, simple, and awkward grammar to clients. Additionally, by placing quotation marks around 'authority people' he

bracketed the phrase, and suspended its legitimacy. His quotation marks imply there is something else, which he can see, at work behind the way 'clients perceive workers.'

4 Cruikshank (1985) and Wharf (1985) have addressed the lack of preventive services in child welfare. Additionally, over the past fifteen years the National Council of Welfare has consistently linked poverty to neglect (April, 1990; December, 1979; March, 1975).

5 C.R. Smith, in the British text *Adoption and Fostering: Why and How*, outlines her belief that 'separation, as such, is not usually the critical variable in causing distress or developmental problems' (C.R., Smith, 1984: 39), nevertheless, she notes that children in care report feeling 'alone, confused, frightened, and unable to control what was happening to them' (ibid.: 40).

6 Although Shulman speaks of 'making a demand for work' as 'gently attempting to involve the client actively in the engagement' and that 'the demand is synthesized with the worker's ability to express some genuine empathy with the client situation' (1992: 94; 1984: 44), apprehending a client's child ensured that a client became 'involved' in 'engagement.' As Carniol has observed, the 'demand for work' made by social workers is often 'one-sided,' as there is no reciprocal capacity for clients to make 'demands for work' of their social workers (1990: 60).

7 Clients often talk about their social workers in negative and derogatory ways. For example, I was standing around the corner from the front desk of a band office, when a woman entered, failed to see me, and asked the receptionist, 'Where's the prick who wants to see me?' When I introduced myself, saying 'I am right here,' she launched, undaunted, into a verbal attack.

8 The child's age is an important variable governing the social worker's determination of degree of risk. Young children are understood to be more vulnerable than older children. Determination of what constitutes a young child is a complex process, as it demands that the social worker assess the child's verbal abilities, the child's assertiveness, the child's ability to tell others, the child's relation to his or her mother, the child's resources for support, the other members of the household, the actual nature of the abuse, and, finally, the child's chronological age. Thus, a twelve-year-old victim who speaks out to assert her rights, with a mother who believes her story, with older siblings in the home, might be returned to a home where an offender still lives. Conversely a twelve-year-old child with less-developed verbal and assertive skills,

lacking mother's support, and without other resources in the home, would probably not be returned.

9 Many social workers assume that more time with clients will result in better work, and, hence, more effective resolution of clients' problems. I argue that the professional mode for constructing problems and for acting on those problems is itself problematic and itself contributes to the durability of problems. Thus, more time with clients, although possibly more rewarding for social workers, would not necessarily in itself result in better practice or significant improvements in clients' lives.

7 PRODUCING REPORTS

1 Media interest in cases of child abuse and neglect, particularly those resulting in the death of a child, makes social workers very cautious about not treating calls as reports. For example, the death of Michael Jack on 21 November 1984, in British Columbia, made headlines for several weeks. His death, and the sensationalism surrounding the case, resulted in the dismissal of both the social worker assigned to the case and the immediate supervisor. The case was presented in blaring headlines on the front page of the *Province* on 13 January 1985 as 'MHR Ducks Queries: Tot's Death Riddle,' and in the Vancouver Sun on 14 February 1985 as 'Coroner to Probe Tot's Death.' Similarly, the 1988 death of a seventeen-year-old ward of the Awasis child protection agency in Manitoba who froze when sent on a trip back to his home resulted in an investigation of the agency and the creation of a legal enquiry; it also resulted in the loss of several workers' jobs.

2 The husband may even understand that his wife, like his child, needs a parent. Being a parent to both his wife and child invests him with considerable power. From a progressive and feminist standpoint such understandings are clearly inappropriate.

3 In this example, the claim can be examined observationally to produce an objective examination of the child's teeth. Are they 'smashed,' or not? If they are 'smashed' how did this occur?

4 For an excellent analysis and history of Native Indians as members of a working class, see Rolf Knight, *Indians at Work* (1978). The transience I witnessed while working in the north reminded me of accounts I had read about men on the 'bum' during the Great Depression. Alan Mettrick (1985) provides a fascinating first-hand account of tramping about Canada during the 1981 'depression.'

5 Unfortunately, not all provinces provide social workers with the opportunity to employ child in the home of relative agreements.
6 Trocmé reports, 'In Metro Toronto self-referrals accounted for 24 per cent of the families ... referrals by a relative or a non-professional community source accounted for another 12%. Professional referrals account for the remainder' (1991: 72).

8 CHILD PROTECTION WORK

1 Under the terms of the old Indian Act, superintendents of Indian reserves could identify individual Indians who could be prohibited by law from consuming alcoholic beverages. The interdict list was created to alert other officials that certain Natives were particularly troublesome when intoxicated and therefore could be denied the right to purchase alcohol.
2 If the grandparents had agreed to assume custody of the child, the necessity for an apprehension would have been reduced, despite my concerns about an ongoing pattern of neglect. I had many positive reasons for avoiding an apprehension: First, an informal agreement would have avoided the antagonism of the court process. Second, I would not have been credited with another apprehension of a Native child on my caseload. Third, I would have avoided the tedious paperwork and court work associated with an apprehension. Fourth, I would have avoided separating a child from her family. Unfortunately, such informal arrangements have major weaknesses – they can easily be broken. The grandparents could have returned the child to Donna at any time. Donna could have demanded her child back. Donna could have taken her child. If any of these events had occurred, I would have been powerless to intervene. A formal court order, however, provided a legally mandated entry point to provide service to the family and to enforce an intervention strategy, most importantly the safe placement of a child. If I had chosen not to apprehend, I could have been faulted for 'missing an opportunity' to assure protective intervention for the child.
3 Pelton voices the understandings of most front-line social workers when he argues: 'The lower socio-economic classes are disproportionately represented among all child abuse and neglect cases known to public agencies, to the extant that an overwhelming percentage – indeed, the vast majority – of the families in these cases live in poverty or near poverty circumstances' (1978: 610).

4 Increasingly, social workers are expected to demonstrate sensitivity in working with people from different cultures in order to overcome racially discriminatory practices (Culhane Speck, 1987; McKenzie and Hudson, 1985; Close, 1983; Johnson, 1983) engaged in by white professionals. Social workers' response to their history of racism has been to develop a literature that addresses the dangers and difficulties posed to practitioners who must cross racial, cultural, and ethnic boundaries, for example, *Social Casework* (1980) dedicated an issue to analysis of 'The American Indian Today,' and McGoldrick, Pearce, and Giordano (1982) edited *Ethnicity and Family Therapy*. Similarly, see Dubray's work (1985) on 'American Indian values,' and Kelley, who proposes an 'ecological approach' to Indian agency development.

5 For certain 'sophisticated' leaders of the Native Indian community, such accents are regarded as an embarrassment and are an impediment to be overcome through education and training.

6 A central strategy of Alcoholics Anonymous, from which a great many programs for alcoholics are derived, is to teach the alcoholic that there is a 'Higher Power' in life than himself and that he must rely upon this universal power for guidance and to solve his problem (Alcoholics Anonymous, 1976: 45).

7 For example, the 'childhood level of living scale' presented in the text *Damaged Parents* advises social workers to watch for; the 'state of repair of house,' for example, storm sashes present, windows caulked, screen doors mounted, and living room doubles as bedroom; 'negligence,' for example, food scraps on the floor, windows broken without repair, and buttons missing from clothes; 'quality of household maintenance,' for example, dirty dishes in rooms, leaky faucets, ceiling leaks, or dirty bathroom (Polansky et al., 1981: 245–50).

8 Cantwell outlines: 'A neglected child may be identified by observation of his or her flattened occiput and hair rubbed off from excessive lying in the crib' (1980: 185).

9 Harris and Bernstein advise social workers preparing a child neglect case for court that 'the court will long remember a fiery red rash with a pus-like crust, a kitchen with accumulated filth on the floor, or a child whimpering and desolate' (1980: 476).

10 Whenever I or other social workers are in doubt about the health of a child, he or she will be taken to the hospital for examination by a physician. Doubt on such occasions indexes a knowledge about physical health and the risks of illness and injury. For example, I picked up from the RCMP a three-year-old child who had been found wandering

on the street. He had a bruise on his forehead, about an inch in size, and scrapes on his nose. He appeared to be very groggy and tired. These behaviours were taken as possible signs of a concussion. As a result, I did not want to risk placing him in the group home, so I took him to the hospital and requested that the doctor admit him for twenty-four hours for observation. My work on this occasion was accomplished by reading certain particulars into a background knowledge.

11 Donna never did attempt to defend her actions. Perhaps her own shame and guilt, and her sense of being intimidated by a white professional, her parents, and the courts prevented her making arguments before the court in her defence. Indeed, following my first meeting with Donna the next day, I never expected that Donna would defend herself in court, as she presented herself as a very quiet, frightened, and ashamed young Native woman.

12 On one occasion, I responded to a late afternoon call with a relief district supervisor (DS). We arrived at the apartment to find two children, about ages three and four, home alone with no adult present. They were filthy, the apartment was a mess, and questioning proved futile as they were unable to provide a clear story. The DS, whose time was not pressed because she was only doing relief work, insisted that we first attempt to locate the mother. I went next door, spoke with a neighbour, and began phoning places the neighbour thought she could be. After an hour and fifteen minutes of futile search, just as we had decided to apprehend the children, the mother's sister dropped by looking for the children's mother. When we asked if she was prepared to take the children, she agreed to do so. By waiting at the apartment, we had avoided apprehending the children. In this case, the exceptional time flexibility of the relief DS opened up options that are normally not available for front-line social workers. The pressures of work demands often compel front-line workers to engage in 'swoop and scoop' child protection practice.

13 Mundane words like 'beds,' which in daily life refer to simple objects and activities like sleep or relaxation, become organizational terms articulating accounting practices or tracking children and levels of service. Actual beds in the home are administratively transformed into 'abstract' and accountable 'beds' available for placement of 'wards' (either temporary or permanent).

14 Different child protection agencies provide a variety of family support programs that aim to offer intensive contact between identified problem

families and the agency. Social workers hope that by contracting family support services with dysfunctional families, for three or four hours, four or five days a week, these families will learn more appropriate parenting skills and thereby avoid the apprehension of the family's children. Unfortunately, during the 1980s some provinces eliminated family support worker programs as a cost-cutting measure. For an example of this discussion, see the paper by Currie and Pishalski (1984).

9 PRODUCING A FILE

1 Pithouse observes: 'The workers deploy flexible assumptions that cast records as convenient vindications of practice or, alternatively, as superfluous, time wasting and often misleading. In neither context do they view written records as an authentic source of information about their actual practices and personal competence' (1987: 33). Although Pithouse accurately captures many workers' understanding of records, their cynicism, complaints, and suspicions must be understood as a moment of boundary work for constructing a professional identity based on the values of integrity, honesty, objectivity, and truthfulness. Some 'facts' may go unrecorded to conceal actual work from supervisors, for example, providing abortion counselling while working in a Catholic agency, and workers may recognize that the forms they are required to complete inadequately match practice in the field, yet, as professionals, they struggle to develop better records that are congruent and honest, even to the point of risking their jobs.

2 During the period when I worked in child welfare, we could not assume that the child had medical coverage, because of provincial medical insurance premium charges. We knew that many poor and unemployed parents could not afford, or failed to apply for provincial medical coverage. Unfortunately, even when some provinces implemented special programs for low-income earners to provide lower premiums, many poor people remained unaware of these programs (Carroll, Doyle, and Schacter, 1984: 218) and did not apply for medical insurance.

3 See Barton Schmitt's, 'The Child with Nonaccidental Trauma,' Kenneth Feldman's, 'Child Abuse by burning,' and Ruth Kempe et al.'s, 'The Infant with Failure to Thrive,' all in C. Henry Kempe (ed.), *The Battered Child* (1980), for a medical investigation of etiology of injury or syndrome.

4 Similarly, whenever an income assistance client was pregnant and

unable to work, rather than being given the form 'client's inability to work,' which was an extra-billed item, she was instructed to request a signed note from her doctor that attested to the 'fact' that she was pregnant and addressed the approximate delivery date.

5 The 'promiscuity' frame operates in a particularly sexist manner. 'Promiscuity' is a category applied almost exclusively to women. Once understood as 'promiscuous,' Joyce's behaviour is viewed as problematic or pathological. Therefore, she is expelled. Henry, because he is a boy, and because the 'promiscuity' frame does not apply, is understood as 'doing what comes naturally.' Therefore, Henry is allowed to continue to live in the home. The 'promiscuity' frame organizes Joyce's sexuality as pathological, while Henry's is 'normal.'

6 Although I ensured that the child care activity form was completed promptly to ensure payments for foster parents, even then the foster parents would not receive payments until the child had been in their care for one month. Advance payments required the approval of the district supervisor and could only be for a maximum of $100. This was less than one third the monthly rate. We were able to overcome this problem by issuing money to foster parents as a 'clothing allowance' (up to $340). This served as an advance payment.

7 Although social workers may dispute the 'factualness' of a previous worker's assessment, for example that Mr Brown really is schizo-phrenic, they do not dispute that the worker really believed that Mr Brown was schizophrenic. The previous worker's assessment is a matter of documentary record.

10 THE REPORT TO THE COURT

1 The institutional sphere of law is not an area in which I have any expertise or special knowledge, and just as this study has taken up child protection and social work as understandable only as socially grounded and empirically investigated, the same holds true for the sphere of law. As Thompson says, in *Whigs and Hunters*: 'Thus the law (we agree) may be seen instrumentally as mediating and reinforcing existent class relations and, ideologically, as offering to these a legitimation. But we must press our definitions a little further ... For class relations were expressed, not in any way one likes, but through *the forms of law*; and the law, like other institutions which from time to time can be seen as mediating (and masking) existent class relations (such as the Church or the media of communication), has its own char-

acteristics, its own independent history and logic of evolution' (1975: 262). As Thompson observes, there is a considerable difference between the rule of law and the rule of arbitrary extra-legal power. From Thompson, two important insights emerge: First, contrary to the scientific Marxism of Paul Q. Hirst, the study of crime and deviance are not outside the proper concept of a Marxist theory (Hirst, 1979: 204); and, second, the law is not merely reducible to class rule, but rather expresses in its own form the complex social relations responsible for its genesis. An adequate understanding of the law requires a proper empirical investigation of its evolution, a task which is outside of this work.

2 The institutional exercise of the law over people's daily lives expresses the essential nature of law as power. Foucault notes, 'In Western societies since the Middle Ages the exercise of power has always been formulated in terms of law' (1980: 87). Foucault extends this analysis, however, to argue that the law is but one mechanism of power, which since the eighteenth century has been augmented by other mechanisms of power, for example, normalization, codes and 'forms that go beyond the state and its apparatus' (1980: 89).

3 The document ends with a signature of 'A Commissioner for Taking Affidavits for (Province).'

4 Section YY designates the specification of provisions for a Hearing.

5 Social workers often decided to return the child to a parent, and not proceed to a hearing, even when there were legitimate grounds for an apprehension. Sometimes a parent has simply made a bad decision to leave children alone without a babysitter. Sometimes babysitters do not arrive to care for children or have left the children alone. Sometimes the social worker decides there is little continued risk to the child.

6 As the social worker, I had to complete a short term stay form. This ensured that the group-home parent was paid for the few hours of work required to care for the lost child.

7 Some jurisdictions do not require a report to the court, instead the social worker makes an application for a hearing within four days of the apprehension. As a result, many apprehensions do not get counted as such because the social worker simply returns the child and is not required to proceed to court.

8 Note that these provisions constantly repeat the phrase the 'parent apparently entitled to custody.' This wording tacitly articulates the social worker's problem of becoming embroiled in custody disputes.

Disputing parents will report one another to the child protection authorities to advance their claims to the children. Yet, the mandate to become involved in these disputes does not rest with child protection workers. It rests with family relations workers situated in probation offices. It is inappropriate for child protection workers to become partisan allies of a parent struggling for custody. They cannot normally apprehend a child from one parent and turn it over to another. The provision that the child be returned to the parent 'apparently entitled to custody' means that the child be returned to the parent from whom it was apprehended.

9 Our judge was known to comment when he received an affidavit that was paper-clipped, not stapled, to a report to the court with: 'The Affidavit is not attached to the Report.'

10 The detail and care in the preparation and completion of the report to the Court was structured by the day of the apprehension. If the child was apprehended on a Tuesday, and court was held the next day, the worker had to scramble frantically to prepare the report, to ensure that it was heard the next day to meet the requirement to hear a case within seven days of the apprehension. If the child was apprehended on a Wednesday, however, the worker had an entire week to assemble her report to the court.

11 Because this case study is based on my experience in a small town, each lawyer or law firm had a file, which was maintained at the court registry for correspondence.

12 The authority of the court does not begin or end in the practical accomplishment of symbol and ceremony of those who perform the court, but rather is reinforced and buttressed through the operation of the police, the jails, the federal prisons, and, if necessary, by the army itself. Indeed, in cases regarding criminal matters, a police officer or sheriff is necessarily present to guard the accused.

13 C.B. Macpherson, when speaking of democratic theory argued that 'all roads lead to property' (1973: 121). By this he meant that any discussion of freedom, liberty, and rights must be understood within the social relations that construct such qualities as forms of property. He outlined that property within capitalist society has elevated 'extractive powers,' (property in capital), rather than the 'development powers' (property in common, property in quality of life, property in freedom). Macpherson artfully connects what we recognize as civil rights to a historical process that generated property in labour, a possibility which could only arise in a capitalist society (1973: 130).

14 This section allows the court to proceed to an immediate hearing. This requires consent of the parents, the child protection agency, and, if the child is a 'status Indian,' the band.

15 Clause (b) implies the possibility of disagreement between the judge and the child protection agency. There remains the possibility for a verbal reprimand, however, ultimately the court is required by legislation to issue an order that sanctions the actions of the child protection agency. The process is similar to that noted by Pollner in his analysis of a traffic court, wherein a judge aware of the 'inferentially established' possible solutions to the problem of a disjuncture or puzzle, viz. reprimanding the police officer for hallucinating, incompetence, or being drunk, 'explicitly precludes other possibilities which are at least candidate solutions given that the defendant's version has been selected as the version' (1974: 53). Similarly, the judge in family court is required to offer solutions to puzzles that sustain the warrant of the social worker's actions even in those cases where there is disagreement.

11 THE HEARING

1 The documentary affirmation of the reality of parentage and paternity gives truth to O'Brien's insight: 'Paternity, then, is not a natural relationship to a child, but a right to a child. "Right," of course, is a political concept, which makes no sense in anything other than a socio-legal-political context' (1981: 54).

2 The judge in our community maintained an almost inflexible adherence to the letter of the law. On one occasion a woman appeared before the court who refused to reveal the name of the father of her child. Additionally, the registration of live birth provided no information regarding the father. His Honour insisted that 'biology dictates that every child has to have a biological mother and father.' However, because of the woman's determination, he was forced to waive service on the father.

3 For the administration of the Young Offenders Act, an important moment of the proceeding is 'proving age.' Proving age requires that the social worker or probation officer produce the registration of live birth and swear that this child now before the court is the person indicated in the registration. This activity envelopes a presently unfolding situation into the criteria of a documentary reality. It allows the people in the court to engage in the work of subsuming this juvenile's situation within the terms of the act.

4 Pollner, to explicate the operations of 'mundane reasoning' and the practices of 'mundane reasoners,' formulates the notion of 'incorrigible propositions' (1974: 43), which he proposes comprise a foundation for sense-making activities. Such incorrigible propositions are the 'common-sense' recognition that there is an everyday and real world, that within this 'real world' standpoints are interchangeable – hence, intersubjectivity is possible, but that from time to time there will be disagreements about what actually happened in this real world. These disagreements, however, can be posed as 'puzzles' that are themselves suggestive of candidate solutions.

5 For example, when I apprehended Johnny Quincy Jr, I knew that he was 'entitled to be registered' under the Indian Act. His mother, Ruth, and father, John, were both 'Status Indians' and members of the Red River Band. When John married Ruth, she applied to transfer from the band list where she was registered (Salt Lake Band) to the band list of her husband (Red River Band), despite the fact that the family continued to live on the Viking Reserve. Curiously, Johnny Jr did not appear on the Viking Band list where he lived, nor on his father's band list (Red River). When I tried to find out where Johnny Jr was registered, I discovered that he had been born out of wedlock. Johnny Jr was registered under the Salt Lake Band where Ruth had been registered before she married John. Through her life Ruth had had minimal contact with this band. The Salt Lake Band was that of her father, whom she had never known, as he died shortly after her birth. Ruth's mother had come from another band, the Viking, where she lived after her husband's death. To confuse the situation further, when Ruth was three years old her mother remarried a man from the New Dawn Band. Although the family continued to live on the Viking Reserve, Ruth's parents were legally registered as members of the New Dawn Band. Both Ruth and her mother failed to apply to have their own children transferred to the list of the band where they lived and where they felt they belonged.

6 Subpoenas are used usually to compel those parents who are reluctant to appear in court to do so. This occurs most often with fathers accused of sexual abuse or parents accused of abuse. Less frequently subpoenas are used to ensure the presence of witnesses, particularly 'expert' witnesses who require a subpoena to legitimize travel or time away from regular duties.

7 Despite appearing in court regularly over a two-year period, I recall only one occasion where the judge ruled in favour of the client and

against my recommendation. My experience was not unusual, as other workers with considerably more years in the field reported that they may have 'lost' only one or two cases.

8 This position was euphemistically renamed the 'opportunities worker.'

9 For example, when the 'Community Involvement Program' funding was cut, the result was the cessation of employment programs throughout our region during the last half of the year.

References

Alexander, P. (1985). A systems theory conceptualization of incest. *Family Process*, 24: 79–88.

– (1986). Procrustes was himself tortured: a reply to 'The procrustean bed.' *Family Process*, 25: 305–8.

Allen-Meares, P., and Lane, B.A. (1987). Grounding social work practice in theory: Ecosystems. *Social Casework*, 68: 515–21.

Althuser, L. (1971). *Lenin and philosophy and other essays*. New York: Monthly Review Press.

– (1977). *For Marx*. London: NLB

Alcoholics Anonymous. (1976). *Alcoholics anonymous: The story of how many thousands of men and women have recovered from alcoholism* (3rd ed.). New York: A.A. World Services.

American Psychiatric Association. (1994). *Diagnostic and statistical manual of mental disorders (DSM IV)*. Washington, DC: Author.

Anderson, C. (1982). The community connection: The impact of social networks on family and individual functioning. In F. Walsh (ed.), *Normal family processes*. New York: Guilford Press.

Anderson, L., and Munoz, X. (1986). *Flowers through the sand: The experience of women in an affirmative action program*. Winnipeg: Women's Research Advisory Committee.

Anderson, R.E., and Carter, I. (1984). *Human behavior in the social environment: A social systems approach* (3rd ed.). New York: Aldine.

Aronson, N. (1984). Science as a claims making activity: implications for social problems research. In J.W. Sneider and J.I. Kituse (eds.), *Studies in the sociology of social problems*. Norwood, NJ: Ablex.

Atherton, C.R., and Klemmack, D.L. (1982). *Research methods in social work: An introduction*. Toronto: D.C. Heath.

Atkinson, J.M. (1978). *Discovering suicide: Studies in the social organization of sudden death*. London: Macmillan.

Attneave, C.L. (1976). Social networks as the unit of intervention. In P. Guerin (ed.), *Family therapy: Theory and practice*. New York: Gardiner Press.

Auerswald, E.H. (1968). Interdisciplinary versus ecological approach. *Family Process*, 7: 205–15.

Babbie, E. (1983). *The practice of social research* (3rd ed.) Belmont, CA: Wadsworth.

Badgley, R.F. (Chairman). (1984). *Sexual offences against children: Report of the Committee on Sexual Offences against Children and Youth*. Ottawa, Ontario: Government of Canada.

Baily, T.F., and Baily, W.H. (1983). *Child welfare practice*. San Francisco: Jossey-Bass.

Banton, R., Clifford, P., Frosch, S., Lousada, J., and Rosenthall, J. (1985). *The politics of mental health*. London: Macmillan.

Barlow, D.H., and Hersen, M. (1984). *Single case experimental designs: Strategies for studying behavior change* (2nd ed.). Toronto: Pergamon.

Barlow, D.H., Hayes, S.C., and Nelson, R.O. (1984). *The scientist practitioner: Research and accountability in clincial and educational settings*. Toronto: Pergamon.

Barth, R.P., and Blythe, B.J. (1983). The contribution of stress to child abuse. *Social Service Review*, 57: 477–89.

Bartlett, H.M. (1970). *The common base of social work practice*. Washington: National Association of Social Workers.

Baudrillard, J. (1975). *The mirror of production*. St Louis: Telos Press.

Benjamin, A. (1981). *The helping interview* (3rd ed.). Boston: Houghton Mifflin.

Bernardes, J. (1985). 'Family ideology': Identification and exploration. *Sociological Review*, 33: 275–97.

Biestek, F.P. (1957). *The casework relationship*. Chicago: Loyola University Press.

Bloom, A.A. (1980). Social work and the English language. *Social Casework*, 61: 332–8.

Boehm, W.W. (1958). The nature of social work. *Social Work*, 3: 10–19.

Bolger, S., Corrigan, P., Docking, J., and Frost, N. (1981). *Towards socialist welfare work: Working in the state*. London: Macmillan.

Bologh, R.W. (1979). *Dialectical phenomenology: Marx's method*. London: Routledge and Kegan Paul.

Bourgault, D., and Meloche, M. (1982). Burnout or dying of exhaustion like a chameleon on a kilt. *Social Worker*, 50: 109–15.

Brill, N.I. (1985). *Working with people: The helping process*. New York: Longman.

British Columbia. (1980). *Family and Child Service Act*.

British Columbia Department of Social Welfare. (1968). *Annual report of the Department of Social Welfare for the year ended March 31, 1967*. Victoria, BC: Queen's Printer.

Callahan, M. (1984). The human costs of restraint. In W. Magnusson, W.K. Carroll, C. Doyleg, M. Langer, and R.B.J. Walker (eds.), *The new reality: The politics of restraint in British Columbia*. Vancouver, BC: New Star.

Camden, E. (1984). *If he comes back he's mine: A mother's story of child abuse*. Toronto: Women's Press.

Canada. (1989). *Criminal Code* (Pocket ed.). Toronto: Carswell.

Canada. (1982). *Young Offenders Act*.

Cantwell, H.B. (1980). Child neglect. In C.H. Kempe and R.E. Helfer (eds.), *The battered child* (3rd ed.). Chicago: University of Chicago Press.

Capen Reynolds, B. (1942). *Learning and teaching in the practice of social work*. Silver Spring, MD: National Association of Social Workers.

Carkhuff, R.R. (1983). *The art of helping*. Amherst, MA: Human Resource Development Press.

Carlson, B.E. (1984). Causes and maintenance of domestic violence: An ecological analysis. *Social Service Review*, 58: 569–87.

Carniol, B. (1992). Structural social work: Maurice Moreau's challenge to social work practice. *Journal of Progressive Human Services*, 3: 1–20.

– (1990). *Case critical: The dilemma of social work in Canada* (2nd ed.). Toronto: Between the Lines.

Carroll, W.K., Doyle, C., and Schacter, N. (1984). Medicare at risk. In W. Magnusson, W.K. Carroll, C. Doyle, M. Langer, and R.B.J. Walker (eds.), *The new reality: The politics of restraint in British Columbia*. Vancouver, BC: New Star.

Carter, B., Papp, P., Silverstein, O., and Walters, M. (1986). The Procrustean bed. *Family Process*, 25: 301–4.

Close, M.M. (1983). Child welfare and people of color: Denial of equal access. *Social Work Research and Abstracts*, 19: 13–20.

Cloward, R.A., and Piven, F.F. (1975). Notes toward a radical social work. In R. Bailey and M. Brake (eds.), *Radical social work*. New York: Pantheon.

Cohen, S. (1985). *Vision of social control: Crime, punishment, and classification*. Oxford: Polity Press.

Collier, K. (1984). *Social work with rural peoples: Theory and practice.* Vancouver: New Star.

Combs, A.W., Avila, D.L., and Purkey, W.W. (1978). *Helping relationships: Basic concepts for the helping professions* (2nd ed.). Toronto: Allyn and Bacon.

Compton, B.R., and Galaway, B. (1984). *Social work processes* (3rd ed.). Homewood, IL: Dorsey Press.

Cruikshank, D.A. (1985). The Berger Commission Report on the Protection of Children: The impact on prevention of child abuse and neglect. In Kenneth Levitt and Brian Wharf (eds.), *The challenge of child welfare.* Vancouver: University of British Columbia Press.

Culhane Speck, Dara. (1987). *An error in judgement: The politics of medical care in an Indian/white community*. Vancouver: Talon Books.

Currie, J., and Pishalski, F. (1984). Loosening the fabric: The termination of the family support worker program in British Columbia. *Journal of Child Care,* 1: 59–73.

Daley, M.R. (1979). 'Burnout': Smoldering problem in protective services. *Social Work,* 24: 375–9.

Darrough, W.D. (1978). When versions collide: Police and the dialectics of accountability. *Urban life,* 7: 379–403.

Deglau, E. (1985). A critique of social welfare theories: The culture of poverty and learned helplessness. *Catalyst,* 33–53.

de Montigny, G.A. (1980). The social organization of social workers' practice: A Marxist analysis. Unpublished MA thesis, OISE, Univeristy of Toronto.

Dinkmeyer, D., and McKay, G.D. (1976). *Systematic training for effective parenting.* Circle Pines, MN: American Guidance Service.

Dolgoff, R.L. (1981). Clinicians as social policy makers. *Social Casework,* 62: 284–92.

DuBray, W.H. (1985). American Indian values: Critical factor in casework. *Social Casework,* 66: 30–7.

Elgin, P. (1979). Resolving reality disjunctures on Telegraph Avenue: A study of practical reasoning. *Canadian Journal of Sociology,* 4: 359–77.

Falconer, N.E., and Swift, K. (1983). *Preparing for practice: The fundamentals of child protection.* Toronto: Children's Aid Society of Metropolitan Toronto.

Feldman, K.W. (1980). Child abuse by burning. In C.H. Kempe and R.E.

Helfer (eds.), *The battered child* (3rd ed.), Chicago: University of Chicago Press.

Ferguson, K.E. (1984) *The feminist cage against bureaucracy*. Philadelphia: Temple University Press.

Foucault, M. (1970). *The order of things: An archaeology of the human sciences*. New York: Random House.

– (1973). *The birth of the clinic: An archaeology of medical perception*. (A.M. Sheridan, trans.). London: Tavistock. (Original work published 1963).

– (1980). Truth and power. In C. Gordon, L. Marshall, J. Mepham, and K. Soper (eds. and trans.), *Power/knowledge: Selected interviews and other writings, 1972–1977*. New York: Pantheon.

Freed, A.O. (1978). Client's rights and casework records. *Social Casework*, 59: 458–64.

Freudenberger, H.J., and Richelson, G. (1980). *Burn-out: The high cost of high achievement*. Garden City, NY: Anchor Press.

Garfinkel, H., Lynch, M., and Livingston, E. (1981). The work of a discovering science construed with materials from the optically discovered pulsar. *Philosophy of Social Science*, 11: 131–58.

– (1967) *Studies in ethnomethodology*. Englewood Cliffs, NJ: Prentice-Hall.

Gelles, R.J. (1975). The social construction of child abuse. *American Journal of Orthopsychiatry*, 45: 363–71.

Germain, C.B. (1981). The ecological approach to people–environment transactions. *Social Casework*, 62, 323–31.

– (1982). *Social work practice an ecological perspective*. The ninth annual Easton-McCarney memorial lecture. Waterloo, Ontario, Faculty of Social Work, Wilfred Laurier University, September.

– (1991). *Human behavior in the social environment*. New York: Columbia University Press.

– and Gitterman, A. (1986). The life model approach to social work practice revisited. In Francis J. Turner and Katherine Kendall (eds.), *Social work treatment: Interlocking theoretical approaches*. New York: Free Press.

Gil, D.B. (1970). *Violence against children*. Cambridge, MA: Harvard University Press.

Gitterman, A., and Germain, C.B. (1976). Social work practice: A life model. *Social Service Review*, 50: 601–10.

Goffman, E. (1959). *The presentation of self in everyday life*. New York: Doubleday Anchor.

Goldstein, H.K. (1969) *Research standards and methods for social workers* (rev. ed.). Northbrook, Il: Whitehall.

Gordon, W. (1969). Basic constructs for an integrative and generative conception of social work. In G. Hearn (ed.), *The general systems approach: Contributions toward an holistic conception of social work.* New York: Council of Social Work Education.

Gough, I. (1979). *The political economy of the welfare state.* London: Macmillan.

Gramsci, A. (1971). The intellectuals. In Q. Hoare and G.N. Smith (eds. and trans.), *Selections from the prison notebooks of Antonio Gramsci.* New York: International.

Green, B.S. (1983). *Knowing the poor: A case-study in textual reality construction.* London: Routledge and Kegan Paul.

Griffith, A.I. (1984). Ideology, education, and single parent families: The normative ordering of families through schooling. Doctoral dissertation, University of Toronto.

Haley, J. (1976). *Problem solving therapy: New strategies for effective family therapy.* San Francisco: Jossey-Bass.

Harris, J.C., and Bernstein, B.E. (1980). Lawyer and social worker as a team: Preparing for trial in neglect cases. *Child Welfare,* 59: 469–77.

Haselkorn, F. (1978). Accountability in clinical practice. *Social Casework,* 59: 330–6.

Hearn, G. (ed.). (1969) *The general systems approach: Contributions toward an holistic conception of social work.* New York: Council on Social Work Education.

Hegel, G.W.F. (1967). *The phenomenology of mind.* (J.B. Baillie, trans.). New York: Harper Torchbooks.

Hepworth, D.H., and Larson, J.A. (1986). *Direct social work practice: Theory and skills* (2nd ed.). Chicago: Dorsey.

Hepworth, H.P. (1985). Child neglect and abuse. In K.L. Levitt and B. Wharf (eds.), *The challenge of child welfare.* Vancouver: University of British Columbia.

Hirst, P.Q. (1979). *On law and ideology.* London: Macmillan.

Hoffman, L. (1992). A reflexive stance for family therapy. In S. McNamee and K.T. Gergen (eds.), *Therapy as social construction.* London: Sage.

Holbrook, T. (1983). Notes on policy and practice: Case records: Fact or fiction? *Social Service Review,* 57: 645–58.

Hollis, F. (1972). *Casework: A psychosocial therapy* (2nd ed.). New York: Random House.

Howe, E. (1980). Public professions and their private model of professionalism. *Social Work*, 25: 179–91.

Hume, D. (1969). *A treatise of human nature*. (E.C. Mossner ed.). Harmondsworth, England: Penguin.

Jellinek, E.M. (1960). *The disease concept of alcoholism*. Highland Park, NJ: Hillhouse.

Johnson, L.C. (1986). *Social work practice: A generalist approach* (2nd ed.). Toronto: Allyn and Bacon.

Johnson, P. (1983). *Native children and the child welfare system*. Toronto: Canadian Council on Social Development and James Lorimer.

Johnson, T.J. (1972). *Professions and power*. London: Macmillan.

Kadushin, A. (1972). *The social work interview*. New York: Columbia University Press.

– and Martin, J.A. (1988). *Child welfare services* (4th ed.) New York: Macmillan

Kagle, J.D. (1983). The contemporary social work record. *Social Work*, 28: 149–53.

– (1984). Restoring the clinical record. *Social Work*, 29: 46–50

Karger, H.J. (1981). Burnout as alienation. *Social Service Review*, 55, 270–83.

– (1983). Science, research, and social work: Who controls the profession? *Social Work*, 28: 200–5.

Katzer, J., Cook, K.H., and Crouch, W.W. (1982). *Evaluating information: A guide for users of social science research* (2nd ed.). Don Mills, Ont.: Addison-Wesley.

Keller, E.F. (1985). *Reflections on gender and science*. New Haven: Yale University Press.

Kelley, M.L., McKay, S., and Nelson, C.H. (1985). Indian agency development: An ecological practice approach. *Social Casework*, 66: 594–602.

Kempe, R.S., and Kempe, C.H. (1978). *Child Abuse*. Cambridge: Harvard University Press.

– Cutler, C., and Dean, J. (1980). The infant with failure to thrive. In C.H. Kempe and R.E. Helfer (eds.), *The battered child* (3rd ed.). Chicago: University of Chicago Press.

Kimelman, E.C. (1983). *Interim Report: Review committee on Indian and Metis adoptions and placements*. Winnipeg: Community Services and Correction.

Klaus, M.H., and Kennell, J.H. (1982). Mothers separated from their new-born infants. In G.J. Williams and J. Money (eds.), *Traumatic abuse and neglect of children at home* (abridged ed.). Baltimore, MD: Johns Hopkins University Press.

Knight, R. (1978). *Indians at work: An informal history of Native Indian labour in British Columbia, 1858–1930*. Vancouver: New Star.

Kovel, J. (1981). *The age of desire: Reflections of a radical psychoanalyst*. New York: Pantheon.

Kress, G., and Hodge, R. (1979). *Language as ideology*. London: Routledge and Kegan Paul.

Laclau, E., and Mouffe, C. (1985). *Hegemony and socialist strategy: Towards a radical democratic politics*. New York: Verso.

Laird, J. (1985). Working with the family in child welfare. In J. Laird and A. Hartman (eds.), *A Handbook of child welfare: Context, knowledge, and practice*. New York: Free Press.

Larson, M.S. (1977). *The rise of professionalism: A sociological analysis*. Berkeley: University of California Press.

Latour, B., and Woolgar, S. (1979). *Laboratory life: The social construction of scientific facts*. Beverley Hills, CA: Sage.

Leonard, Peter. (1990). Fatalism and the discourse on power: An introductory essay. In Linda Davies and Eric Shragge (eds.), *Bureaucracy and community: Essays on the politics of social work practice*. Montreal: Black Rose Books.

Lee, J.A. (1980). The helping professional's use of language in describing the poor. *American Journal of Orthopsychiatry*, 50: 580–3.

Lewis, R.G., and Ho, M.K. (1975). Social work with Native Americans. *Social Work*, 20: 379–82.

Lipsky, M. (1980). *Street-level bureaucracy: Dilemmas of the individual in public service*. New York: Sage Foundation.

London Edinburgh Weekend Return Group. (1979). *In and against the state*. London: Pluto Press.

Lynch, M. (1985). *Art and artifact in laboratory science: A study of shop work and shop talk in a research laboratory*. London: Routledge and Kegan Paul.

McDougall, D. (1985). Children's rights: An evaluation of the controversy. In K.L. Levitt and B. Wharf (eds.), *The challenge of child welfare*. Vancouver: University of British Columbia Press.

Macpherson, C.B. (1973). *Democratic theory: Essays in retrieval*. Oxford: Clarendon Press.

McNamee, S., and Gergen, K.J. (eds.). (1992). *Therapy as social construction*. London: Sage.

Maidman, F. (1984). Child protection: Issues and practice. In F. Maidman, S. Kirsh, and G. Conchelos (eds.)., *Child welfare: A source book of knowledge and practice*. New York: Child Welfare League of America.

Marx, K. (1987). *Capital: A critical analysis of capitalist production, Vol. 1*. (S. Moore and E. Aveling, trans., from 3rd ed. edited by F. Engels). Moscow: Progress.

– (1969). *The 18th Brumaire of Louis Bonaparte*. New York: International Publishers.

– and Engels, F. (1976). The German ideology. In *Karl Marx, Frederick Engels: Collected Works*, vol. 5, *1845-47*. New York: International Publishers.

Maslach, C. (1982). *Burnout: The cost of caring*. New York: Prentice-Hall.

May, P.A. (1986). Alcohol and drug misuse prevention programs for American Indians: Needs and opportunities. *Journal of Studies on Alcohol*, 47: 187-95.

McGoldrick, M., Pearce, J.K., and Giordano, J. (eds.). (1982) *Ethnicity and family therapy*. New York: Guilford.

McHoul, A.W. (1982). *Telling how texts talk: Essays on reading and ethnomethodology*. London: Routledge and Kegan Paul.

McKenzie, B., and Hudson, P. (1985). Native children, child welfare, and the colonization of Native People. In Kenneth Levitt and Brian Wharf (eds.), *The challenge of child welfare*. Vancouver: University of British Columbia Press.

Mead, G.H. (1934). *Mind, self, and society: From the standpoint of a social behaviorist*. Chicago: University of Chicago Press.

Merleau-Ponty, M. (1968). *The visible and the invisible*. Evanston, IL: Northwestern University Press.

– (1973). *Adventures of the dialectic*. Evanston, IL: Northwestern University Press.

Mettrick, A. (1985). *Last in line: On the road and out of work ... a desperate journey with Canada's unemployed*. Toronto: Key Porter Books.

Minuchin, S. (1974). *Families and family therapy*. Cambridge: Harvard University Press.

Mitchell, A. (1985). Child sexual assault. In C. Guberman and M. Wolfe (eds.), *No safe place: Violence against women and children*. Toronto: Women's Press.

Mullaly, R.P. (1993). *Structural social work: Ideology, theory, and practice.* Toronto: McClelland and Stewart.
– and Keating, E.F. (1991). Similarities, differences, and dialectics of radical social work. *Journal of Progressive Human Services* 2: 49–79.
Monette, D.R., Sullivan, T.J., and Dejong, C.R. (1986). *Applied social research: Tool for the human services.* Montreal: Holt, Rinehart, and Winston.
Nachmias, D., and Nachmias, C. (1981). *Research methods in the social sciences.* New York: St Martin's Press.
National Council of Welfare. (1990). *Fighting child poverty.* Ottawa.
National Council of Welfare. (1979, December). *In the best interests of the child: A report by the National Council of Welfare on the child welfare system in Canada.* Ottawa.
National Council of Welfare. (1975, March). *Poor kids: A report by the national council of welfare on children in poverty in Canada.* Ottawa.
Ng, R. (1988). *The politics of community services: A study of an employment agency for immigrant women.* Toronto: Garamond.
Nietzsche, F. (1961). *Thus spoke Zarathustra.* Harmondsworth: Penguin.
Noble, J. (1979). 'Class-ifying' the poor: Toronto charities, 1850–1880. *Studies in Political Economy: A Socialist Review,* no. 2, 109–28.
O'Brien, M. (1981). *The politics of reproduction.* London: Routledge and Kegan Paul.
O'Connor, J. (1973). *The fiscal crisis of state.* New York: St Martin's Press.
Oliver, M. (1990). *The politics of disablement.* London: Macmillan.
Palmer, B.C. (1987). *Solidarity: The rise and fall of an opposition in British Columbia.* Vancouver: New Star.
Parton, N. (1985). *The politics of child abuse.* London: Macmillan.
Pelton, L. (1978). Child abuse and neglect: The myth of classlessness. *American Journal of Orthopsychiatry,* 48: 608–17.
Pfohl, S. (1985). Toward a sociological deconstruction of social problems. *Social Problems,* 32: 228–32.
– (1977). The 'discovery' of child abuse. *Social Problems,* 24: 310–23.
– & Gordon, A. (1987). Criminological displacements: A sociological deconstruction. In *Body Invaders: Panic sex in America.* Arthur Kroker and Marilouise Kroker (eds.), Montreal: New World Perspectives.
Phillipson, C. (1982). *Capitalism and the construction of old age.* London: Macmillan.
Pincus, A., and Minahan, A. (1973). *Social work practice: Model and method.* Itasca, IL: F.E. Peacock.

Pithouse, A. (1987). *Social work: The social organisation of an invisible trade*. Aldershot, England: Avebury.

Polansky, N.A. (ed.). (1960). *Social work research: Methods for the helping professions*. Chicago: University of Chicago Press:

–, Chalmers, M.A., Buttenwieser, E., and Williams, D.P. (1981). *Damaged parents: An anatomy of child neglect*. Chicago: University of Chicago Press.

–, Gaudin, J.M., and Kilpatrick, A.C. (1992). The maternal characteristics scale: A cross validation. *Child welfare*, 71: 271–80.

Polanyi, M. (1967). *The tacit dimension*. Garden City, NY: Anchor Books.

Pollner, M. (1974). Mundane reasoning. *Philosophy of the Social Sciences*, 4: 35–54.

Polsky, N. (1969). *Hustlers, beats, and others*. New York: Anchor Books.

Poulantzas, N. (1978). *Political power and social classes* (T. O'Hagan, trans.). London: Verso.

Province. (1985). MHR ducks queries: Tot's death riddle. Vancouver, 13 January 1985.

Radbill, S.X. (1980). Children in a world of violence: A history of child abuse. In C.H. Kempe and R.E. Helfer (eds.), *The battered child*. Chicago: University of Chicago Press.

Rai, G.S. (1983). Reducing bureaucratic inflexibility. *Social Service Review*, 57: 44–58.

Rein, M. (1970). Social work in search of a radical profession. *Social Work*, 15: 13–33.

Roy, D.F. (1959–1960, Winter). 'Banana time': Job satisfaction and informal interaction. *Human Organization*, 18: 158–68.

Ryan, W. (1976). *Blaming the victim* (rev. ed.). New York: Vintage Books.

Saleebey, D. (1992). Biology's challenge to social work: Embodying the person-in-environment perspective. *Social Work*, 37: 112–18.

Saulnier, K. (1982). Networks, change, and crisis: The web of support. *Canadian Journal of Community Mental Health*, 1: 5–23.

Schmitt, B.D. (1980). The child with nonaccidental trauma. In C.H. Kempe and R.E. Helfer (eds.), *The battered child*. Chicago: University of Chicago Press.

Schutz, A. (1973). On multiple realities. In M. Natanson (ed.), *Alfred Schutz collected papers: The problem of social reality*, vol. 1. The Hague: Martinus Nijhoff.

Schwartz, W. (1961). The social worker in the group. *The social Welfare Forum*. Official Proceedings, 88th Annual Forum, National Conference on Social Welfare. New York: Columbia University Press.

Seabury, B.A. (1985). The beginning phase: Engagement, initial assessment, and contracting. In J. Laird and A. Hartman (eds.), *A handbook of child welfare: Context, knowledge, and practice*. New York: Free Press.

Seligman, M.P. (1975). *Helplessness: On depression, development, and death*. San Francisco: Freeman.

Selye, H. (1956). *The stress of life*. New York: McGraw-Hill.

Shulman, L. (1984). *The skills of helping: Individuals and groups* (2nd ed.). Itasca, IL: F.E. Peacock.

Shulman, L. (1992). *The skills of helping: Individual, families, and groups* (3rd ed.). Itasca, IL: F.E. Peacock.

Sigurdson, E., and Reid, G. (1987). *External review into matters relating to the system of dealing with child abuse in Winnipeg: Final report*. Winnipeg: Manitoba Department of Community Services.

– (1990). *Child abuse and neglect: The Manitoba risk estimation system*. Winnipeg.

Silverman, P. (1978). *Who speaks for the children? The plight of the battered child*. Don Mills, Ont: Musson Books.

Silvers, R.J. (1977). Appearances: A videographic study of children's culture. In P. Woods and M. Hammersley (eds.), *School experience*. London: Croom Helm.

Simmons, J. (1965) Public sterotypes of deviants. *Social Problems*, 3: 223–32.

Simons, R.L., and Aigner, S.M. (1985). *Practice principles: A problem solving approach to social work*. New York: Macmillan.

Simpkin, M. (1983). *Trapped within welfare: Surviving social work* (2nd ed.). London: Macmillan.

Siporin, M. (1975). *Introduction to social work practice*. New York: Macmillan.

Smith, C.R. (1984). *Adoption and Fostering: Why and How*. London: Macmillan.

Smith, D.E. (1974). The social construction of documentary reality. *Sociological Inquiry*, 44: 257–67.

– (1978). *The ontological domain of ethnomethodology*. Unpublished manuscript, Ontario Institute for Studies in Education, Toronto.

– (1979). Using the oppressor's language. *Resources for Feminist Research* (Special publication 5): 10–18.

– (1981) On sociological description: A method from Marx. *Human Studies*, 4: 313–37.

– (1983). No one commits suicide: Textual analysis of ideological practices. *Human Studies*, 6: 309–59.

Smith, D.E. (1984) Textually mediated social organization. *International Social Science Journal*, 36: 59–75.

– (1987). *The everyday world as problematic: A feminist sociology*. Toronto: University of Toronto Press.

– (1990). *The conceptual practices of power: A feminist sociology of knowledge*. Toronto: University of Toronto Press.

Smith, G.W. (1990). *Policing the gay community*. In Roxana Ng, Gillian Walker, and Jacob Muller (eds.), *Community, organization, and the Canadian state*. Toronto: Garamond.

Smith, J.E. (1984). Non-accidental injury to children – I: A review of behavioural interventions. *Behavioural Research and Therapy*, 22: 331–47.

Specht, H. (1986). Social supports, social networks, social exchange, and social work practice. *Social Service Review*, 60: 218–40.

Spinetta, J.J., and Rigler, D. (1982). The child-abusing parent. A psychological review. In G.J. Williams and J. Money (eds.), *Traumatic abuse and neglect of children at home* (abridged ed.). Baltimore, MD: Johns Hopkins University Press.

Steele, B. (1980). Psychodynamic factors in child abuse. In C.H. Kempe and R.E. Helfer (eds.), *The battered child* (3rd ed.) Chicago: University of Chicago Press.

Stein, R.E.K. (1982). A special home care unit for care of chronically ill children. In M. Bryce and J.C. Lloyd (eds.), *Treating families in the home: An alternative to placement*. Springfield: Charles C. Thomas.

Straus, M.A. (1980). Stress and child abuse. In C.H. Kempe and R.E. Helfer (eds.), *The battered child* (3rd ed.). Chicago: University of Chicago Press.

Sudnow, D. (1964). Normal crimes: Sociological features of the penal code in a public defender office. *Social Problems*, 12: 255–76.

Summit, R., and Kryso, J. (1978). Sexual abuse of children: A clinical spectrum. *American Journal of Orthopsychiatry*, 48: 237–51.

Therborn, G. (1980). *The ideology of power and the power of ideology*. London: Verso.

Thomas, R.K. (1981). The history of North American Indian alcohol use as a community-based phenomenon. *Journal of Studies on Alcohol*, 9 (Supplement): 29–39.

Thompson, E.P. (1963). *The making of the English working class*. New York: Vintage.

– (1975). *Whigs and hunters: The origin of the Black Act*. New York: Pantheon.

- (1978). *The poverty of theory and other essays*. New York: Monthly Review Press.

Trocme, Nico. (1991). Child welfare services. In Richard Barnhorst and Laura C. Johnson (eds)., *The state of the child in Ontario*. Toronto: Oxford University Press.

Tudiver, N. (1979). *Ideology and management in the social services*. Paper presented at the annual conference of the Canadian Association of Schools of Social Work, Saskatoon, Sask., June.

Turner, D., and Shields, B. (1985). The legal process of bringing children into care in British Columbia. In K.L. Levitt and B. Wharf (eds.), *The challenge of child welfare*. Vancouver: University of British Columbia Press.

Van Stolk, M. (1978). *The battered child in Canada* (rev. ed.). Toronto: McClelland and Stewart.

Volosinov, V.N. (1973). *Marxism and the philosophy of language* (L. Matejka and I.R. Titunik trans.). New York: Seminar Press. (Original work published 1930).

Walker, G.A. (1981). *Women, the state, and the family: Ideology and professional practice*. Unpublished manuscript. School of Social Work, Carleton University, Ottawa.

- (1986). Burnout: From metaphor to ideology. *Canadian Journal of Sociology*, 11: 35–55.

- (1990). *Family violence and the women's movement: The conceptual politics of struggle*. Toronto: University of Toronto Press.

Walsh, F. (1982). Conceptualizations of normal family functioning. In Froma Walsh (ed.), *Normal family processes*. New York: Guilford Press.

Ward, E. (1984). *Father-daughter rape*. London: Women's Press.

Warry, W. (1991). Ontario's First Peoples. In Laura C. Johnson and Dick Barnhorst (eds.), *Children, families, and public policy in the 90's*. Toronto: Thompson Educational Publishing.

Wasserman, H. (1971). The professional social worker in a bureaucracy. *Social Work*, 16: 89–95.

Weber, M. (1978). *Economy and society: An outline of interpretive sociology*, vol. 2. (G. Roth and C. Wittich, eds.). Berkeley: University of California Press.

Wharf, B. (1985). Preventive approaches to child welfare. In K.L. Levitt and B. Wharf (eds.), *The challenge of child welfare*. Vancouver: University of British Columbia Press.

- (1993). Rethinking child welfare. In B. Wharf (ed.), *Rethinking child welfare in Canada*. Toronto: McClelland and Stewart.

Wheeler, S. (1976). Problems and issues in record-keeping. In S. Wheeler (ed.), *On record: Files and dossiers in American life*. New Brunswick, NJ: Transaction Books.

Will, D., and Wrate, R.M. (1985). *Integrated family therapy: A problem-centred psychodynamic approach*. London: Tavistock

Willis, P. (1977). *Learning to labour: How working class kids get working class jobs*. Westmead, England: Gower.

Wilson, S.J. (1980). *Recording guidelines for social workers*. New York: Free Press.

Wittgenstein, L. (1958). *Philosophical investigations* (3rd ed.) G.E.M. Anscombe, trans.). New York: Macmillan.

Woolgar, S., and Pawluch, D. (1985). Ontological gerrymandering: The anatomy of social problems explanations. *Social Problems*, 32: 214–27.

Wright, L. (1982). The 'sick but slick' syndrome as a personality component of parents of battered children. In G.J. Williams and J. Money (eds.), *Traumatic abuse and neglect of children at home* (abridged ed.). Baltimore, MD: Johns Hopkins University Press.

Yelaja, S.A. (1985). Introduction to the social work profession. In S.A. Yelaja (ed.), *An introduction to social work practice in Canada*. Scarborough, Ont.: Prentice-Hall.

Young, T. (1982). Book review: Damaged parents: An antomy of neglect. *Social Service Review*, 56: 160–5.

Zastrow, C. (1985). *The practice of social work* (2nd ed.) Homewood, IL: Dorsey.

Zimmerman, D.H. (1976). Record-keeping and the intake process in a public welfare agency. In S. Wheeler (ed.), *On record: Files and dossiers in American life*. New Brunswick, NJ: Transaction Books.

Index